DATE DUE

NOV 29 1988		
		FEB 10 2003
MAY 16 1988		
SEP 30 1991		APR 07 2003
OCT 1 1992		AUG 09 2003
FEB 25 1993		AUG 24 2010
NOV 12 1993		DEC 2 2013
AUG 26 1994		
JUN 18 1999		
Nov 14 2000		

#47-0108 Peel Off Pressure Sensitive

THE
COLLECTED
POEMS OF
CHARLES
OLSON

THE
COLLECTED
POEMS OF
CHARLES
OLSON

Excluding the *Maximus* poems

Edited by George F. Butterick

University of California Press / Berkeley Los Angeles London

University of California Press
Berkeley and Los Angeles, California
University of California Press, Ltd.
London, England
Printed in the United States of America
1 2 3 4 5 6 7 8 9

Library of Congress Cataloging-in-Publication Data
Olson, Charles, 1910–1970.
   The collected poems of Charles Olson.
   I. Butterick, George F.   II. Title.
PS3529.L655A17   1987   811'.54   86-14652
ISBN 0-520-05764-3 (alk. paper)

CONTENTS

INTRODUCTION

Charles Olson, who was born in 1910, did not publish his first poems until 1946, several years after what would prove to be the middle of his life. Indeed, from all the known evidence, he did not even begin writing poems until twenty-nine years old. Before then his overriding ambition had been to be a Melville scholar, a man of letters, a "writer." Even in college he published only newspaper editorials, book reviews, and a single play. What prompted him to try his hand at poetry? Most likely, as with many poets, it was a gradual awakening, an evolution, rather than an incident along the road to Damascus or a Caedmonic dream. One can be sure it was not encouragement from his early mentor, Edward Dahlberg, who had such an antipathy to modern poetry. Nor was it a directive from Ezra Pound, whom Olson began visiting in 1946, for he had already written many of the poems in the early pages of this edition. We may never know for certain. All he ever said was that it was overhearing the talk of Gloucester fishermen as a boy, on summer evenings, that made him a poet. It never even occurred to me to ask. He just seemed so completely and classically a poet, filling out the role as he did any space or company with his physical and imaginative presence. There was—and is—hardly room for thought of him otherwise.

There is, therefore, no section of juvenilia in this collection, although some of the earliest poems in their apparent simplicity are those of a beginner. But this is no problem: he was always, like his Melville, a "beginner—and interested in beginnings." It was not until 1949, with the writing of "The Kingfishers," and 1950, with the publication of his manifesto "Projective Verse," that he was set irrevocably on his course. There might be said to be three periods of Olson's poetic development, even though this collection is not divided so neatly: the initial years through 1948, or until he began his association with Black Mountain College and including the annunciative "La Préface," his first "postmodern" poem; the middle period, beginning with "The Kingfishers" and corresponding roughly to his stay at Black Mountain, during which time the *Maximus* poems were launched; and the period from around 1957, when he returned to Gloucester from Black Mountain, until the end of his life (although the final years, beyond 1964, were given over almost exclusively to *Maximus*).

Nor is this a collection, like some poets' *Collected Poems,* of previously published volumes intact and in order of publication. Olson did not necessarily conceive of his work that way and, more important, three-quarters of the roughly four hundred poems presented here were never published in his lifetime. Upon his death, he left not only the final third of his *Maximus* epic unpublished but also a sizable body of other writings, including an unusually large number of unpublished poems, many equal in quality to those published during his lifetime. It was his understanding that they would eventually be published, although as with *The Maximus Poems* he left few specific guidelines. And since the earlier most comprehensive volume of his separate poems, *Archaeologist of Morning,* had been allowed to go out of print by its publisher, this occasion, part of the larger design of making his complete writings available, was viewed as the opportunity to bring all his non-*Maximus* poems worthy of pre-servation into one large collection. If Olson had a reputation as a major shaper of twentieth-century poetry before this work was available, how much greater his promi-nence will be when the full extent of his accomplishment is made known. For it is as a poet, not as teacher or theorist or influence alone, that he must be judged and by which his reputation lives or wanes.

Even the imposing *Maximus Poems,* which have been made available in a separate volume by the University of California Press (1983), do not demonstrate the full scope of his powers. Unlike the poems of that epic series, the poems presented here are not localized in Gloucester (though a few have Gloucester as subject or setting) and are not successively forwarded by the voice of Maximus. Rather, they are more self-contained impulses. There are smaller series within them, such as *O'Ryan* or *'West',* but most are isolate bursts or swarms, some intensely lyric, others broader and more encompassing. Whether widely or narrowly occasional, their occasions are all their own. All bear the stamp of Olson's unmistakable authority. Some are charms, others are blasts, ferocities. If he had worked in more traditional forms, there might be more traditional names for them. In fact, he was forging the tradition of what Pound had called the "new" and Williams the "American"—yet he himself had the persistent sense he was working in thematic areas as far back as Homer and Hesiod, the Hittites and Sumerians, the earliest Indo-European road-warriors, Pleistocene forebears, the aboriginal earthlings, Terrans, Gaeans themselves—areas of human occupation inexhaustible to any age.

The poems collected here are from the full course of Olson's career and include all those non-*Maximus* poems the poet himself published during his lifetime. Readers will find such familiar and influential classics as "The Kingfishers," that successor to "The Wasteland"; the probing, hammering, and above all triumphal "In Cold Hell, in Thicket"; and the deeply personal yet archetypal "As the Dead Prey Upon Us." The many unpublished poems left behind at the time of his death are mostly from among his extensive papers at the University of Connecticut Library, but also from holdings in other institutions and in private hands, wherever these have been discoverable. They embody the widest (and sometimes wildest) range of human interests, from the cosmic to the comic to the economic. They extend from one-word poems (anticipating by a number of years, perhaps, Aram Saroyan's famous "eyeye") to the magnificently rolling antiphon beginning "The chain of memory is resurrection . . . ," or "Conqueror," whose lines are so long they can only be doubled-up at the margin. The voice in each is impassioned or hushed, urgent or generous, raised to exhortation, ringing off the ionosphere, or lowered to an earthy jest. None of the poems are without risk.

As in editing the final volume of *The Maximus Poems,* I have gone through Olson's papers repeatedly, including his notebooks, correspondence, and the books in his library (where poems on folded sheets have been found, as well as some written on flyleaves and in margins).[1] A determined effort was made to gather together all known manuscripts in the preparation of this edition. Editors in whose publications poems appeared were contacted where possible, as were the significant correspondents throughout Olson's career. Public repositories throughout the United States and Canada were approached for previously unknown manuscripts, variant texts, texts for collation, and in order to secure dates for undated manuscripts. I received helpful responses from all the institutions known to have Olson materials. Over the past fifteen years, I have generally kept my eyes open. There may be occasional strays left to be found, of course, although I am confident there are no sizable hidden caches, no lost masterpieces. A few poems undoubtedly remain buried among the poet's water-damaged materials in Connecticut,[2] including perhaps two from mid-1951 entitled "Composed of Distinct Parts or Discontinuous Elements" (unless that is an early title for "A Discrete Gloss") and "Not So Much Movement as Its Lack"— both mentioned in July 1951 letters to Robert Creeley but which do not otherwise survive.

The present collection contains almost four times the total number of non-*Maximus* poems published during Olson's lifetime and collected in *Archaeologist of Morning* (1970). In those terms alone, *Archaeologist of Morning,* out of print since 1977, is plainly not the full extent of the poet's accomplishment or his poetic canon. Although useful at the time, it was not an authorized edition in the usual sense, for Olson had no active role in its making, aside from urging that it be done (or at least that some such large collection of his poems be made). It is doubtful he gave any

1. See the introductions to my *A Guide to the Maximus Poems of Charles Olson* (Berkeley: University of California Press, 1978) and *Editing the Maximus Poems* (Storrs: University of Connecticut Library, 1983).

2. Described briefly in my introduction to *Charles Olson & Robert Creeley: The Complete Correspondence* (Santa Barbara: Black Sparrow Press, 1983), V, vii; see also my "Modern Literary Manuscripts and Archives: A Field Report," *Credences,* n.s., 1:1 (1981), p. 84.

personal supervision to the volume: it was still being assembled while he was dying and was published posthumously. It was, in fact, no more than an opportune collection. He did not approve the selection of texts, made no decisions as to textual variants or whether any of the assembled pieces might be better considered prose or additional *Maximus* poems, and did not provide any instructions on the order of the selections, although all these questions had been raised with him. Publisher Barry Hall of Cape Goliard Press had proposed in November 1969 to bring the assembled manuscript to Gloucester some time after Christmas that year, but by then it was too late. Olson died in New York on 10 January 1970.[3]

Moreover, the text itself of *Archaeologist of Morning* is not very reliable. A comprehensive survey reveals more than eighty errors, relatively minor but of varying degrees, such as "the" for "that" or "freatherwork" for "featherwork," "indicated" for "indicted," "might" for "night," "experimental" for "experiential," and omitted (or inserted) punctuation. In some cases, the volume was based on corrupt texts, simply collecting already inadequate printings, such as the *Resuscitator* printing of "Buffalo Ode." Individual texts were unauthorized, as was the order of poems. Indeed, one poem ("Queen Street Burle-Q") attributed to Olson was actually by another poet, owing to the lack of clarity in its original little magazine presentation. In addition, an early and undoubtedly inferior version of "ABCs (3)" was used instead of Olson's preferred version as found in *The Distances*. Likewise, a premature version of "The Praises" was allowed with four lusterless lines—"It is the use, it is the use / you make of us, the use / you make of / you!"—which dissipate the ending and which had in fact been omitted by Olson in *The Distances* (nor are they present in his *Selected Writings*). Again, at least three other pieces may better be considered prose notes ("*place; & names,*" "you can't use words as ideas . . . ," and "A Note for Anyone Able To"). And although the order of poems is generally chronological—based in part, it would seem, on an early "working plan" for *In Cold Hell*—there are many troublesome exceptions; nor is the order according to date of publication. In other words, *Archaeologist of Morning* may be considered irrelevant for preparing a definitive edition of Olson's collected poems.

Occasionally, in the present edition, variant versions of a poem have been included. While this is not intended to be a variorum edition in which all known versions of a given text are printed, in a limited number of cases it has been impossible

---

3. A complete collected poems outside of *Maximus* had been proposed to Olson earlier, in 1968, by Donald Allen (with the present editor to serve as coeditor). Olson found the suggestion agreeable, although contractual arrangements required that Cape publish the volume (Allen to Richard Seaver, 9 September 1968, in Grove Press archive, Arents Library, Syracuse).

or even undesirable to judge which version of a poem is the preferred or "superior" version. In this category are such poems as "Conqueror," "my poor dumb body . . . ," the delicate poems beginning "The perfume / of flowers! . . . ," "The Writ," and "The Americans." These are cases in which both versions are *equally* interesting as poems and, although obviously related, each has its own distinctive, autonomous value, so that the effect on the reader is that of a whole new poem. From these few examples the reader also has the opportunity, and without the redundancies of a variorum edition or cumbersome textual apparatus, to study the effectiveness of changes made by the poet while at the same time gaining some sense of the poet at work.

Every effort has been made to provide an authoritative text for each poem included—the text the poet himself preferred, insofar as that has been possible to ascertain. The last volumes that Olson himself approved—outside of *O'Ryan 1–10* (1965) and *'West'* (1966), which are self-contained series and included here as such—were *The Distances* (1960) and *Selected Writings* (1966), which included sixteen non-*Maximus* poems.[4] Before these volumes, there were only the original *In Cold Hell* from 1953—the record of Olson's cares and deliberations concerning which can be found in his correspondence with Cid Corman and Robert Creeley—and the five poems in *Y & X* (1948), photoreproduced without any textual changes in 1950.

This leaves the many separate poems originally published in magazines or as broadsides and collected only in *Archaeologist of Morning*. Because of the large number of discrepancies noted by the editor in magazine texts when preparing the collected *Maximus Poems* (only fourteen such poems out of seventy-seven corresponded exactly to their original manuscripts or finally published versions), it was appropriate to routinely seek confirmation here, too, by comparing proofs, manuscripts, other published versions, and tape-recorded readings. It was possible to track down original manuscripts sent editors for approximately half the poems in *Archaeologist of Morning;* the rest may be irretrievably lost. Most notably absent are the manuscripts of eleven poems that Cid Corman published in *Origin* but which do not survive

4. If one counts the 1967 reprint edition of *In Cold Hell, in Thicket,* it can be said that that volume constitutes the last appearance during the poet's lifetime of some of his most important poems. No proofs of that edition seem to have survived, however, and there is considerable doubt whether Olson actually read any in the first place. He provided only a single instruction regarding the text (concerning the final lines of the poem "ABCs"), in a letter to publisher Donald Allen. Allen recalled (in a 13 October 1983 letter to the editor) that Olson "took little or no interest" in the reprint, while Andrew Hoyem, who printed the volume for Allen's Four Seasons Foundation, likewise felt "it's probable that Olson did not even see the galley or page proofs and that Don Allen took responsibility for final approval of the pages" (letter, 8 December 1983).

among Olson's letters at the University of Texas, although five other relevant manuscripts do; nor are they among the later *Origin* materials at Indiana University or at Kent State, while Corman himself reports no knowledge of where they might be.

All changes made in the present texts from previous publications are a result of comparison with the full array of primary textual resources. About three dozen changes were necessary, mostly in magazine and newspaper appearances. For example, there were eleven errors in the *Resuscitator* printing of "Buffalo Ode" (not counting the three in the first installment corrected by Olson for reprinting). These were mostly minor matters ("Fordham" for "Fodham"), although the omission of the word "early" unnecessarily roughened the following line: "at a date early enough to raise two important questions"; and the humorous tang of "just fer enough" was lost in "just far enough . . ." The *Gloucester Daily Times* printing of "An 'Enthusiasm'" alone contained nine errors. *The Distances,* on the other hand, was such a remarkable job of editing and production that I have discovered only five places needing adjustment: a "he" for "be" in "In Cold Hell, in Thicket" (line 1.12), a "his" (referring to Hart Crane) instead of "this" in "Letter for Melville 1951" (line 29 from the end), an "it" for "is" in "Anecdotes of the Late War" (line 4.1), the substitution of a "the" for an "and" in "As the Dead Prey Upon Us" (line 2.9), and the indentation of the final nineteen lines of "The Librarian." In one instance I have arbitrarily made an alteration in the text. In the final poem of the volume, the very first line ("A big fat fly . . .") did not begin with a capital letter in the original manuscript.

The poems have been arranged chronologically, disregarding the individual volumes they may have appeared in previously. Unlike Robert Duncan, for example, Olson did not compose by "books." Consequently, both published and unpublished poems have been integrated, thereby creating a new, more comprehensive canon. Dates are given for each poem in the textual notes at the end of the volume. Only a small percentage of the poems were explicitly dated by the poet in manuscript; dates for the rest had to be earned in the usual fashion—from internal and external evidence. Mentions of poems by title in the poet's correspondence or in notebooks were immediately helpful, as were contemporary allusions within the texts. In his "Key West II" notebook from early 1945, for example, Olson kept a record of which poems had been sent out—and, for the most part, rejected. "Law" was probably written during the time that Olson worked for the Office of War Information in Washington, that is, 1942 to 1944, since also on the typescript is a note from "Lew," probably Lewis Frank, with whom he shared an office (see *Muthologos,* I, 110 and 124). "The Town" was based on a newspaper account from about 2 June 1945 of the Nazi destruction of Lidice, and "The Gonfalon Raised Tonight" draws upon a 7

April 1958 article on youth gang violence in *Time* magazine. An early version of "The Boat" was dated only "29th / 54," although the poem was discovered to be based on the finding of the pharaoh Cheops' solar barge in the great pyramid at Giza in late May of that year, thus providing a more definite date.

Other dates were more complicated to attain. An undated typescript of an early version of "A Lustrum for You, E.P." titled "Lustrum," with folds in it as if once mailed, is signed "John Little." It has a note typed in the margin quoting Ezra Pound in June 1945—a quotation, however, that actually was found in a November 1945 article on Pound. This evidence ordinarily might have provided a date for the poem. A letter from Olson to critic Malcolm Cowley in Chicago's Newberry Library, however, reveals that the original version had been sent to the *New Republic* earlier than either of those dates, actually in March or April of that year (the marginal note was then a late addition)—and also that the pseudonym "John Little" (a chuckle on the part of the six-foot-seven Olson) had been used by the poet to preserve his anonymity, and therefore effectiveness, with the Justice Department, should it be possible to work on Pound's behalf upon his return to the United States from Italy for trial. Still another poem, titled "Examples" in one version, was dedicated to a Richard "Bridgeman"—finally realized to be "Bridgman," since teaching at Berkeley and who in response to an inquiry acknowledged meeting Olson at Dartmouth in April 1962, thus enabling a close date for the poem.

At one point, the lower part of the *e* on Olson's typewriter failed to register upon each striking, at the same time leaving an impression of the underscore two spaces above. By checking dated typescripts with the same feature, it was possible to calculate inclusive dates for this condition and thus to assign approximate dates for otherwise undatable manuscripts. Often approximate dates were achieved by noting the watermarks of the various kinds of paper used. A chart of stationery and typing bonds used by the poet was drawn up, together with respective dates (again achieved from other, dated manuscripts). In a number of cases, however, where a poem appears on unwatermarked paper—notably such early poems as "Fable for Slumber," "The House," and "Hymn to the Word," or others from the early to mid-fifties like "The Civil War" or "The Connection"—only broadly approximate dates were possible. Sometimes, especially when there were no watermarks or other observable characteristics, only the immediate context of a manuscript's discovery amid other dated or datable materials provided inclusive dates. In these cases, I placed the poems at the beginning of their possible time frame rather than at the end.

The chronological order posed something of a problem at times, especially in cases where a poem was first written at one date and then revised several months or even years later. In these cases—except for the poems identified by Olson at various times as being among his "earliest" (specifically, "Atalanta" and "White Horse")—it seemed most reasonable to position poems at the date of their last major rewriting. Thus, poems such as "Other Than," "La Torre," "The Dry Ode," and "The Binnacle," which were all extensively revised after their original writing, are placed at their later dates. The strictly chronological arrangement is not always in the reader's best interest, however, when it comes to variant versions of a poem; in this case a logic other than the rigidly mechanistic is called for. This alternate logic is readily apparent in placing "You, Hart Crane" and "Birth's Obituary" (revised some four years later) or the two versions of "Conqueror" (one written in January 1948 in California, the other a revision made at least four months to more than a year later in Washington) side by side at their earlier dates, where the similarities and differences can be appreciated, rather than having them separated by several pages of intervening poems. The same logic applies to the two versions of "The Writ," one apparently written in 1956, the other revised the following February. More problematic in this regard are the three versions of "The She-Bear," separated by as many as seven or even twelve years (March 1950 to sometime between 1957 and 1962), although the resulting versions are not in fact radically different. "New England March," on the other hand, is so different from "Purgatory Blind" that I thought it best to allow them their respective (and respectful) distance.

There are other necessary exceptions to blind chronology: the three "ABCs" were written at different times, with other poems intervening, yet are published here together as they were in *In Cold Hell* and *The Distances*. The poems from *'West'* likewise are kept together, since Olson considered them a series, although one unpublished stray, "A Part of the Series on the Paths," is allowed its own place, since it was never published by the poet with the rest of the series (for reasons given in note 7 below). Generally, however, poems are placed in an order that goes from the general to the particular. Thus, a poem from "ca. 1948" appears before one dated simply "1948," which in turn appears ahead of ones dated "ca. January–February 1948" and "January 1948" and "9 January 1948." Poems dated more broadly "ca. 1948–1950" are placed after those dated "ca. 1948" but before those from "1948." Finally, when two poems appear with the same date, they are arranged alphabetically for the sake of consistency.

The only alternative overall arrangement that makes any sense would have been to divide the poems into the volumes they were originally collected in, with the uncollected poems following or interspersed chronologically between books. In such instances, however, does a later volume supersede an earlier? And what happens when there is an overlap—as in the case of "La Préface," which is in *Y & X* and *In Cold Hell* but not in *The Distances,* or "Other Than" and the other twelve poems that were in *In Cold Hell* but not in *The Distances?* It gets confusing. In addition, the making of Olson's books were never clear-cut affairs. Beyond *Y & X,* it might even be suggested that he did not always make his own books with overwhelming decisiveness. The uncertain time he had making *In Cold Hell* is evident in his letters to Cid Corman and especially his letters to Creeley from 1952 to 1953; but even *The Distances* was a complicated matter. Olson eliminated nineteen poems from that volume, which actually was to be a collected poems, including many of the poems from *In Cold Hell.* This was in August 1960, after the book had already been set in type, while reading the galleys and suffering a change of heart.[5] Most significant, Olson—

5. Olson's original selected poems with Grove—the manuscript of which was prepared in the summer of 1958—even included sections from *Maximus.* The making of *The Distances* is also very instructive in terms of the care Olson demanded for his texts. In returning the corrected galleys to Grove (now among Donald Allen's Olson materials at the University of Connecticut Library), Olson wrote in August 1960 (this and other letters cited are in the Grove Press archive at Syracuse):

> The main problem, as you will see, is the single space leading *throughout.* It's too much. *Please* show the printer that his own work (in the anthology 'New Am Verse' [i.e., Donald Allen's *The New American Poetry 1945–1960*]—I assume it's the same printer) is the measure of the difference.
> (I have no idea what this involves to change it, but so crucial is it that I will have to see another proof—though that could be page proofs (expected anyway?)

Grove did the best it could, following Allen's encouragement, without resetting the entire volume, but the results still left Olson dissatisfied. On 9 October he wrote the publisher an ultimatum of despair: "Please suspend any further press work on my book THE DISTANCES, until I have seen complete proofs: some of the poems as printed and photo-reduced . . . no more resemble the poems as I wrote them as if they were somebody else's. . . . The adjustments in space which have been made since throw the poems off worse than they were before." He continues strongly: "In any case as is I could not possibly approve this volume as being mine." (Allen, on the other hand, felt "the page proofs look very *good!* to me"—his letter to Grove, 13 October.) Publisher Barney Rosset's response (12 October) appears to have assuaged the poet (Olson's concerns may have been those familiar ones of artistic self-doubt on opening night), for he writes Rosset again on 24 October—after having gone through the further torment of eliminating even more of the early poems—to thank him for his explanatory letter:

> I regret very much there had to be so much doing about it, but if you realize that it had an enormous spread of time in it—from 1946 to 1959, 13 years of poems—you may be able to see the problem it presented to me, a curious one not ever experienced before, and, I should guess, a rather unusual one.
> I did also want you to recognize that at no time was Don anything but on the ball, and that all the fuss was due to the above situation I was in, not at all he.

Poets regularly make selections from their work from over a longer stretch than thirteen years, of course; but of interest here is Olson's determination regarding the reproduction of his texts—an anxious exactitude that might not have been as fully expected in light of other patterns in his life.

unlike those poets who have built their collected poems volume by volume, incorporating earlier books relatively whole—did not himself preserve *Y & X* in *In Cold Hell,* nor *In Cold Hell* in *The Distances.* There is then, no precedent from that quarter, the poet's own example.

I never discussed with Olson, poem by poem, whether he would have wanted all of these poems published, but there was clearly never any overall objection. The *Maximus* poems were most on his mind the years I knew him, but he spoke of other accumulations among his papers waiting for attention, including the "Special View of History" lectures, the "New Sciences of Man" materials, *The Post Office,* and his letters with Robert Creeley. He also spoke of the unpublished poems as if someday they would all see the light of day. The collected published poems first had to be dealt with, since he had a contract outstanding with publisher Jonathan Cape, and these became *Archaeologist of Morning.* As already indicated, it could hardly be argued that that volume comprised the only poems Olson ever wanted collected, since it was published posthumously with little if any personal supervision. He seemed to have accepted, however, the notion of preserving relatively obscure and previously uncollected poems in *Archaeologist;* at least, nothing that he was told concerning the collection brought him to his feet growling. Whether that can be taken as tacit approval, or just postponement of involvement until the book was far enough along to be worth worrying about, cannot be known.

More convincing evidence is that he wanted other poems published at various stages of his career, especially in the early years, but for a variety of reasons (most often, their rejection by editors) this did not occur. The work became buried like the levels of Troy under the accumulation of the day's or the week's activity. Dozens of the unpublished early poems presented here for the first time had been sent out for publication, but were turned down. For instance, "She," "She, Thus," "Birth's Obituary," "The Night," "Her Dream, Half Remembered," "Ballad for Americans," and many others from the early and mid-forties were refused by, variously, *Harper's Bazaar, Partisan Review, New Republic, Sewanee Review, Virginia Quarterly Review, New Directions, Atlantic Monthly, Nation,* and *Foreground,* among others. The entire "Enniscorthy Suite" was sent to *Harper's* but only one section, "Lower Field," was accepted. The ballad "Willie Francis and the Electric Chair" was rejected by People's Songs, Inc., in New York. "The Kingfishers" had been turned down by the *Hudson Review,* among other places, before it was published by Robert Payne in *Montevallo Review.* There is little likelihood that Olson saw the early rejections as definitive, knowing full well how literary rejection can be a matter of the deepest subjectivity and haphazard temporality, not a conclusive measure of the quality of a submission.

The nature and history of Olson's publishing practices—the early rejections, the later somewhat casual and unstrategic efforts, the lack of obvious careerism—support the inclusion of the previously unpublished poems. After 1951 there is no evidence that Olson put himself forward in the usual sense of submitting his work to editors unknown to him. (*Origin,* it might be said, marked the turning point.) All his later publications were in response to requests rather than a result of actively entering the lists, playing the numbers, sending out manuscripts complete with an "SASE." He served his apprenticeship in the 1940s, with a success rate of perhaps five percent. Eventually, his work was no longer rejected, though in rare cases an editor could not or would not use everything sent. Robert Payne turned down "A Man Who Is Not St. Francis" (a later version of "Applause") and "The Collected Poems Of" for the *Montevallo Review;* Tambimuttu rejected "The Bride" for *Poetry London–New York,* accepting other poems but misplacing the manuscripts. After the matter was discussed with Donald Allen, "The Gonfalon Raised Tonight" and "Rufus Woodpecker . . ." were both held back from Olson's collected poems that Grove Press eventually published as *The Distances.* And as late as 1961, Hugh Kenner, who had requested work from Olson for the *National Review,* passed up "Across Space and Time." (It was then published by Gerrit Lansing in his magazine *Set.*) In other words, Olson himself tried to publish many of the poems published here, desired to have them published at one time, so it may not be entirely relevant to ask whether he would have wished them included in his *Collected Poems.*

I, too, might have withheld the three-line poem beginning "Indian trinity . . ." from July 1967, were it not for the discovery that Olson—while acknowledging the poem as "slight"—sent it out for publication with the request, "don't at all think the 'slightness' of this is an imperviousness." [6]

The poet also intended to publish others of the poems made public here for the first time, but for special considerations or circumstances. He writes to John Wieners, for example, then editing *Measure:* "*The Writ* (promised earlier) but I remember myself that Villiers [the magazine's English printer, also early printer of *Origin*] can't set a wide one for the life of 'em." Again, M. L. Rosenthal accepted "A 2nd Musical Form, for Dave Young" for the *Nation,* although in the transition to a new poetry editor it never saw print and the manuscript was lost.

---

6. Note to the editor of the Washington University student literary magazine, *Freelance* (at Washington University Libraries), although the poem was apparently never published. That the poem also depends in part on a relatively inaccessible reference—"Etchimin," another name for the Passamaquody Indians of Maine—makes it even less a candidate for widespread enjoyment.

Moreover, a number of the poems published while Olson was alive were not originally published with his explicit intentions or approval. "These Days," for instance, had been sent as part of a letter to William Carlos Williams, as a greeting and sign of creative life, and forwarded by him to a magazine editor, who decided to print it. Another, beginning "pitcher, how . . . ," was originally given informally to Fielding Dawson at Black Mountain for his birthday in 1951 and not published until 1958, when Dawson was editing a little magazine and wanted Olson represented. Robert Creeley on his own initiative sent "The Red Fish-of-Bones" to *Poetry* as a place that might pay a little to the needy Olson. (Subsequent appearances in that magazine were the result of the direct invitation of editor Henry Rago.) Jonathan Williams used "For a Man Gone to Stuttgart . . . ," written for him in 1953 while he was in the U.S. Army Medical Corps, to "inaugurate" his *Elegies & Celebrations* (1962), writing Olson afterwards. *"For my friend"* had been given to John Clarke in Buffalo, who later published it in the *Magazine of Further Studies,* returning the manuscript to Olson.

Many other poems were sent to friends, itself a kind of publishing. Ezra Pound, Corrado Cagli, Ben Shahn, Caresse Crosby, Edward Dahlberg, Frances Boldereff, Monroe Engel, Robert Creeley, Frank Moore, Jean Riboud, Robin Blaser, Donald Allen, Philip Whalen—all received copies of poems not otherwise published. Two early poems, "Atalanta" and "White Horse," were sent to the Guggenheim Foundation for his file as examples of his work. Later, in the 1960s, Olson sent or gave poems to friends like Edward Dorn or Ed Sanders, knowing they would be published. Again, the history of Olson's relationship with his writings strongly argues that his *Collected Poems* should not be limited to only those poems which by force of circumstance had been published during his lifetime.

Many of Olson's poems went unpublished simply because they were overlooked, lost to the day's accumulation, the compulsion to keep on with it, pushing around the "bend" of the "nest" or "next second" (as he writes in "I, Maximus"), which when fulfilled makes a perfect whole. Until then, it is the process that counts, even if the path occasionally seems tortuous. Many manuscripts were withheld not because Olson doubted their value, but because they were misplaced or the time was not right for a retrospective pause. (Every poet loves a "run," a hot streak.) Some sense of the situation is given in Olson's 24 April 1961 letter to LeRoi Jones (at Simon Fraser University Library): "And wot happens when I take my clothes off last night? I knock a pile of papers (mss.) on to the floor—& I am staring at my poem to you on Election Day After Afternoon ["The Hustings" from November 1960]—by god, I'm going to see again if etc." He may never have found enough time or "etc." to his satisfaction, but there is no doubt that "The Hustings," in both its versions, is a significant poem.[7]

In this regard, Olson's attitude toward publishing becomes increasingly like that of Frank O'Hara, with manuscripts stuffed in drawers or entrusted to the care of friends. As John Ashbery observes in his introduction to *The Collected Poems of Frank O'Hara:* "That [this volume] should turn out to be a volume of the present dimensions will surprise those who knew him, and would have surprised Frank even more. Dashing the poems off at odd moments . . . he would then put them away in drawers and cartons and half forget them. Once when a publisher asked him for a manuscript he spent weeks and months combing the apartment, enthusiastic and bored at the same time, trying to assemble the poems. Finally he let the project drop, not because he didn't wish his work to appear, but because his thoughts were elsewhere." Olson did less "dashing off" of poems than O'Hara, perhaps, but he was just as reluctant to relax his drive for the sake of the temporary satisfaction of a literary reputation. He was not a skillful manager of his affairs in the corporate sense, an orchestrator or manipulator of a career. If anything, he failed in the other extreme. His ceaseless, uncompromising independence cost him publishing offers, professional posts, reading tours, academic exposure—all the conventional steps toward a successful public career. Not that he was above press-agentry, for he could provoke drama and invoke a style like the best of the rest, but he wanted recognition on his own terms. And those terms always involved the work, not the legend.

---

7. Another example occurs in a letter, ca. 15 August 1964, to Robert Kelly, then editing *Matter* (among Kelly's papers in the Poetry Collection, SUNY Buffalo): "I've been through everything and the damned poem, beautiful though I think it was—using Hurrian directly with Englese is GONE! Unless somewhere in all this paper river I will fish it out *later*." (The poem, probably either "'home,' to the shore . . ." or "Her Headland . . ."—both from March 1964—was found among the poet's papers after his death and included in *The Maximus Poems.*) Still another reflection of the condition of Olson's manuscripts can be had from the following letter to Donald Allen from Gloucester, 31 May 1966 (Literary Archives, University of Connecticut Library), concerning the poem "A Part of the Series on the Paths":

My *dear* Don,
   I am stuck, very much, because a missing page of *mss* I remember decisively was on the back of a letter written to you *possibly* from Wyoming [though it cld have been 1963 here]

—I am equally almost positive I asked you once   & not too long after   to check & either copy or return the passage on the reverse to me [I enclose the kind of A&P block paper it was written on
   —wld you blessedly & graciously do it again for me? I need it actually for a potential *book*—& am shrieking from the thought I *cannot* restore the style or content of it [It *was* on a *fierce* & *very local Kentucky* pair of *Brothers* . . .

HELP ME AS MUCH AS YOU *POSSIBLY* CAN. A <u>PLEA</u>!!

Olson's entire publishing history indicates there is sufficient justification for making these poems available, even though he expressed no explicit wish for their publication. The poems will speak for themselves, of course, but one of the surprising things is the range of material as well as styles, quite in addition to the fascination of viewing a poet's development over thirty years. Some of the early work might be considered preliminary, youthful, even though written when the poet was in his thirties—but it is absolutely necessary in terms of displaying his full development. In his beginnings (many of the early poems show the influence of Yeats and Blake), he simultaneously represents and strains against the poetic inheritance he was born into, until erupting in 1950 to help shape the era with an ars poetica of his own.

Not every poetic fragment among Olson's papers has been included here. As many as three hundred poems and scraps have been left behind, not counting those which will appear in a volume of auxiliary *Maximus* poems. Some were too fragmentary, others illegible; some were painfully trite or belabored, offering only an unrewarding woodenness, undeveloped sentiment, flatness without challenge. They are unsuccessful as poems by a variety of criteria, but above all when measured by the standard of Olson's previously published poems as well as by his statements on poetics—not only "Projective Verse," but other public statements such as "A Foot Is to Kick With," "A Later Note on Letter #15," or "you can't use words as ideas. . . ." Unlike the poems included here, they would be of interest only to the most specialized scholars and otherwise of no advantage to Olson's reputation or to the world of poetry at large.

Relatively few poems had to be abandoned to oblivion on the basis of legibility. In only one poem, the final poem, was there any uncertainty that the text could be presented exactly as Olson conceived it, although in two other instances—identified in the textual notes at the end of the volume—it was necessary to forgo the poet's illegible emendations in order to preserve at least his basic, original typed text. The same standards offered in my *Editing the Maximus Poems*, pp. ix–x, for evaluating unique holograph manuscripts, obtained in preparing this edition: "A manuscript . . . had to be legible, ninety-eight percent, say, legible. If it was handwritten, it had to be able to be transcribed with certainty, not only as far as individual words were concerned, but also the poet's intended order of lines and sections. . . . Moreover, no crucial words—those upon which the success of the poem depends—could be out of reach."

A number of poems identifiable as alternate or withheld *Maximus* poems have been set aside, as mentioned, for a separate volume in accordance with the poet's wishes. Some were published by Olson, such as "a Dogtown Common blues" and "The Ridge," but most were not. It was not always the easiest distinction to make, since a number of the unpublished poems concern persons and places occurring in *The Maximus Poems,* yet may not be properly part of that series. I based my decisions on the degree of independence from the sequence a poem seemed to exhibit. "The Librarian" confused Olson himself in that regard when it was first written. The "rat-hole" poem, focusing on Gloucester inventor John Hays Hammond, Jr., is another good example. Olson did not consider it a part of the *Maximus* series at the time of its writing in March 1960 or later when assembling *Maximus Poems IV, V, VI.* The poem seems to be limited to a study of Hammond. Despite direct echoes of *Maximus* materials, such as references to Cashes Ledge and John Smith's poem "The Sea Marke" and the recurrent "dogs," the subject remains Hammond himself and his bid for im-mortality, rather than Gloucester or more related concerns of Maximus. The later "Ferrini—I" from January 1963 is yet another example, despite the fact that Vincent Ferrini is very much a "person," as Olson writes, of *The Maximus Poems* and an inte-gral part of Gloucester life. On the other hand, the following poem titled "On Stop-ping Looking Out" strongly depends on its association with "On first Looking out through Juan de la Cosa's Eyes" from *Maximus,* as well as with the withheld *Maxi-mus* letters from 1954–1955, "The Land-Songs of Maximus," "On David Ingram," and "Further Stories of the Islands and the Roads" (see *OLSON,* no. 6, Fall 1976, pp. 35–43):

> Juan de la Cosa, Cabeza de Vaca, David Ingram—me.
> He walked with his eyes, he walked in his flayed skin, he walked
> The blue on lighter blue of receding ranges,
> water on water, the courses of buffalo,
> and rivers, some snows, before there were so many men the trace
> got obliterated. Now to restore
> the double path, the world
> and any man's mother, until
> he can look into
> himself, stare
> at the fire, rouse himself
> via himself, give out
> what is in. What is
> in?

Shared references or a shared allusion are not enough. Otherwise the "sonnet" (as Olson called it) "I'm With You" would be as much a part of the *Maximus* series as the La Cosa poem, drawing as they both do from Keats's "On First Looking into Chap-man's Homer."

Thus poems with the spirit as well as the references of Maximus were held aside for a volume of their own, along with "'light sits under one's eyes . . .'" from *Archaeologist of Morning,* now that it is realized how little a role Olson had in the making of that collection.[8] From *Archaeologist of Morning,* I have also withheld three pieces as being prose rather than poetry, reserving them for the anticipated collection of Olson's various notes and essays: *"place; & names,"* which Olson himself called "prose" in a note to LeRoi Jones from about January 1962 (now at the Arents Library, Syracuse University); "A Note for Anyone Able To," which despite its lineation (ambiguous at best) is a straightforward prose note, written as such to Robert Kelly, then editing *Matter,* and signed "'Outis"; and, finally, "you can't use words as ideas. . . ."

Another fragment in *Archaeologist of Morning* had originally been excerpted by John Wieners from an April 1957 note to him from Olson and printed in *Measure* as "of WOMEN." This too has been withheld, even though it may appear to work as a poem (it is certainly succinct and suggestive enough). The full note, written on both sides of a small sheet of *Black Mountain Review* notepaper (a photocopy in the editor's possession made possible by Wieners), begins:

> how goes eet?
> Wot abt this black magic
> #2—yes?
> stress

8. The poem beginning, "When I think of what Fitz Hugh Lane didn't do . . ." (*Archaeologist of Morning,* p. [226]), given the (unauthorized) title "'light sits under one's eyes . . .'" by the editor of the *Gloucester Times,* where it first appeared, is definitely a *Maximus* poem; it is not one bit different from the long "I'm going to hate to leave this Earthly Paradise . . ." (*Maximus,* pp. 592–596), written earlier that August and called a *Maximus* poem when published by Olson in *Stony Brook.* It will be inserted in the collected *Maximus Poems,* following p. 596, at the earliest opportunity. In editing *The Maximus Poems* for the University of California Press, it had been assumed that *Archaeologist of Morning* was an authorized volume, one in which Olson had directly approved the selections, and consequently that its poems were not eligible for inclusion in *Maximus.* It has since become apparent that was not the case, however, so the necessary change will be made. The poem in question, therefore, does not appear in the present volume. The poem "Rocking Meter over Desolation" has likewise been withheld for the volume of alternative *Maximus* poems.

Two poems from *Archaeologist of Morning* with Gloucester as subject or setting have been retained in this volume: "An 'Enthusiasm,'" celebrating the Gloucester painter Fitz-Hugh Lane, and the oft-remembered, because least typical, *"Scream"* to the editor of the local newspaper—both originally published primarily for local attention in the *Gloucester Daily Times.* Not quite *Maximus* poems, because of the specificity of their address (more specific and topical than even Maximus!), they at least remind the reader that Olson, like Williams before him, was a decidedly local writer and drew strength from the universalization (no matter he hated the term and the concept) of the particular.

Finally, a version of "The Binnacle" titled "Maximus, home again, crying out, to all" will appear in the auxiliary *Maximus* volume, so that the same essential poem will appear in both volumes, reminding one of the ultimate interrelation of Olson's concerns.

silk stockings. ————&
  panties
        all lure,
  and sorcery
  is the I Ching
  in John Cages . . .

This is followed by Olson's instruction to turn the sheet over, where the message continues. The text with a crude drawing of a hand, photoreproduced by Wieners in *Measure,* resumes and can be accurately transcribed as follows (there are three misreadings in the *Archaeologist of Morning* printing):

WHITE HANDS
(on the ladies'
white legs—*no*
dirtiness LEFT
    Thus magic
    is not for, or for only,
    the PRIESTS

Wieners found the note instructive, writing Michael Rumaker on 29 April 1957: "Olson writes in No: 2 I must stress silk stockings, panties, white hands on the ladies white legs . . . ," and he also quotes the note in full in a letter to Edward Dorn, 30 April 1957 (both letters in Literary Archives, University of Connecticut Library). If Olson had acknowledged the excerpt or approved its later use as a poem, the piece would have been readily included here. Since he did not, it must be relegated to the poet's collected letters.

On the other hand, "The Story of an Olson, and Bad Thing" has been included here even though Olson himself seemed uncertain as to its nature. (See *Editing the Maximus Poems,* p. xvii, n. 3; he also left the piece out of the original edition of his collected poems which became *The Distances*.) The somewhat ambiguous three-liner beginning "turn now and rise . . ."—with its vague echo of the Sumerian-inspired motto of the magazine *Origin*—has also been kept. Not only does an original handwritten manuscript survive among Olson's papers, but he thought enough of it to copy it out a second time and pointedly send it to a magazine editor for publication, no matter how disproportionate it may seem standing alone.

The following persons and institutions were extremely generous in providing copies of texts for publication or comparison. Above all, I wish to thank the University of Connecticut's Homer Babbidge Library, which has the responsibility of caring for

Olson's extensive papers. I am also deeply indebted to the Archive for New Poetry, University of California, San Diego (Michael Davidson, Edith Jarolim); Archives of American Art, Smithsonian Institution; Bancroft Library, University of California, Berkeley (Peter E. Hanff); Beinecke Library, Yale University; Robin Blaser; Butler Library, Columbia University (Kenneth Lohf); Harvey Brown; Robert Creeley; Robert Duncan; Monroe Engel; George Arents Reference Library, Syracuse University (Kathleen Manwaring); Robert Hogg; Humanities Research Center, University of Texas (Ellen S. Dunlap, Cathy Henderson); Mary T. Knollenberg; Gerrit Lansing; Lilly Library, Indiana University (Saundra Taylor); Ralph Maud; Kenneth McRobbie; Frank L. Moore; Morris Library, Southern Illinois University; Henry A. Murray; The Poetry Collection, State University of New York at Buffalo (Robert Bertholf); Wilmott Ragsdale; Reed College Library (Martha Bergquist); Jean Riboud; Merton M. Sealts, Jr.; Simon Fraser University Library (Percilla Groves); State University of New York at Stony Brook Library (Evert Volkersz); Gael Turnbull; University Research Library, UCLA (James Davis); Washington University Libraries (Holly Hall, Timothy Murray); Philip Whalen; John Wieners; and Jonathan Williams.

I would also like to thank the following for help with textual clarification and dating: Donald Allen; Richard Bridgman; Gerald Burns; Cid Corman; Fales Library, New York University (Frank Walker); Andrew Hoyem; Kent State University Libraries (Dean H. Keller); Newberry Library, Chicago (Carolyn A. Sheehy); University of Delaware Library (Dolores Altemus); and University of Pennsylvania Library (Neda M. Westlake).

In addition, the following provided recordings of Olson reading that were also helpful in establishing texts: American Poetry Archive, San Francisco State University (Gordon Craig); Beloit College (Marion Stocking); Fielding Dawson; Goddard College Learning Aids Center; Kemp Houck; Robert Payne; Poetry Collection, State University of New York at Buffalo (Karl Gay); Poetry Room, Harvard College Library (Stratis Haviaras); and Fred Wah. Each helped assure the accuracy of this edition.

Finally, Eric Purchase was of essential help with the proofreading, and Barbara Ras skillfully guided the manuscript through press.

George F. Butterick

THE
COLLECTED
POEMS OF
CHARLES
OLSON

Purgatory Blind

Between the river and the sea,
Annisquam and Atlantic
Boundaries,
The moors of doubt and self-mistrust maintaining
A perilous structure of land against the flood.

Over all the gulls,
White, hungry, gray,
Insisting
In flight or rest
Their toughness.

He, restless,
Wingless,
Hungry for more than ravage, food or flight.

Today the waters
Sea, sky, river
Overwhelm the fragile land.
Moon's swollen tides,
A Hercules, force him upward
Antaeus torn from the ground.

How, down?
What wings to descend?
Where, warm and tender earth?
When gull to be?

Between the creek and sea
The moor.

You, Hart Crane

Space—shroud and swaddle—you wore,
transcontinental blood of Indian girl,
beat of your dream. Fledged by the modern,
new Archeopteryx, you Hart Crane
drank the poison as Crockett the cloud,
tall man's thirst

I remember your death, reject all answers.
Noon, tall time, at Orizaba stern you stood.
In ecstasy of wake you who made a bridge leaped

Birth's Obituary

Plane's flight your helix, transcontinental blood
Of Indian girl, fledged by the modern,
New Archeopteryx, you Hart Crane
Flew where others falter.

I remember your death, and reject all answers.
Noon, high time, at Orizaba stern you stood.
In ecstasy of wake you who made a bridge leaped!
Span made act, your death another Myth propelled.

Space, our shroud and swaddle, makes each a navigator.
Cathay lies where we must go, and if you end
In channel as another did in chains,
Oh Hart, wave-right you are!

You drank the poison as Crockett the cloud,
Tall man's thirst. After slake of sea,
Gyre on your tongue the tempest of the moon
Loud in your throat the wings of the sun.

Atalanta

Atalanta ran swift course
the inward tender of her foot
fire upon my source

Leda lay beside the sea
made Michelangelo of me

        Her draiad eyes, naiad arms
        ended the body of a boy's alarms

White Horse

White horse he was, to her black foal.
Behold! they were desire
They wooed, against a world in shoal
feared their fire.

He grew more human,
less woman she,
image approached
animality.

With grace he asked
return to world;
reply and hate,
to a tree she curled.

Fire Is

Fire is
where flame lives!
Cockleshell and cockleheart!

Where man is most
in woman lost!
Cockleshell and cockleheart!

Light is where
the night is bare!
Cockleshell and cockleheart!

Love is dark
and love is bleak, o!
cockleshell, o!
cockleheart!

Fable for Slumber

An animal dwelt
In the body of a child.
Animal and child,
The man was wild.

The child asked all,
His appetite huge.
The world so small
Gave subterfuge.

Who failed the child
The animal struck.
In a world too mild
The man was amok.

His hate a tooth,
His word a claw,

His anger truth
His ego law.

The child of love
Made man of hate,
The frustrate child
The animal ate.

Hymn to the Word

Cock and cunt
cock and cunt
Take your joy
O take your joy!

Fuck and bunt
fuck and bunt
Lay the night
O lay the night!

Lock and bite
lock and bite
Draw the blood
O draw the blood!

Suck and tongue
suck and tongue
Drain all lust
O drain all lust!

Lock and bite
suck and tongue
fuck and bunt
cock and cunt
O

Tomorrow

I am Gilgamesh,
an Ur world is in me
to inhabit.

Race of waters run
in the blood
red with the fathers.

They told me of flood,
of the earth dissolved,
of drowned mountains.

I live in the land
and know people,
see love recur.

They said the heart
knows no evolution:
it is as it was when it is.

They called me Gilgamesh
and gave me Ur
where I dwell.

The House

The land outside, and the night is the enemy's.

I watched their night descend and cause our eyes
to scatter like small animals. I saw the invaded land
separate, break up to islands in a flood then to be
surrounded easily by their arms.

I am in this house with many people whom I love
though none I intimately know. I pass from room to
room offering a solace they, nor I sitting among them,
need. They are aware as I there is night and no land
beyond the circle of light this kerosene lamp sweetens.

Nor they nor I speak for their eyes are quiet,
do not scatter.

Inside this house we sit and no longer does it
seem to matter that, without, there is no man between
the black of water and of night.

By Cure of—Sulfa

See where, gathered, the wharves
at the Sign of the Wheel crawled
the lobster —father! o

The red brick in the trap soaked
in gasoline over Oceanwood the sign
of the Dog Hot   —o schooner!

And the tercentenary the clam caught
you shall live conjunction of
father, son & sardine sandwich
o! Gloucester!

Law

Blackstone is gone.
They laid his unwieldy weight
in a crate
rolled the ton through the gate
and carried him away.

Man shall have new law
man shall have new law!

A Lion upon the Floor

Begin a song

Power and the abstract
distract a man
from his own gain

Begin a song of six cents

foul his eye
deprive his hand upon a nape and hip
of kiss beak claw
—a lion upon the floor

Sing a song

Let the salt in
begin
cut the heart open
the blood will run with sun
the wind will put the belly back
and the rain the roar below

Sing a song of six cents
sing a song of seven seas

The tall grass green
the muscle in the sea
an axe to cut a continent
an ox to walk a sky

Sing a song of six cents
sing a song of seven seas
give a girl to each man
to put him on his knees

Lion, spring!

Sing, Mister, Sing

Hills are grey elephants
the sun is a prince
the plains is an ocean
Bigmans pants

       pound the earth, pound the earth
       I dance, I dance

The prince is astride
the grey hills glide
the ocean's a tide
Bigmans hide

       round the earth, round the earth
       I ride, I ride

Ride and prance
brag and dance
round the world, round the world
Bigmans chance

The K

Take, then, my answer:
there is a tide in a man
moves him to his moon and,
though it drop him back
he works through ebb to mount
the run again and swell
to be tumescent I

The affairs of men remain a chief concern

We have come full circle.
I shall not see the year 2000
unless I stem straight from my father's mother,
break the fatal male small span.
If that is what the tarot pack proposed
I shall hang out some second story window
and sing, as she, one unheard liturgy

Assume I shall not.
Is it of such concern when what shall be
already is within the moonward sea?

Full circle: an end to romans, hippocrats and christians.
There! is a tide in the affairs of men to discern

Shallows and miseries shadows from the cross,
ecco men and dull copernican sun.
Our attention is simpler
The salts and minerals of the earth return
The night has a love for throwing its shadows around a man
a bridge, a horse, the gun, a grave.

Pacific Lament

In memory of William Hickey, a member of
the crew of the U.S.S. *Growler,* lost at sea
in February, 1944.

Black at that depth
turn, golden boy no more
white bone to bone, turn
hear who bore you weep
hear him who made you
deep there on ocean's floor
turn
as waters stir;
turn, bone of man

Cold as a planet is
cold, beat of blood no more
the salt sea's course
along the bone jaw white
stir, boy, stir
motion without motion
stir, and hear
love come down.

Down as you fell
sidewise, stair to green stair
without breath, down
the tumble of ocean
to find you, bone
cold and new among the ships
and men and fish askew.

You alone o golden boy no more
turn now and sleep
washed white by water

sleep in your black deep
by water out of which man came
to find his legs, arms, love, pain.
Sleep, boy, sleep
in older arms than hers,
rocked by an older father;
toss no more,
love;
sleep.

She

You are to me, love, half family half tree
You go in two directions, double my joy
Swift away and sure at home, Atalanta and Penelope

Less the latter than her quality
Men have not made the image of:
A permanence, a skill we only value now
That women, as a rule, not only cannot cook, my love
But cannot—rhyme—as well!

It is not chastity and tricks
But taste and wonder, knacks
Of trees and wind, hills and their covering
Contour of earth and undersurge of sea

You are to me, love, these, a simile
To run around my metaphor

And laugh, and jibe with glee
The bulk of my magnificence
The consequence of me!

She, Thus

The bottom of the air is disturbed as with an undertow
Breathing is difficult, and though the winds blow
Heaviness is upon me.

      His strictures tighten, bind my wonder
      cramp the questions of my flesh, and the thunder
      of his voice makes my ear huddle like a child.
      Only in sleep do I belong to myself.

      I cannot recapture the play I need
      the run and nonny of a sun and sea.
      I am too quick for his slow pace
      and my blood, errant if slight
      Atalanta race
      guys his deliberate course.

      I drop my apples. He stops, admires.
      Something he fails to do hurts like wires.

      I intent, a bird, ask if this be love
      He, turtle wise, knows, huge appetite on move

I work and, inside, prick myself, a needle
I waste, and call myself a weed, a nettle
And yet I know I am as lovely as a flower
as subtle as the image in the pool
a queen of love, fashioned for misrule.

In the meadow where he wooed me
on that rock I caught.

I look back and there, apt, he comes
Where are the other ones?
He does not seem to run the faster
and yet, I do not know, he is the master.

O make the wind blow sweeter
O make the air be light
for I would have my breath again
and be your love tonight!

The Night

I waked, and sat out the watch, the night.
With a full moon the land was bright.

> I had disliked them both, flight doctor, engineer
> the latter a pulp crammed with 'sir'
> and Medical Dick, theatric, stuffed with career
> dead men in his mouth, and a sex leer

At three the baby cried in the house next door.
The white dog fed her pups at four.

I disposed of their argument: cold or dry run
with the warhead in, the QED
is a hit, and death

In the neighborhood at six there was an unheard stir.
Men's feet scratched the street in half an hour.

I remembered an accident on a city street:
the human body broken is a doll of flesh.
They said it was a hand at the water's break
disclosed the pilot in the mangrove mesh.

Motors roar in the predawn dark.
Cannon at seven sound the end of sleep.

In the morning she said my skin was soft
my eyes brown, and round like a boy's
my flesh pink: it was the night.

A Translation

from Havelock Ellis

This was her dream:

I had gone to bed worried with the troubles of the day,
and full of fierce revolt against society.
I tried to soothe myself with thoughts of him, away.

I do not know at what hour of the night
I seemed to find myself, quite sudden, naked

in a sweet place round with sun
and full of joy to walk alone thus bathed in light.

And as I walked my skin grew firm, my breasts regained
Their beauty and their youth. With one thing only was I stained:
on my body the wrinkles of childbirth still remained.
Which my hands from instinct tried to hide
While my heart so gently to me cried:

"They are the wounds of the war to which women go;
  he cannot but love you so."

Then I knew.
And knew that I could tell him:
there is this corner in the world
where we may walk quite naked without shame.

Thus did she dream.

Her Dream, Half Remembered

A Translation from Havelock Ellis

There, quick, a crowd was on me. Jugglers, giants,
Sullen hunchbacks, tumbling dwarfs. Acrobats whirled,
And I was full of fear of the returning world.

But there was one, a man, small, erect, all bronze
His copper skin patina to my eye

Who watched me dance, with half descent and bound
From holly tree to sunwhite shadowed ground.

He held the flute he played with serpent arms,
And kissed me as I floated down with knees apart
Cubed and motleyed like some clown, astart.

Ballad for Americans

We have no history

Anglo
mechanico
Klaxon
saxon
yes
—a horn for the past to blow
into our empty ear

do you hear
Kabotchnik?
no?
don't you know about
the Battle of Bunker Crop?
that's OFFICIAL, hunk!
or how the rude (you) farmers stood
at Conk Bridge and Lax Green?
Antidiedem? Bull's Fun?
Yeah, the Rebels yelled to see the Yankees run

you got another story, eh?
so's the South—her story
and she's stuck with it:
licked
she began

Who says America's not begun
—see how we run!
we always win
watch the other guy lose
we call it history, boys
make a lotta noise
whattaya mean, no joys
jeezus
whaddaya want, toys?

I could tell you a story
it ain't in the books
What do you say about my woman's looks?
that's important, see
I'd always won until she licked me,
yeah,
she gave me the gettysburg

get it? (swing it)
I got a history
you got a history
the South's got a history
and we'll all get a history when we get the gettysburg!

Key West

"Just the kind of a guy who
used to play the piano
in the whore houses
when I was a kid,"

was what Sully said.
He had me pegged.

"You'd think, from the size of him
he'd be a stevedore," was Canby's idea.
"But he don't know any more about low poker
than a hog does about the Bible!"

At first they figured I was F.B.I.
Ditto three sailors at the Cuban place
where I went for bollos and fried salami.
"Listen, jerk, nobody don't work
in a dump like this in war."
"If he don't, he must be queer"

or

—an FBI piano player

in a whore house

New England March

Annisquam
Atlantic
river, sea
roar
with the moon tide

The moor,
frantic,
rots with flood

Over all the gulls
white
hungry
gray

Lower Field—Enniscorthy

The sheep like soldiers
black leggings black face
lie boulders
in the pines' shade
at the field's sharp edge:
ambush and bivouac

A convocation of crows overhead
mucks

in their own mud and squawk
makes of the sky
a sty

A bee is deceived
takes the rot of a stump
for honeycomb

Two black snakes cross
in a flat spiral
the undisciplined path

Report: over all
the sun

Said Adam

I

The day red like the cardinal
color, not song
(his song the day's inadequate whippoorwill)

Dusk the whiskered bird
(no flight—or light)
from the ground sharp the sound:
whip-poor-will!
whip-poor-will!

Night, and still the bees
the large linden hums a honey loom

their work a wind,
no color no light.

II

Day and night we humans wander
without color without light
aimless as cattle feed
without wind without flight.

This tree does not bend its neck
needs not to,
goes upward year in and dark
at ease, absurd, in nature's round.

Cortex and spine,
bulls we are
caught in habit
prevented by a fence
from our desire.

III

All else moves easily
bee and flaming bird
tree, light and whipping song.
We lumber
make enigma
lack what we want
locked in what we have.

Our choice like the shades of green
but we limit spring
lose the joy of our short season
refuse the color
leave the light no place to go.

Cry why
do we have to choose
can we not feed and run
as bee and bull
wear red and sing
as whippoorwill?

IV

In the night
the whiskered song whips out:
whip-poor-will!
whip-poor-will!
whip-poor-will!

Burial Ground

The slug and the rat possess the dead.

The earth is red
the grass is green:
this is said
to dish the spleen

The ant and stone
grant peace to the bone.

The wind is the same
the sun is the sun:
this is the tone
put an end to moan

    Make me no memory
    make me no tomb
    let them have the cemetery
    I'll take the womb

Enniscorthy Suite

I. The Dry Lot

Atop the down pasture
the wind the wind
incessant in the trees
a shore
pours
a distant sea

One side (the south) is still, then snap, the woods!
craw
bob white bob white
still
huhwheep tzuz, eep eep eep
snap
the woods!

The red road down the north
quiet as a road
lazy in the sun
knowing its own worth

      This is the dry lot, this is the dry lot
      the long slope, sweep, sleep
      up green up green
      green to begin
      green each year anew
      green atop and down
      unceasing green

The long earth the red earth
longer than blood
between the wood and the road
the wind and me

II. Lower Field

The sheep like soldiers
black leggings black face
lie boulders
in the pines' shade
at the field's sharp edge:
ambush and bivouac

A convocation of crows overhead
mucks
in their own mud and squawk
makes of the sky
a sty

A bee is deceived
takes the rot of a stump
for honeycomb

Two black snakes cross
in a flat spiral
the undisciplined path

Report: over all
the sun

III. Bottom Land

The barley's bent beards shine
the oats stand green
spring, it is the spring
green and green

The barley's bent beards shine
the oats a darker green
spring, it is the clover
love and lover

Spring, it is the barley
spring, it is the oats!
Spring, it is the one time,
Sing, springtime!

IV. The Family Plot

Burn the grass as the ground the grave
the sun stays green, the live alive

Turn the soil as the worms the dead
the wind is young, the rain is red

Gray is the stone, dark is the tree

The dead are alone
the live are alone

Alive and alone at Enniscorthy

The Town

I

Sheep graze where the cemetery was
where the houses were the wheat grows
o mourn the town

> There is a photo:
> the church with bulbous spires
> the school
> houses of white stone
> poppies and a street

Stones in the stubble
wheat and rubble
o mourn the town

> We know what the people did:
> worked in the fields
> part time in the mines

It is necessary to understand:
now, where the town was, it is empty earth
a mere contour of yellow clay
alone like a pasture in the sun
part planted to wheat
part feed for sheep and bee

> They stripped the men and slaughtered them.
> They took away the women and children.
> They left not one stone standing of 112 buildings.
> Of 667 people only 2, women, are known to be alive.

2

Three years it lay
now, the third spring after, there is a space cleared
25 feet square without rubble
with two dirt mounds flattened
on each two lines crossed
white pebble by pebble

> They marched the men naked to the cemetery
> shot them in rows of 10
> did not bury them in the cemetery
> (today it is a field of clover)
> instead, had the tombstones hauled away
> later, in what had been the center of the town
> had a hole dug
> not big enough
> stuffed and pressed the bodies in, ploughed
> turned the earth over

It is not known if the square now cleared, and the hole, correspond.

3

There is another photo a family group
a father, mother, two brothers, a sister-in-law and child.
What became of the sister-in-law and child is not known.

It started at night on a Tuesday in June.
We in the next village heard the first shots at 4 a.m.
rifles, machine-guns, pistols.
It kept up until 8.

The first fire was started at 7:30.
It was the mayor's house, the rest burned for three days.

They they came to our village
told us to open our windows
there would be explosions
would break our panes.
They brought up artillery and shelled the town.
This lasted a whole day.
Planes circled
watched the shells burst.

They brought Jews from a concentration camp
made them bury the dead.

4

Pieces of stone
scattered in the wheat
part of the church
part of the school
trouble the feet
the wind and the sheep
who mourn the town

Afternoon

A tiger came
out of the forest
where macaws
and monkeys
scream

Profoundly
he walked
across the field
to the white river
and sat down
in the sun

Behind the green
he saw the blue
behind the blue
the red

In the woods
a bird of paradise
flowered

Quietly the tiger
ate the sun

2 Propositions and 3 Proof

The Propositions:

1

He is a good workman.
It is enough to say.
A man is his work
and what a man is
can you tell a tree

2

The blood is a season
like the running sap
the root? memory coursing
the round rings reach out restrain
o cylinder of air
grow leaf bough green gray
the bark stays dark

The Proof:

1

Three sit though the figure is one.
The scene the Cafe Tabourey
The time the night before All Soul's Day
The year 1873.
Dramatis personae: none

masks? my face needs no enlargement
it means exactly what I have said
literally and completely, in all respects.

my voice? I gave it hell to sound against.
They do not hear.

drama, no. I know no such accomodation.
I am no longer an other. Je est.

Three sit. That boy this man the Abyssinian. One.
without ghost. 10. as platinum is.
The clothes? bateau blue. The cheeks: pink hollow brown.
Platinum eyes consult the red sea

2

Space—shroud and swaddle—you wore.
transcontinental blood of Indian girl
beat of your dream. Fledged by the modern
new Archeopteryx, you Hart Crane
drank the poison as Crockett a cloud.
Tall man's thirst.

I remember your death, reject all answers.
Noon, high time, at Orizaba stern you stood.
In ecstasy of wake you who made a bridge leaped

3

King Tching T'ang's inscription read:

AXE   TREE   SUN

The AXE to put away old habit

New as the young grass shoot,
wrote Kung, interpreting TREE

Look to a constant renovation LOOK to
as each new day
look: the sun!

on his bathtub:

AXE   TREE   SUN

A Lustrum for You, E.P.

I

So, Pound, you have found the gallows tree
you with your thumb at your nose
the word in your mouth dirty, and otherwise.

They'll cant your body, canto maker.
Sudden, and your freckled neck will break
as others', nameless, broke.

There was Booth's collaborators in a gray Washington snow
after another war.
Matthew Brady's camera slanted, one by one, to each adjustment
                                        of the noose.

Or do they shoot you now

2

You wanted to be historic, Yorick.
Mug the mike with your ABCs
you even made Sligo Willie sneeze:
revolutionary simpleton.
Ezra Pound, American.

Sing out, sing hate.
There is a wind, mister
where the smell, o anti-semite
in the nose is as
vomit, poet.

I quote: in a modern city the live man feels
or perceives this sort of thing as the savage
perceives in the forest.

3

You are your own best witness.
These are not the great days.
No hunt, sir, and what you take for bays,
Propertius, are the rattle of cans.

4

Listen, Montana, you've been right about a lot, sure.
The Civil War did drive everything out of the American mind,
you and Martin Van Buren included.
You have also said, a propos Jefferson and/or Pound: the
real life in regular verse is an irregular movement UNDER-
NEATH.

Private gain is not prosperity, but that the treasure of
a nation is its equity?

Yes, if a man isn't willing to take some risk for his
opinion, either his opinions are no good or he's no good.
Remember Heine? You have admired him. He walked through
a revolution too. He didn't have his eyes left, and he
wasn't as gay as you. It was paresis laid him low. (What
got you?) He left what he called his mattress grave and
found his way, blind, through the bullets in the street,
it was 1848, to the Louvre. He did it, he took the risk,
to have another look at Venus. What were you looking at
in a broadcasting studio?

5

There is a court
where order, traitor
—you stood with the lovers of ORDER
    19 years on that case/first case
keeps the fragrance of,
sometimes in the palm of a hand
also on street corners,
hyacinth and burnt feathers

Where the wind is a warm breath
it does not smell of flesh in a furnace

6

The sentence reads: lover of the obscene
                        by the obscene undone

                        fecit, Pound fecit

The Winter After

Bitter winter

Rain
Rain down, all moving things
Blind, with care as under-
ground go by each
Turned in
claws across the day
curled in their dark intent
go where?
> will rain
> does the sun
> will rain put out
> does the sun know
> will rain put out the fire,
> the bitter fire?

Winter wind
City wind
enters the bones
as fear comes
blows down as men move
weak
the next corner colder than the bones are cold

> Cold, when the fire comes
> the wind will make
> will the wind
> the fire higher
> will the wind be left
> or the heat be too much for the wind and the rain?

Wet snow
the wet street slow to let it gather
as men the death ahead
it falls as night exists
inhabiting itself
falls, whitens roof, pavement, ground
and if men stir

  or do the ashes also burn
  when men ignite the nitrogen of air?

Marry the Marrow

Marrow unvisited,
And then, visited,
The bones gone and the needed waters' return:
A tight relax as of the sea
Against the land
In flood.

Structure! least steel, most liquid:
The Annisquam and the Atlantic
At high fulfilled the land,
Brimmed and eased it.
Stretched fabric across the hips of the earth,
French cut,
Discovering the global curve beneath.

(Death is the untensed, the rigid,
What the worms enjoy,
Wood,
Naught.)

("There's tricks i' th' world,"
And disaster,
And so with love.)

But there's instancy.
And to lie in wait for it,
And to seize it,
It is to justify the stars.

Annul the Milky Way we do.
But then, quick as star's fall,
Your Cassiopeia and Charles' Wain do burn.

There's structure in the heavens.
Sickness is, to let the clouds decide.
Sometimes we make the sky.

Shall we string and tense the marrow more?

There Was a Youth
Whose Name Was Thomas Granger

I

From the beginning, SIN
and the reason, note, known from the start

says Mr. bradford: As it is with waters when
their streames are stopped or damed up, wickednes
(Morton, Morton, Morton)
here by strict laws as in no place more,
or so much, that I have known or heard of,
and ye same more nerly looked unto
(Tom Granger)
so, as it cannot rune in a comone road of liberty
as it would, and is inclined,
it searches every wher (everywhere)
and breaks out wher it getts vente, says he

Rest, Tom, in your pit where they put you
a great & large pitte digged of purposs for them
of Duxbery, servant, being aboute 16. or 17. years of age
his father & mother living at the time at Sityate

espetially drunkennes & unclainnes
incontinencie betweene persons unmaried
but some maried persons allso
And that which is worse
(things fearfull to name)

HAVE BROAK FORTH OFTENER THAN ONCE
IN THIS LAND

2

indicted for ye same) with
a mare, a cowe, tow goats, five sheep, 2. calves
and a turkey (Plymouth Plantation)

Now follows ye ministers answers

3

Mr Charles Channcys   a reverend, godly, very larned man
who shortly thereafter, due to a difference aboute baptising
he holding it ought only to be by diping
that sprinkling was unlawful, removed him selfe
to the same Sityate, a minister to ye church ther

in this case proved, by reference to ye judicials of Moyses
& see: Luther, Calvin, Hen: Bulin:. Theo: Beza. Zanch:
what greevous sin in ye sight of God,
by ye instigation of burning lusts, set on fire of hell,
to proceede to contactum & fricationem ad emissionem seminis,
        &c.,
& y^t contra naturam, or to attempt ye grosse acts of

4

Mr Bradford: I forbear perticulers.
And accordingly he was cast by ye jury,
and condemned.

                It being demanded of him
the youth confessed he had it of another
who had long used it in old England,
and they kept catle togeather.

44

And after executed about ye 8. of Sept^r, 1642.
A very sade spectakle it was; for first the mare,
and then ye cowe, and ye rest of ye lesser catle,
were kild before his face, according to ye law
Levit: 20.15.

and then he him selfe

           and no use made of any part of them

Trinacria

Who fights behind a shield
Is separate, weak of the world
Is whirled by sons of self, sown
As teeth, a full armed crop
Sprung from no dream
No givers of a fleece
Who bring their dragon blood inside
Reality, half slain

There is a sword. If not so armed
A man will hide within himself
The armed man too, but battle
Is an outside thing, the field
Its own reward, reality

        Join sword and shield, yield
        Neither ground, contend

45

And with one stroke behead
The three, the enemy

Then, like a Greek, emboss
The shield with legs, and boast
Of mighty ancestry.

La Préface

The dead in via
        in vita nuova
                in the way
You shall lament who know they are as tender as the horse is.
You, do not you speak who know not.

     "I will die about April 1st . . ." going off
     "I weigh, I think, 80 lbs . . ." scratch
     "My name is NO RACE" address
     Buchenwald   new Altamira cave
     With a nail they drew the object of the hunt.

Put war away with time, come into space.
It was May, precise date, 1940. I had air my lungs could breathe.
He talked, via stones   a stick   sea rock   a hand of earth.
It is now, precise, repeat. I talk of Bigmans organs
he, look, the lines! are polytopes.
And among the DPs—deathhead
                 at the apex
                     of the pyramid.

Birth in the house is the One of Sticks, cunnus in the crotch.
Draw it thus: (   ) 1910 (
It is not obscure. We are the new born, and there are no flowers.
Document means there are no flowers

and no parenthesis.

It is the radical, the root, he and I, two bodies
We put our hands to these dead.

The closed parenthesis reads: the dead bury the dead,

and it is not very interesting.
Open, the figure stands at the door, horror his
and gone, possessed, o new Osiris, Odysseus ship.
He put the body there as well as they did whom he killed.

Mark that arm. It is no longer gun.
We are born not of the buried but these unburied dead
crossed stick, wire-led, Blake Underground

The Babe
the Howling Babe

The Dragon-Fly

Noon. The tall trees uphold the sky
The wind makes a sea of the ripening rye.
But the sun is the element of the dragon-fly:

The oats are green, green is the rye
The great green is the dragon-fly

A round moon makes of the night a stage
Sets down spaced black trees as properties
Peoples the lawn with swans and arabesques:

But the black of the wing of the dragon-fly
Plants the night in the middle of the rye.

Epigraph to *Call Me Ishmael*

O fahter, fahter
gone amoong

O eeys that loke

Loke, fahter:
your sone!

Lalage!

The legs of Lalage toss, and toss, and toss
(l'esprit de femme)
against the canvas of the circus sky

The legs of Lalage whip, and whip, and whip
lie open as they turn, play
on bed of air, go straight, snap shut, curl
to make short thigh, stir
(as tho she dreamed)
her body's plange the new gratuity

Lalage! Lalage! her legs une porte aux bras
her arms une pointe, her act le grand tourner
her swing inverted fouette
on stage of revolutionary night

Or call her Lalagea and go back
to Horace and an image of a love
and sing, en rond en rond, as time does turn
as she turns, high, by single arm and ring
Sing: Lalage! Lalage! the legs of Lalage!

The Return

The dying of the day in the dying of the year
is wanhope.
The sun–deserted air, and the heart, hear like a huge ear
the kids and grackles.
The heart hurts
in the crevice which night will narrow.

Still
over the heads of things the sun throws spears.

The buildings wear their roofs and chimneys well,
wild you might say.
And we look up at the gold tree tops
as children will.

Bagatto

à Corrado

Double, double, twice the face
Tarot pool and tarot race

The MAN of MAGIC, beginning, prime
Number 1, major arcana, master of rime

Causer of terror, maker of sense
He'll read you the answer, whatever the tense

He sits at his table with crossed legs and tools
Observing the structures but, breaking the rules

He perfected his craft in a workmanlike manner:
a cup, a shoe, and awl, and a hammer

He raises his left hand to throw down the dice
The measure of fate: the event, and the price

His eye is green, his sleeve is red
He comes out of humus, of leaf and, the dead

His hat is a nimbus, infinity
Out of unsure man, by authority

He will will you your power, refract you your light
If you'll mount the tower, and not dread the height

For beneath the surface his twin is revealed
Together the key to what is concealed

Trouble, trouble, face to face
Tarot race in watery place

"Double, double, root and branch . . ."

Double, double, root and branch
Tarot dance is tarot chance

Birth in the house is the 1 of STICKS
the crotch, gashed, of a dark green tree
(the gash the flame that falls like a leaf).
Held in the hand: the lengthened arm of power
of sway achieved, by act on object, fire.
As suit it is a subtler story, of magics
black, and white. For Sticks are negative

obstacles, misfortune, sickness, loss
antinomy of Swords, the positive, what you profess.
As Swords your soul & goal, Sticks are adversative
the oppositions in events your self must meet
and match, if it will thrive, and make you king.
Born of this need, presented to this thing
adversity, you take the sword, fight, retreat,
return, strike out again, beat back the stick
and, in the winning of the field, declare your fortune
and your fate. For as the green tree shall be hewn
so struggle is the tarot law, attack
the sign of birth, strife the mark of life.

        Double, double, strife and trouble
        Man is chance and man is rebel.

The Fool

His number is zero, or twenty-one
Precedes the magick, or ends its run.
And here is significance, lost to those
Who scholiasts are, and follow their nose.
For this is no youth, silly and fey
Who drifts along in any old way.
And if the sense of this man is lost
It's due to the sickness with which we are crossed.

Beggar he is, and blessed with the mask:
he wears his arrogance, addressed to his task.
The motley, yes, the holes, the hunger
But no man, nor woman say he wrong her
He walks free, by field, or precipice, by swamp
To catch the light, or pain, and mock at pomp.
And what he follows he intends to find
Be it locked in other men, or in the wind.

The green man, they called him, in another time
When spring was open and life a mime
And men were foolish with little cause
And women—with no cause at all
He worked his havoc with a look and a call
And we all ran after—"down with laws"

Or wanderer, troubadour, disguised prince
He'll tell you a tale to make you wince
Or lead you a figure to cause you to dance
While the dull ones stand by and look askance.

Our father, we pary thee, Pantaloon
Who art in your attic an antique-antic
To give us this day our double Fool
And forgive us our Clown and Harlequin
As we our young Virgin, Columbine.

So come, great fool, all in your season
And spice our selves with your unreason
For we are in our own impasse
And need your holy foolishness!

À Constance, This Day

As swift and dying as the forms of flame
As brilliant, love

To hold the heart firm in the midst of same
To keep its eyes
And see as love sees

To lose its grasp, inevitable, and we not to blame
If it relight, when tinder, coal demand
As love can

It is its swiftness in which love asserts its claim
Our rudimentary feet, or wings, do follow after
And elementary forms all we do gather

And if it die, go down, as can a flame
Can you, or I, give love another name?

The Moebius Strip

Upon a Moebius strip
materials and the weights of pain
their harmony

A man within himself upon an empty ground.
His head lay heavy on a huge right hand
itself a leopard on
his left and angled shoulder.
His back a stave, his side a hole into the bosom of a sphere.

His head passed down a sky (as suns the circle of a year).
His other shoulder, open side and thigh maintained,
by law of conservation of
the graveness of his center,
their clockwise fall.
Then he knew, so came to apogee
and earned and wore himself as amulet.

I saw another man lift up a woman in his arms
he helmeted, she naked too, protected as Lucrece by her alarms.
Her weight tore down his right and muscled thigh
but they in turn returned upon the left
to carry violence outcome in her eye.
It was his shoulder that sustained, the right,
bunched as by buttocks or by breasts,
and gave them back the leisure of their rape.

And three or four who danced,
so joined as triple-thighed and bowed and arrowed folk
who spilled their pleasure once as yoke
on stone-henge plain.
Their bare and lovely bodies sweep, in round
of viscera, of legs
of turned-out hip and glance, bound
each to other, nested eggs
of elements in trance.

X to the Nth

for F.Z.M.

Steorra, stir
by the bird's whir
entrail and flight:
auspex, speak!

Mixed, fixed
here in the middle place
choked
locked in event.
The answer to exteriors is to polish them.
Break, and polish 'em.

The tresor is hid.
Dig, I want a fool
to bury the hanged man,
and two women to put their hand on him
(neither one a papess)
to tell a fact when they see one.
Actually there are two, and they know it:
a coin, a quantity and a gout.
The answer to Grave's disease is
the grave, the question, have you enough chaos, man,
to make a world? (A.E. to Joyce, a Dublin street, 1910)

Sir, it's a wicked pack of stars you have!
(C.O. to C.C., Second Ave., spring, 1946)

The Green Man

Go, fool, and hatch of the air
a blue egg.
And the night will be there, the Twins
a different thing.

And you? can hang your plough
from a gold bough,
your tongue
on any branch,
and follow after.

Follow, fool, your stick and bag
and each furious cloud.
Let those who want to, chase a king.

And you who go when the green man comes
who leave your fields,
go as the dog goes at his heels
ahead, aside, and always after
be full of
loud laughter

     Of bitter work, and of folly
     cockatrice and cockolloly
     furiously sing!

Canto One Hundred and One

The earth is for the living OR
the earth is the dead man's land. BOTH
depending upon the way you look at it.

I have looked at the earth. You and I have Troilus' vantage:
(from the seventh sphere or
back of the warhead of a rocket)
its features are as clear and as obscure as the moon's to us.
Diomed is Diomed, pocked.
And Cressid still a whore.
We are come far
and are
nowhere.

Once upon a time we planted the dead and got a season.
These days, we don't raise a likely crop.
At harvest man turns out to be a weed, at best a vetch
tolerable fodder.
It comes to this: nor Mars nor Cadmus nor did Jason
sow the teeth whence came this dragon brood.
The teeth were caries-ridden,
and fell out.

It's cause, it's cause for a large act of simplification.
If I got the facts straight, pitchblende
used to be, served well as, the source of the color orange
for the potter, a quiet trade.

    The earth for the living AND the dead, I say.
    I for one prefer a dye to a gold-filled denture.
    You take Siegfried
    I'll settle for things as they were.
    Hey, mister, got a seed?

Your Eyes

Your eyes of draiad speak
    of winter melancholy
And the old gods weep
    for modern folly

They know your naiad arms will lift
    with the green spring
And sing as old gods did
    hey ding a ding

It is not you, their creature
    for whom they weep
It is the others round you lost
    to a season's rape

So bear your melancholy
    of winter, or of spring
For of your rocks and hair and holly
    the old gods sing.

R^2

Undo time's work
as that old Roman wizard could
restore
a knee   a part of thigh   a tip of horn   an eye

what had corrupted off
some ancient bronze

Or speed, at multiples to speed
and catch again, regain
what light had made its shape upon
an Antony retained   one monstrous rape preserved
Tlascalan girl   a Philippi
or wild Phoenician bird

In the Hills South of Capernaum, Port

I

As salt, keep your savour
as light be not obscured.

The old commandments hold,
I would intensify them:

not to kill, yes, but also not without cause
to take anger
or to say Raca to your brother, or, thou fool

adultery, commit it not, nor even in your heart
nor put away your wife
saving for the cause of fornication

swear not, nor by earth, for it is God's footstool
nor by your head
for you cannot make one hair white or black

eye for eye, no. Give your enemy your coat
cheek also
and go two mile with him

The sun rises. And on the just and the unjust
the rain comes down.
The idea is to be perfect.

2

Nor sound the trumpet of what you do
be not public when you pray, nor repetitious
and when you fast
wear no long face.

The light of the body is the eye, let it be clear.

And be clear too concerning treasures and/or masters
any double allegiance. Take the natural for base
assume your nature as a bird his or the grass.
The life is more than meat, the body than clothes.

3

Nor judge, nor give what is holy to dogs
give gifts largely, as a father might
what man, if his son ask a fish, gives a snake?

Few find, but do you look for, enter, the narrow gate
Watch out for the false, the wide ones, frauds

Men do not gather grapes where thorns are
make wine with their feet in that place
find figs in thistles or tulips

The proposition is this:
a good tree and a rock
or
a foolish man, and sand.

       He taught them as one having authority.

A Spring Song for Cagli

There is a boy who walks with a fish.
Where there is gravity all motion goes into the center.

We have discovered the shaft, where the boy is
or the god no longer buried, now the light can come in.
See, man, yourself turned inside out, put back again!
Look in, pick up the fish, and go along.

We call you, say: go down
It is not
        in the world
             as it seems.

Kiss his hand, or Leonardo's skirt if you are Raphael.
Obey the law by which you stand upon the earth.
It is no easy act, who made it
by which we stick to what is ours.

Willie Francis and the Electric Chair

Now the preacher told Willie when he said his last prayer
"You're a lucky fella, Willie, to be goin' to the chair
Most don' know and some ain't ready
But you is lucky for you know you're goin' to die"

      O Willie didn't burn, O Willie didn't burn
      When the good Lawd arranged it to be Willie's turn

Now they walked sad Willie right into the room
It was shiny and clean as a new store broom
They sat down Willie right up in the air
And Willie knowed it was a bad chair

      O Willie know'd, O Willie knowed
      O Willie knowed it was a bad chair

They strapped Willie in to that bad chair
And everything went all dazey in the air
The white folks watchin' went swingin' in a swing
Away back they'd go and then they'd swing in

      O Willie was in, O Willie was in
      He was goin' to pay for his black sin

He tried to remember what the preacher had said
He tried not to think he'd just be dead
There was just one thought and it curled and curled
It was "Willie, you're goin' out'a this world"

Sometimes he thought it so loud that it hurt
And when they put his head in the big black bag
It hurt and it hurt and his head was a rag
All locked up in that black bag

O Willie was in, O Willie was in
In the black bag with the loud thinkin'

Now some folks say that dyin' is gold
And some folks say it's hominy grits
But Willie's been close and he oughter know
He says it's black, not gold or white

O Willie's been close and he oughter know
He says it's black and that oughter go

Th'electric man said "Goodbye" to Willie
Just as tho' he were puttin him on a bus to the city
And the way he said it, Willie tried to reply
But he couldn't get a word out no matter how he try

O Willie, O Willie, o don' you try
For the good Lawd's arranged it that you won't die

His mouth felt full of cold peanut butter
He couldn't say "Goodbye," he couldn't even mutter
Th'electric man listened and Willie tried to answer
But his tongue got stuck in the peanut butter

O Willie, O Willie, O don' you try
For the good Lawd's arranged it that you won't die

Now Willie sat straight and Willie sat still
He says that chair makes you "plum mizzuble"
He sat up straight and he sat up still
He says that chair makes you "plum mizzuble"

Then the moment came when the switch was thrown
And there was Willie all on his own
He took it straight and he took it still
That he lived through it was the good Lawd's will

He felt a burning in his head
He felt his left leg go like red
His lips puffed out and he rocked the chair
But he didn't fry when he sat there

> O Willie didn't fry, O Willie didn't fry
> So all you people, don' you cry

He said he saw a lot of lights
Blue and pink and little green speckles
The kind that shine in a rooster's tail
When he greets the morning from the nearest rail

> O Willie didn't fail, O Willie didn't fail
> When he saw the speckles on the rooster's tail

He jammed his feet against the floor
When he went right up to death's big door
He jumped against the straps they swore
To prove that Willie needn't burn once more

"O electric man, O cut me free
The straps they are a cuttin' me!
O electric man, O let me breathe
This big black bag is smotherin' me!"

They cut Willie free, they took him to court
Th'electric man said the current was short
And now they've gone to the big, big bench
To decide if the preacher saw Willie blanch

> O Willie are you free, O Willie are you free
> It's what ten good men now shall see

When Willie was asked what he'd do if free
He said he would a preacher be

But if he gets life a cook he'll be
And serve sidemeat in the penitentiary

> O Willie be free, O Willie be free
> The best damned cook in the penitentiary

When the preacher asked "Did it tickle like I said"
Willie answered "Yes, but it hurt in the head"
O Willie didn't die, O Willie didn't die
He's alive to hear and say "Goodbye"

> O Willie didn't die, O Willie didn't die
> He's alive to hear and say "Goodbye!"

Move Over

Merchants.   of the sea and of finance

(Smash the plate glass window)

The dead face is the true face
of Washington, New York a misery, but north and east
the carpenter obeyed
topography

As a hand addresses itself to the care of plants
and a sense of proportion, the house
is put to the earth

Tho peopled with hants, New England

Move over to let the death-blow in,
the unmanned or the transvest, drest
in beard and will, the capillary

Seven years with the wrong man,
7 yrs of tristus and vibullation.
And I looked up to see a toad. And the boy sd:
"I crushed one, and its blood is green"

Green, is the color of my true love's green
despite
New England is
despite her merchants and her morals

A Fish Is the Flower of Water

You who follow Henry Thoreau
beware

Forbear to drive life into a corner
and think to trap her
She will slip away like any girl

Men curiously without appetite
want wild muskrat meat

Landscape, Without Color

The train carries me swiftly by, yet
I stay
The train carried me swiftly away, yet
I stay
And the crane stands as he stood

The water up to that intolerable claw of his raised leg
the crane stands as he stood

The long-necked geese fly down the slough, competent, organized
still new
the speed of their most irritating flight still doubled by the rushing train

The undirected, unstill gulls blast the marsh in memory as in fact
Unlocated, wild, there and not there, watching, intact
not relative
as geese and crane
to train and time

       The marsh the water
       pilings which cannot stand straight
       stand still, hold in the mind

       The crane is of bronze
       the geese are arrows
       gulls stones which scream

       And what was not seen
       what the crane without moving waited for
       the gulls talked about
       the geese were directed towards

       What passed, that
       I shall not forget

Only the Red Fox, Only the Crow

You who come after us
you who can live when we are not
make much of love

You to whom the spring can return
when we will merely correlate a worm
enjoy the envy
in this blind glance

You who shall have the earth,
and one another,
the government of noon,
do not fail us, dance

We shall not know, but you
remember this: the two-edged worth
of loveliness
The night's for talking and for kissing

And when, on summer field
two horses run for joy
like figures on a beach
your mind will find us,
as we have found,
within its reach.

    This, then, under the leaves
    or under snow,
    you who come after us,
    we send you for envoy:
    make most of love.

All You Can Do

because a woman

suffers differently

from a man

        (do you know grief?

        do you crave,
        from desire,
        to wipe it all out?)

all you can do

is to put forth the hand

of your flesh

"Put him this way . . ."

Put him this way:
as red-hot an arrow as a man can be,
and bound in the family like an iron ring

Say the ring was so iron,
because there was no more a father present
than there was in the case of Christ

And suppose all outside the ring is called
"the world," all that ("ithyphallique")
which did out-rage

For there are two movements observable:
the arrow strikes and strikes the iron,
but it does not go out, it cannot.
What happened was, the world, by resonance,
came in.
And that included
Africa, money-making.

The other movement is why he is a subject
worth consideration: Rimbaud (je est, he sd.)
knew so much because that arrow
in repulse cross and criss-crossed
one core of such reality
he burned it clear, without
destroying it.

Not by impulse but by repulse
he totally pierced
childhood.

And the only price was,
when he returned home to his mother and his sister,
whom he had never left,
he had a gangrenous leg.

It was as though it were from rubbing too long
on iron.

Conqueror

Gulls on the grass / and the odor of live worms / and worms dead on the walk.
Nature deranged
(mine as well)
feeding irregularly.

The answer is easy. We know where the grass is.
But der Weg   tough as we are   a path is not   stirbt   easy to get the foot on
          mister gull.

We know the stupid ones are dead. They cover the smell of the rain
which is a way of saying a knowledge of the most elementary things.

A man, a revolution proceeds out of, a man, the root curiosity, the process
          question, and the end
a method. His motion will be less clear, at least double in direction, himself ahead
and backward as he goes. He starts where the path died.

There are some several rains, and different kinds of deaths, but at this particular
          time no more than one path
the pity of it. They have got us to this extremity, the fuckers and the boobs.
          Cry shit
and leave em   they aint worth our time   walk on em.

If a man is a matter of what consequence in consequence he is an object.
The fear, I take it, comes from the notion he is a three letter word.
We are no longer very interested   a gas by any other name

a man   a stool   a glass   a gull

if for no other reason than
it is better a worm get us in the end

but I can think of another / this morning / as I walk from breakfast to work.

Conqueror

Gulls on the grass   and the odor of live worms   and worms dead on the walk
Nature deranged   mine as well   feeding irregularly

It is easy to put the alternative. We know where the grass is. But der Weg—
tough as we are   a path is not   stirbt   easy to get the foot on   Mister gull.

We know the stupid ones are dead, they cover the smell of the rain,
which is a way of saying, a knowledge of the most elementary things

A man, a revolution proceeds out of a man, the root curiosity, the process
      question, and the end
a method. His motion will be less clear, at least double in direction, himself
      ahead and
backward as he goes. He starts where the path died.

There are some several rains and different kinds of death but, at this particular time,
      no more than one path,
the pity of it. They have got us to this extremity, the fuckers, the boobs. Cry shit
and leave em   they aint worth our time   walk on em.

If a man is a matter of what consequence in consequence he is an object.
The fear, I take it, comes from the notion he is a three letter word.
We are no longer very interested
a gas by any other name   a man   a stool   a glass   a gull
if for no other reason than
it is better a worm get us
in the end

February 10, One Year Too Late

To move time back to where it was before I blundered
and lost the only patrimony I could ever steal!
O! that I had such lever in my hand to wield!

To gain again the days and nights I wasted,
concerns which now have washed away,
when all I had to do was plot the theft
so only she who found the hoard would know.

Accomplice: fate, who only once gives beggars such a chance!
To be myself my patron! To purchase time by simple larceny!
O! that I were not what I am, or that this agenbite might end.

For gall of all is this one doubling thought:
had I the lever in my hand and this year back
would I, without this suffering, know.

The answer is not time. The fault is me.
And I again, again, again, shall plundered be.

"Elements of clothes . . ."

Elements of clothes, an arm and hand the head of a cock
turning, a cube and torso tour en l'air
a fish, free, the milieu man
facts, facts, fable et couleur

A crowd in a forest of the city make
attention turned as heads which hear demand
the green republic now renewed

But the mount of the mass
objects as feathers piled
holds

the shining scales of space are worn
rough as a cat's tongue
delicately

Igor Stravinsky

An Homage

On the edge of woods
(as we are)
the advance, retreat of both
man as nature, nature as more than man
the sounds
tempi
fable
struggle-borne

On the edge of man
a horn   a hooded step
by two white ropes an Echo led
to this levitican point

On the edge
tympanum and unicorn
telluric cube
he the balance—
And the scale   the hounds
man, and the maiden both, torn

On the edge of woods
rock   water
(peacocks in the sun)
a cello rubs itself against a tree.

Troilus

Love is not present now,
has flown
            is not a state so separate as we think
that men and women breed by kiss and glance
            no dance
outside the modes and figures of that trance,
the full intent

That love at least must live
is lie we practice to protect
what we inherit, breath,
unwilling to admit
the large wrongs bring
love also down to
death

Why should love live
when all that should enforce it fails
this side of meaning
                                tearing off
what love alone is key to, form
that feature nature wore
before man turned her, woman, whore;
when matter stood so many objects clear
not use, delight the round of human year

Love is not love with end, with objects lost.
Means wither. Bodies, gestures fall.
                                All nature falls!
The path, are blown along the path papers, dust
cloth (strips which give no clue
dropped without care
picked up, lamely, at a dare)

The path, love is the path.
                                And in the forest calls, calls!
We shall answer, find.
                                But if love now is lust
or mere drift back
better we know, and say
we do not know the way

The way, love is
the way!

Siena

Awkwardness, the grace
the absence of the suave

At once/ a boy walks out of his father's house
a field planted to angles & infinity goes off
/ and above/ the boy enters the desert to meet
the Christ
        He meets the Christ

Lazarus is raised by a glance

Two men cast a net / a third stands on the shore
The sea is grass, and the fish,
as large as the boat, are
flowers. The boat is
as a child carves
wood. He on the shore is
the Christ
        The Christ is a fish

Nicholas hovers over the city walls

Wolves came in close in those days
or tore the farmer's child. But shall we say
miracles are not necessary now
to stop marauders?
Clare, Francis be
our protection
        at sea/ before the sultan/ death

From the trough of the wave where only our heads show
the ship a postcard sunk in hillocks thru which swim
a man wrenched round to point at him who like a haloed stump
raises his hand above us
          we   who are awkward   ask

Sans Name

Called death, is darkness

the house that afternoon a full round O
the play a good one, not long enough

sound sennet, or a march, they all go off
the street lights don't come on

a tiger's heart wrapt in a player's hide

Li Po

The fire makes noises like snow on wet panes

The fire makes its effort to keep out the cold

The fire is less master of the cold night than the snow

Tanto e Amara

I have heard the dread song I had not heard
in the middle of life, I had not heard.
I was all eyes, all things were, now they are blind
and I am, I crawl, do not know where I go

You who have heard will understand
death is a remote beginning.
I am rudimentary.
I grow a heart.

I stumbled when I saw, knew high passage, persons
one imperial nature whose conclusion was
nothing, it is nothing.
I know now it was nothing.

The wise man said, nothing dieth
but changing as they do one for another show
sundry formes. He lieth. I cannot have back my mother.

In the grave, before the dirt goes, will go my love.
And what shall I be, which forms will plague me then
where shall I go, in what ditch pour what blood to hear
her voice, the love I hear, that voice now mingled
in the song,
the song of the Worms?

Name-Day Night

What it is to look into a human eye

men   what they are   who
of a sudden of a night in a room
a room not so different from this in which I recollect
(along the floor, circles of lamp light intersect)
start up, join hands, a kerchief joins them, their eyes
follow the pattern of their leader's feet
(their order)
they dance

what it is   what it is to say wherein it lies

where beauty lies
                            that men containeth
                                                    at this hour

Came 2 am the three men sang
one led (as in the dance) he of Peloponnesus
he sang of love, a narrative of man and maid

their meeting   what the youth said
the night left out   the morning, final stanza, key

then proudly (as he had danced) the Macedonian
he sang of war most hieratically: Turks defeated
and, at each turning of the song, pistols shot off

None sang of death. I marked then, and ask now
what light it is shines in their eyes, what source
their gusto hath;
this name-day night these men of Greece disclose
their eyes shine from outside, take light, shine
from nature, partake her common force, shine
by addition, separation, what is cruel
are not monocular, shine
by death its recognition, multiply
by life its shortcoming, shine
these eyes of night their sons and daughters know not of

And the hour tells what it is
              what delight it is
                        that maketh modest man

La Chute

my drum, hollowed out thru the thin slit,
carved from the cedar wood, the base I took
when the tree was felled

o my lute, wrought from the tree's crown

my drum, whose lustiness
was not to be resisted

                              my lute,
from whose pulsations
not one could turn away

                              They
are where the dead are, my drum fell
where the dead are, who
will bring it up, my lute
who will bring it up where it fell in the face of them
where they are, where my lute and drum have fallen?

La Chute II

If you would go down to the dead
to retrieve my drum and lute
a word for you, take my word
I offer you directions

Do not wear a clean garment
they below will dirty you
they will mark you
as if you were a stranger

Nor rub yourself with oil
the finest oil from the cruse.
The smell of it will provoke them
they will walk round and round
alongside you

Carry no stick. At least
do not raise it,
or the shades of men will tremble,
will hover before you

Pick up nothing to throw, no matter the urging.
They against whom you hurl it will crowd you,
will fly thick on you.

Go barefoot. Make no sound.
And when you meet the wife you loved
do not kiss her
nor strike the wife you hated.
Likewise your sons. Give the beloved one no kiss,
do not spit on his brother

Behave, lest the outcry shall seize you
seize you for what you have done
for her who, there, lies naked
the mother
whose body in that place is uncovered
whose breasts lie open to you and the judges

in that place
where my drum and lute are

La Chute III

The mother, the pleasure. To return is
to advance, to ravin, to hunt
is more than the beginning, to enter
is more than the womb

                  the hell
is the present descent, the hell
is the guilty present, the descent
is not to the past, the descent is
the pursuit, the desire and the door

For the door is the second birth
the crime none no longer dare
not the advance by the womb of the mother
the advance by the mother's hair

Dura

To come to the look in the sacrificer's eyes

the archaic sought, the harshness
unsought

        And the eyes which should burst
do not.

The Kingfishers

What does not change / is the will to change

He woke, fully clothed, in his bed. He
remembered only one thing, the birds, how
when he came in, he had gone around the rooms
and got them back in their cage, the green one first,
she with the bad leg, and then the blue,
the one they had hoped was a male

Otherwise? Yes, Fernand, who had talked lispingly of Albers & Angkor Vat.
He had left the party without a word. How he got up, got into his coat,
I do not know. When I saw him, he was at the door, but it did not matter,
he was already sliding along the wall of the night, losing himself
in some crack of the ruins. That it should have been he who said, "The kingfishers!
who cares
for their feathers
now?"

His last words had been, "The pool is slime." Suddenly everyone,
ceasing their talk, sat in a row around him, watched
they did not so much hear, or pay attention, they
wondered, looked at each other, smirked, but listened,
he repeated and repeated, could not go beyond his thought
"The pool   the kingfishers' feathers were wealth   why
did the export stop?"

It was then he left

2

I thought of the E on the stone, and of what Mao said
la lumiere"
               but the kingfisher
de l'aurore"
               but the kingfisher flew west
est devant nous!
                 he got the color of his breast
                 from the heat of the setting sun!

The features are, the feebleness of the feet (syndactylism of the 3rd & 4th digit)
the bill, serrated, sometimes a pronounced beak, the wings
where the color is, short and round, the tail
inconspicuous.

But not these things were the factors. Not the birds.
The legends are
legends. Dead, hung up indoors, the kingfisher
will not indicate a favoring wind,
or avert the thunderbolt. Nor, by its nesting,
still the waters, with the new year, for seven days.
It is true, it does nest with the opening year, but not on the waters.
It nests at the end of a tunnel bored by itself in a bank. There,
six or eight white and translucent eggs are laid, on fishbones
not on bare clay, on bones thrown up in pellets by the birds.

                 On these rejectamenta
(as they accumulate they form a cup-shaped structure) the young are born.
And, as they are fed and grow, this nest of excrement and decayed fish becomes
                 a dripping, fetid mass

Mao concluded:
           nous devons
                nous lever
                     et agir!

3

When the attentions change / the jungle
leaps in
            even the stones are split
                        they rive

Or,
enter
that other conqueror we more naturally recognize
he so resembles ourselves

But the E
cut so rudely on that oldest stone
sounded otherwise,
was differently heard

as, in another time, were treasures used:

(and, later, much later, a fine ear thought
a scarlet coat)

                "of green feathers   feet, beaks and eyes
                  of gold

                "animals likewise,
                  resembling snails

                "a large wheel, gold, with figures of unknown four-foots,
                  and worked with tufts of leaves, weight
                  3800 ounces

                "last, two birds, of thread and featherwork, the quills
                  gold, the feet
                  gold, the two birds perched on two reeds

gold, the reeds arising from two embroidered mounds,
one yellow, the other
white.

       "And from each reed hung
         seven feathered tassels.

In this instance, the priests
(in dark cotton robes, and dirty,
their dishevelled hair matted with blood, and flowing wildly
over their shoulders)
rush in among the people, calling on them
to protect their gods

And all now is war
where so lately there was peace,
and the sweet brotherhood, the use
of tilled fields.

4

Not one death but many,
not accumulation but change, the feed-back proves, the feed-back is
the law

       Into the same river no man steps twice
       When fire dies air dies
       No one remains, nor is, one

Around an appearance, one common model, we grow up
many. Else how is it,
if we remain the same,
we take pleasure now
in what we did not take pleasure before? love
contrary objects? admire and/or find fault? use
other words, feel other passions, have

nor figure, appearance, disposition, tissue
the same?
>   To be in different states without a change
>   is not a possibility

We can be precise. The factors are
in the animal and/or the machine the factors are
communication and/or control, both involve
the message. And what is the message? The message is
a discrete or continuous sequence of measurable events distributed in time

is the birth of air, is
the birth of water, is
a state between
the origin and
the end, between
birth and the beginning of
another fetid nest

is change, presents
no more than itself

And the too strong grasping of it,
when it is pressed together and condensed,
loses it

This very thing you are

II

>   They buried their dead in a sitting posture
>   serpent   cane   razor   ray of the sun

>   And she sprinkled water on the head of the child, crying
>   "Cioa-coatl! Cioa-coatl!"
>   with her face to the west

Where the bones are found, in each personal heap
with what each enjoyed, there is always
the Mongolian louse

The light is in the east. Yes. And we must rise, act. Yet
in the west, despite the apparent darkness (the whiteness
which covers all), if you look, if you can bear, if you can, long enough

     as long as it was necessary for him, my guide
     to look into the yellow of that longest-lasting rose

so you must, and, in that whiteness, into that face, with what candor, look

and, considering the dryness of the place
     the long absence of an adequate race

     (of the two who first came, each a conquistador, one healed, the other
     tore the eastern idols down, toppled
     the temple walls, which, says the excuser
     were black from human gore)

hear
hear, where the dry blood talks
     where the old appetite walks

               la piu saporita et migliore
               che si possa truovar al mondo

where it hides, look
in the eye how it runs
in the flesh / chalk

     but under these petals
     in the emptiness
     regard the light, contemplate
     the flower

whence it arose

with what violence benevolence is bought
what cost in gesture justice brings
what wrongs domestic rights involve
what stalks
this silence

what pudor pejorocracy affronts
how awe, night-rest and neighborhood can rot
what breeds where dirtiness is law
what crawls
below

III

I am no Greek, hath not th'advantage.
And of course, no Roman:
he can take no risk that matters,
the risk of beauty least of all.

But I have my kin, if for no other reason than
(as he said, next of kin) I commit myself, and,
given my freedom, I'd be a cad
if I didn't. Which is most true.

It works out this way, despite the disadvantage.
I offer, in explanation, a quote:
si j'ai du goût, ce n'est guères
que pour la terre et les pierres.

Despite the discrepancy (an ocean   courage   age)
this is also true: if I have any taste

it is only because I have interested myself
in what was slain in the sun

I pose you your question:

shall you uncover honey / where maggots are?

I hunt among stones

Epigon

in whose heart it
burns

Beauty hath
two forms

in the hidden wood, in
the room, sleep

Lady, who
art

birth is as green and rock
as magic ring and hummock by

wearing water. Birth
is a euphemism, two eyes
is more accurate: it is the mortal which matters,
from which I now spring

intent,
the measure

Nature,
is proved again

I am
of use

blood has to be spent, this boreal heath warmed
out from this faery circle   (in the November sun
creatures present, including the angelic orders, ordering)
to take on the demons, to regain
first principles, crying
redeem, redeem
the dead

you,
who art awake!

The Laughing Ones

they
are the light-hearted races,
enjoy nothing so much, obviously,
as the cracking of skulls (Troy's fields
were covered with 'em

their mortality
is altogether pervasive, these
chillun of the sun

the earth (the Others
call it darkling)
they flee. Persephone
is never of their making,
Demeter neither. Women
are delights, things to run with, equals
—small game they slay

it is true: the sun breeds slayers, makers of spring
and slayers. (There it is: Celts,
light, light, thin with it
And only in love with the dark,
which they never know. How
can they? their blood
does not go down, it
races out! And they like it—
out! They only remember
what space has had her arms around.

You dark men root in woman as a cave, they
(the splinters)

want to dance, only to dance
& slay. They
are without suspicion, stupid, gay, think
the world is a banquet leading not to conversation but
a scrap!

O

what shall men do with these empty-heads
before they destroy us? what shall you do, you
who favor the beat
not the color of
blood?

what shall we do to bring them down, the laughing ones
who do not have beautiful teeth?

The Praises

She who was burned more than half her body skipped out of death

Observing
that there are five solid figures, the Master
(or so Aetius reports, in the *Placita*)
concluded that
the Sphere of the Universe arose from
the dodecahedron

whence Alexander,
appearing in a dream to Antiochus,
showed him
And on the morrow, the enemy (the Galates)
ran before it,
before the sign, that is

I

By Filius Bonacci, his series, rediscovered Pisa 1202, we shall attack,
for it, too, proceeds asymptotically toward the graphic and tangible, the law
now determined to be
phi

      its capital role in the distribution of
      leaves   seeds   branches on a stem (ex.,
      the ripe sun-flower)

      the ratios $\frac{5}{8}$, $\frac{8}{13}$
      in the seed-cones of fir-trees,
      the ratio $\frac{21}{34}$
      in normal daisies

      Pendactylism is general in the animal kingdom.
      But crystals . . . there, pentagonal forms or lattices
      do not, can not appear

      So we have it: star and jelly fish, the sea urchin.
      And because there is an ideal and constant angle which,
      for leaves and branches on a stem, produces
      the maximum exposition to light, that light vertical,
      fruit blossoms   the briar rose   the passion flower
      But lilies   tulips   the hyacinth, like crystals . . .

      Here we must stop   And ponder   For nature,
      though she is, as you know (so far, that is

97

as it is allowed to a mortal to know) from all points of view
similar to herself, yet minerals . . .

     o, that's not fair, let
     woman keep her jewels, odd man
     his pleasure of her glow, let
     your lady Nephritite
     pumice her malachite, paint
     her lids green against the light

Sd he:

     to dream takes no effort
       to think is easy
         to act is more difficult
   but for a man to act after he has taken thought, this!
   is the most difficult thing of all

2

We turn now to Ammonius,
who was present when Nero was,
who is full of delights,
& who smiles quickly

     the epiphanies, he says, in this case are four:
     1st, to such as begin to learn & to inquire,
     the Pythian response,
     with flute

     (2) when part of the truth is glimpsed, the sun
     (a creature of four-fold eyes and heads,
     of a ram   a bull   a snake   the bright-eyed lion)
     This is little, even though the drum
     is added

When a person has got the knowledge, Ammonius
(and he does not mean to be ambiguous)
confers one overwhelming title:
he says a man may then call himself OF THEBES. He may sing

The last, and triumphant mode, I leave, as he leaves it,
untranslated: when men are active, enjoy thought, that is to say
when they talk, they are LESKENOI. They rage

Which is why what is related must remain enigmatic
And why Ammonius excepts, from these epiphanies,
those who are entirely brutish.

Which brings us to what concerns us in the present inquiry.

Avert, avert, avoid
pollution, to be clean
in a dirty time

                O Wheel, aid us
                to get the gurry off

You would have a sign. Look:
to fly? a fly can do that;
to try the moon? a moth
as well; to walk on water? a straw
precedes you

                O Wheel! draw
                that truth
                to my house

Like pa does, not like sis,
on all detractors, piss, o advertised earth!
And you, o lady Moon, observe my love,
whence it arose

Whence it arose,
and who it is who sits,
there at the base of the skull, locked
in his throne of bone, that mere pea of bone
where the axes meet, cross-roads of the system
god, converter, discloser, he will answer,
will look out, if you will look, look!

3

What has been lost
is the secret of secrecy, is
the value, viz., that the work get done, and quickly,
without the loss of due and profound respect for
the materials

which is not so easy as it sounds, nor
can it permit the dispersion which follows from
too many having too little
knowledge

                    Says Iamblichus:
    by shipwreck, he perished (Hippasus, that is)
    the first to publish (write down, divulge)
    the secret,
    the construction of, from 12 pentagons,
    the sphere

    "Thus was he punished for his impiety"

What is necessary is
containment,
that that which has been found out by work may, by work, be passed on
(without due loss of force)
for use
        USE

"And they took over power, political power, in Gr Greece, including
Sicily, and maintained themselves, even after the Master died, until,
at Metapontum, the mob

"Only Philalaos, and Lysis, did not perish in the fire. Later,
Archytas it was, pupil of Philalaos, who, friend to Plato, initiated him,
and, at Tarentum

4

Which is about what we had to say,
the clues, anyhow

What belongs to art and reason is
                              the knowledge of
                                          consequences
L da V, his notebook:

            Every natural action obeys by
            the straightest possible process

The Babe

Who it is who sits
behind the face,
who it is looks out by both,
by beauty and by truth,
those cheeks, mere Angels side by side
the greater one

Who it is whose eyes
what it is to look where eyes are
where eyes are form, not by lyric, not by absolute
whose eyes at once are maculate and innocent, by mastery
won

Who it is looks, can look
into the smallest thing, and says,
it was made for us both, we are committed
to be just, who says, to the very largest,
none is over us
when we have earned it

Look, in that face,
and read an answer, you
who are alone, what you ask,
that you be justly done by,
that what price you pay be more
than beauty or than truth, be
the recognition that you are
of use

one to another separate, but
the form we make by search, by error, pain
be seen by eyes other than our own

dedicate, thus, one to another, aid:
to offer, able to offer the just act, the act
crying to be born!

"all things stand out against the sky . . ."

all things stand out against the sky
this winter day
all high: the factory stack, truck overpass, the water tower,
the cripple coming toward me on the street, the bridge,
a locomotive's steam, all dry
as twigs are, as the girders are,
all spun, all spidered by
rigueur

or so they seem to my new eyes fresh opened after peril, after
narrow pass of choices painfully pursued
where misstep meant—and action was denied—loss, loss
i could not bear to lose

i greet you, day, with joy, clear
thankfulness, for with what strain
i held the bow, withheld the arrow
you, my heart, only know, you who by the holding lost
how many years

sweet life, that asks such spending of us
when we would be as girls are, boys and dogs
this winter afternoon, who quarrel, hide by trees, whittle,
throw each other, run, stick out their tongues, rassle,
spit words tomorrow will dry up, the life
that's wasted on the young!

"hear my prayer my father . . ."

hear my prayer my father
let an angel here
let an angel there
let an angel all around me
let an angel on top
let an angel on the bottom
let an angel on all four sides
let angels walk
around me

"under every green tree . . ."

under every green tree, sex
is sympathetic
magic
the uncontrolled use
of analogy
characteristic of
early thought

a pillar of gold
and of emerald
hold up
the sky

The Advantage

1

Where do these
   invisible seeds
     settle from?

     And how are men able
       to spore them
         into air?

        For the gains are
        thus communicated.

2

        Shall you say there are not Powers
           when men spring up (like violets, sd Bolyai Farkas)
          on all sides, to the need?

        Men have their proper season, and that season
        its act and image,
         image more than act,
          a rhythm more than image or than act,
        proper to them.

3

So if we now again shall call
   the sun a male,
and give him back the moon
   for mate,

who'll say we're wrong, we
who have endured, to rotting,
the old device, the making
domestic abstract gods
of paled–out humans,
father   mother   son?

will you say
    the root of universe
        is not the root of man,

deny
    the edge of peril
        is the edge of life,

cry down
    the act of touch,
                the dumb thing knocking, knocking
at that door?

These Days

whatever you have to say, leave
the roots on, let them
dangle

And the dirt

        Just to make clear
        where they come from

A Po-sy, A Po-sy

I

aw, piss, and sing, be
robert burns

Or throw an arm up
in the wind, in the wind's eye,
swing the sail, head
downwards

And look up, hear
the curlew (lost), right straight up
a daisy's ass

"There is no more time, bro., no more . . .
t's for tiffins, for the likes of
yoooooooooooou!

Watch out, CITIZENS, they've
got you where it hurts
                    where it
                        hurts.   "O

one of those brothers is, o (repeat)
                    (go on) "my neigh-bor noooW (lyrics
by o–PHEEL–ia: haie high hi!)
                        "one (beat) of (beat)
                        THOOOOOSE
who lived in harlem with everything they ever had (eeeee-
clectic!)

        And they shat in paper bags.

2

SING! in other words, high! like thistles sound, like "O-
jai, o, O-hi, where the lyyyyyr-ick
(low) soooooooules, the (high) faaaaaayk-irs
be, THE
            ooooooooo–RIENT, the AWK–ceedent, oH, GOOOOO
west, o. there's NOOOO
rest, there's
only one nest and it's
west

O, there's
NOOOO rest, there's

            (and repeat and repeat and repeat and reeee-
            PETE!)

3

yes, my friends, this discussion comes to you as free as
paper bags, comes to you
no permissions granted,
leaves cancelled:x
            Ariadne's silk
s'gone back to
mulberrys

work! bro.: 5 minutes
is all that's necessary to get a fact straight.
Or how will you read a maze
when you see you?

look! sucker: i tellya,
a nose is, a nose is
sure it is, just what you think it is
                    WHAT YOU THINK IT IS
                                                wype it,
citizen,
            get on with it
                            The dogs with the fine limbs
are on
                            Here, bro., try to bring an interval down,
at any number of traces
                            See, see, where the blood streams!
And it ain't   in no firmament

4

no   And my thumb
hurts
        ("What are all these snakes
in her hair?"
                    "My god, man, don't you know yr plough
when your hand's on it?")

Try again
to bring her head
round
        (the buoy
is just off yr

plover (lost, also

Who does not fight
will remain unhealed,
no matter how many rains he holds
in his outright palm

5

Pansies, it turns out, was a translation

  Dazies, they call 'em, the high-browns

    Medusahatta

        (And he didn't know it. But his bigger brother
        did. Only, with his bigger brother, it didn't
        matta.)

Sd Mrs Henry Adams of Mr Henry James: "Henry
doesn't bite off more than he can chew, he
chews on more than he has bitten off

  And then there's the one about time,
  wounds all heels

    But it's brooks, brooks who makes the proper current
    ("yr predecessor, my little running water!")

6

In order to be a rock,
start right now ceasing to be
if you are, a twig

        Ophelia Flotsam
                "And feel yourself to be a
                flot-
                sum, and feel yrself to be
                a
                flot   (hold)

                    sum   (continue)

                                        Settle
right down here, prat in the stream

if you want to be distinguishable,

if you want to be

            "from the ELE-
            ment, from the
                        ele-
                        MUNT, o

7

balls! Or the image of
3! Sure! it's all over his work. And why not?

What superior direction do you take?
Where's your fin, your stump, former fish?

    item: The vessel walked right off its course and up on the land.

    "O brothers," he cried, "who, after a thousand toils, have
    gained this point of vantage, smell
    the ground!"

8

Soil is of the matter

    Narcissi are

        And the smallest king of an eye
        is a larger thing than a dollar bill!

She also sd:

make me a mysterious statue

9

So we have it: Alkinoos,
And three blind lice
                    (Ya wanta know how? honest-ta-gawd? Well,
rustle that ivory drape
                    Put your hand on that stucco
                                                Let
yr eye be as light is, when westering, on brick to its east

only
keep a tight hold on
the mast, for
                    must is a fragrance the earth hath

      And we did this incommemorationofhim,
      going as the sea went, with only blood
      for a thread

                    END posy END
                        rime

"here i am, naked . . ."

here i am, naked
naked to you

depth to depth, i too ask:
love is not
a sufficient word

not to an innocent
of the impossible
                    whose desperations
are hidden from them
                        (It was January. She,
                        who would rather die
                        than do anything conspicuous,
                        bought Bergdorf-Goodman's best
                        dress and hat,
                        rode uptown on a bus, undressed
                        to nakedness, left
                        the clothes on the bank, walked,
                        that little delicate lovely woman,
                        straight to the River
                        and drowned)

The only valid contrary
is ice. And does it, too,
consume, in the end,
the consumer, as fire does?

I go by my nose, pushed
from the back, to tell
such stories, to make
a Hymn to She,

and project it against that very Place,
that Huddle of Human under
the Edge of Ice!

Only it is not enough, there
is wildness left out, to kill
and to self-kill!

           (how a god must have wept
             to watch her, creature, take off those clothes
            and go naked down
            to that water!)

We must save, save,
from the waste, the waste!

           (shall we not break ice,
              and make a fire, a fire
              and burn it, burn it,
              for her!   )

invent a word, a word
to be an answer to the eye's knowing,
the 1 of the 8000 eyes of us, our own spies, we who are god's flies,
the 1 that knows the guilt
of the fire!

"It's SPRing AgAIN!"

It is not spring. The furnace
must still be fed, its mouth
yaws, like a whale's, for boats

Yet I am already sprung, my bones
are loose, are full
of breathing holes

    breached bones
    of the green time
    when labor
    is reborn!

    when right on the surface of the ground
    without stems
    the croci flash
    (like eyes)!

    her eyes, opening
    telling you to flower!

2

here's to opening
but not to upward,
to earth
but not to leaf and sap
to her
to her herself
to earth,
to all her closer intervals

to grass   (her hair)
to what stays close
to all that stays
close as the cards she plays
from start to finish
from her breast!

3

spring says,
there are correct extensions
(let you go no further than
your finger tips!)

her trees, for instance,
they come later, are
what's worked for, ask
(for structure)
equal labor

spring says, labor,
what man knows
and not as sweat and brows
(hebraic punishments)
but thing itself
das ding an sing
SING!   the labor of
the THING!   the lesson of

    S P R I N G!

Asymptotes

yup, our disgraces are
our Graces

nor have i a talent,
or a virtue,
to lend

i, too, am retted down, am
mere aroid,
like a cuckoopint decide
i am all spike and bract

for who has time
to undo his ignorance?
have you?
may i stop you,
may i tap you on the shoulder

              say, have you got a match,
              Prometheus?

              what was it like,
              to be bound?

              in your winter, what fed
              on your liver, Ambiguous?

myself, i go by glee,
don't even know the bird
eats me

      (o for a beak,

              (Hail, Claw!

      to be sharp!

The Morning News

"O mister Eckhart! calling
Meister Eck-heart!

"Doctor Strzygowski!"

". . . truly hermetique,
Nothing catholique . . ."

Natura NON morte:
it was a bowl of fruit
(I am no hero and no saint,
nor are we scamps
or crockery-breakers)
a bowl, a golden bowl, in any day,
put out there, on the table, as jewels
were worn, in fact, as the fine birds
were wrought, the pair of peacocks' heads,
say, set with the Syrian garnets

Neither to be eaten, nor

to be made pretty of.

I

"One of the less known names of that Omaha chief known to history as Handsome Slayer was, He-Who-Runs-Away-To-Play-Another-Day. He was one of the founders of that curious Indian society which called itself the Backward Boys. It was a special Plains society, of which the members did everything, including the carrying of a lance and the riding of their horses, backwards.

118

"It was rumored that, and it is now thought that, there were hidden sexual motivations for this strange behavior. It is true, that all Indian life, particularly that of the Plains Indians of North America, exhibits a violence which the modern mind, now that it has been given the proper tools, cannot avoid seeing as repressive in origin. It is only now becoming clear, for example, that the war-whoop, which seemed to the early settlers to be only a device of what we would now call 'psychological warfare,' was, in truth, nothing but an obvious sign of Indian arrestment at a pre-Oedipean level.

"We are just beginning now to do adequate research into this interesting orality."

I remember the day. It was not too many years ago. Spring was on me so (it was a Sunday afternoon, April, perhaps) that I persisted, when my friends insisted, that I come inside and be present while they entertained their girls at cocktails, I persisted in the sun and sat long alone on the grass.

But here is the point. When I did come in I was so caught up in the afflatus of that season

        Aprille with her arrowes sweete
that I sat plump down between the two ladies, and took them both in my arms.

At which point, and since that day (one of the ladies later became the wife of one of my friends) those two buddies of mine have been consistently and hiddenly, my enemies!

        And who shall say
I was not possibly, like that old Indian chief,
p.sy-kick? who'll
deny to this brief vigil of our senses, knowledge
of what's inside us?

(Will you,
old Armourer?

or you,
my Captain of the Hold?

for look! look! where the blood
   has ceased to run
in the collapsed veins!

2

"Though it is Easter, this is, alas,—we must face it, be brave,
remember *all* our Lessons—the day of *no* light. This is, in
short, the Gray Day. All we can do is, quietly, each for
himself, weep."

    Listen, bro. What you better remember is,

    when she passes, you tip your hat!

    We are such trembling vapours

    as trains are run on. Do not count

    the telegraph poles.

    And if you can bounce high,

    do that too, until she cry,

    "Lover, gold-hatted, high-bouncing lover,

    you come over here!"

             (Hold! o Amor-eur!

             I, too, wear
             the Visored Face.)

3

"What desolation! I cannot stand

yr new

civilization!"   (What a shot
                                                   that was!)

    You who have stayed too long at the oar-locks,

    look now—or you'll never see its like again!

    The rails are layed down, and even the engine's

    got its steam up. Don't, Pearl,

    lay yrself across the tracks!

        (And he sped, red-hot, over the seas,

        put a belt around the earth,

        and all this before the Supreme Court could say,

        Dred Scott!)

4

    The sun sat there,
    like a great squash.

    And by god if the two of 'em,
    with their spread fat arses,
    didn't try to squush
    me!

Who the hell are they to say

"Th–is,

is go–ing to beeeeee

a GRRRR–eat

DAY!"

And we used to do it,
at dawn on the deck,
and toss the bucket overboard,
dowsing it a couple of times
to be sure it was clean

What I remember most
is the smell of Shea's tobacco.
And his talking, before breakfast,
of "Kunrudd," as he pronounced it,
of Kunrudd, and that book
whose title he could never get straight.

(Come to think of it, it was Red Flaming who sd,

desolation. I'm not so sure he doesn't show

some of the old blood. For he is, with all his strength,

one of the Boys.

There was this conversation:
"Can you tell a dawn when you see one?"
"Aw, a pock a lips! Gimme no more of yr jaw!"
It reminded me of what the old man used to say:
"Put a tackle on it, it's
hangin',
son!"

5

I gathered what he meant was, the chin. When the chin is large (this is already clear to Fenichel and other excellent doctors like him) it is a sign that there has been too much eating going on, even though it can come just as much from self-satisfaction as from actual cannibalism.

"This is now so apparent that there is no longer any need to study further the institution, among the tribes, of what can best be translated as Saint Stephen's Rite. Stephen is interesting as the founder, as the first one with genius enough to see how necessary it was in a hunting society that a masticatory image be provided to the people so that they might understand what they were doing with their daily lives.

"Like so much of the late Metastatic culture . . . ."

WE BREAK OFF THE INTELLECTUAL PART OF THIS PROGRAM TO BRING YOU A SPECIAL AND MOMENTOUS NEWS BULLETIN!

"Cibola has fallen!

The Anthropophagi are

IN COMPLETE RETREAT!!!!"

AND NOW the poet HAS AN IMPORTANT MESSAGE FOR YOU!

THE POET: "O! seven cities!
That made this country great!
Whose skies, *profumo*, blotted out the sun!

"O! seven cities!

Who once so poisoned all our children that

they opened out, *colombo*, all the West!

"O seven cities! Now

that you lie down together,

fortissimo, deny not,

(o God, Smog of our Fathers)

your glorious wrongs!"

THANK YOU, LAUREATE!

IN ADDITION, AT THIS WAKE-UP HOUR,

WE BRING YOU—
        THE HANDSOME SAILOR!

(*Crowd noises:*   "sesquipedentifrice
sesquipedentifrice   sesquipedentifrice"

and *shouts* of: "Fer cryssake, he
                      won't TALK!

                     "Look! the dope, he
                      STUTTERS!"

and *all:* "KILL 'im, KILL 'IM"

no, citizens,

no

(*musical bridge,* in, & over:

"This is
        th-is is,
                    the NEWooo
Da-YYYYY!"

6

And they cuffed him

And our tears were as gold

"It is cold here
You must go out and bring in some wood
For there is much to be done."

And we obeyed her,
because she was old,
and our mother.

END
broadcast

A Gloss

These days
only the telephone men are spurred,
look, at their hips, prepared.

There was a time
when singers issued from the hand of God holster and gun,
began their business properly aged four,
drew up their language while the world was round
(and sweet as any mother), turned things on their tongue
all milk and honey. And then went out along their growing
full of incest and green fire.

At 14 add syllables for grit, and yawning guilt.
Admit the teeth are now some new-found aids.
Observe: the priest rejected, not the mother.
And all the vocal system glottal stop.

At 18 they discover story, put out their certain hands
all clipper-tape and snarl, grab at the father, find
him at a rape which, like a line-storm, tears
each caught-wire down.

At which point cease, or so the lesson seems to read.
For the shock and the bell are here
where the man-act interposes.
The man and the God are clear,
and a man, if he is to be a man,
must here stand clear.

I'll get a crucible, he said, put all of me in,
dissolve down to one abridgement,
then be lead,
and useful for connections.

But when the place is as raw as rock
a man must fight every instant
to keep himself vertebra, bone
from the neck to the tip of his cock!

Of Lady, of Beauty, of Stream

that rising, of the first, you cause,

so very much as though you bent
over the clearest water, clear
by your bending

and i, the goldenest trout, hiding
near to some very white sand,
came up, up through that very clear water
up through a mouth made of eyes:

and you caught me, caught me, took me
in that strong, that directive hand!

At Yorktown

1

At Yorktown the church

at Yorktown the dead

at Yorktown the grass

are live

       at York–town the earth

piles itself in shallows,

declares itself, like water,

by pools and mounds

2

At Yorktown the dead

are soil

at Yorktown the church
is marl
at Yorktown the swallows
dive where it is greenest,

                                 the hollows
are eyes are flowers, the heather,
equally accurate, is hands

       at York-town only the flies
dawdle, like history,
in the sun

3
at Yorktown the earthworks
braw
at Yorktown the mortars
of brass, weathered green, of mermaids
for handles, of Latin
for texts, scream
without noise
like a gull

4
At Yorktown the long dead
loosen the earth, heels

sink in, over an abatis

a bird wheels

and time is a shine caught blue

from a martin's

back

The She-Bear

o goddess excellently bright

look kindly

on this effort

I

Time, of itself, brings no significant changes

Does time stop me on the street and say,

"Pardon me, mister, which way
is life?"

To shred, pound, wash, decant
in order to begin . . . .

Look, it is at root

a question . . . .

Take fertility, for example, founding it

on quite other associations than you're used to:

        what each carried

        they threw down into springs,

        or on to the carefully colored sand,

                        the men

        their cylinders,

               the women

        annulets

There is a way

to breathe again, the process

not at all so complicated, a matter

of a turn (you asked me:

two blocks left, then

straight ahead)

of an act (disposing,

such as the above)

or this aversion:

        one night a year the priestess,

        not abandoning herself,

        on the contrary

by presentation takes on lovers
collects
a thumb's length of value (coins,
or turquoise pieces), leaves them
to the honor of Mimosa
And goes about the business of her day

(o goddess, receive these, our tokens,
for your light)

2

Agree we call the place
Pelican Rapids

Agree we have a fish hook
and an axe

Agree
a root can be a poison
or a plant, a house
a suffocation
or a frame

On this plateau, agree
we've left marauders
on the plain below

Let us raise a praise for woman,

let us give her brightness back

            "o Black, o dirtied, o

            covered

            o Naked, o wild, o

            thighed

            o Loose, o corrupted, o

            lain on

            o Bearer,

            who has suffered

            chagrin

                o Hair, o Silk

                o Pleasurer

                o Cedar-Box, o

                Wronged

            o Round, o flesh, o

            Answerer

            o Theorist, who would charm

            to save

o Seeker, o Imaginer
of passion

o Caught
in your own snare

o Descender, so rankly
imprisoned, turn aside
the Judges' stare

o Prostitute, Equal, Light, o
Dunged in this same Cave, o Lady
throw off all Crawlers!

Breast-Brilliant, blind
them!

The Cow
and the Patriarch
are gone, the Stable
and the Son

The Presumers, the Forgivers
are done, you have finished them
with the fire
from your eyes

o Lady Below, o Hatcher
o Reminder, we sing of
your pride

The She-Bear (II)

Agree we call the place
Pelican Rapids

Agree we have a fish hook
and an axe

Agree
a root can be a poison
or a plant, a house
a suffocation
or a frame

On this plateau, agree
we've left marauders
on the plain below

Agree, in other words,
we start again

(o goddess excellently bright

　　look kindly on the effort)

I

To shred, pound, wash, decant

Time, of itself, brings no significant changes.
Does time stop me, on the street, and say "Mister,
pardon me. But which way"?

Look. It is at root a question. Or the question

Founding it on quite other associations
than we are used to

　　　　(for ex., what they carried
　　　　they threw down into springs.
　　　　Or onto carefully colored sand.

　　　　　　　　　　　　The men,
　　　　widsom,
　　　　　　　　the women,
　　　　love.

There is a way. The process,
not at all so complicated, a
disposing (as above) or
an aversion:

one night a year,

not abandoning herself,

on the contrary,

       takes on lovers

collects a thumb's length

of value

And leaves it to the honor of Mimosa

and goes about the business

of her next day. Normal.

These are some of the
problems.

II

Lady Mimosa, deliver us

from all mud

keep us at it

Lady, who thought of yourself,

the very brilliance of my flesh

is enough

you are right

You who play it up,
we also have to uncover.
And are stripped,
by our own effronteries

Because you had light,
you have the advantage
of us: what you do by fiat
we come up on, on foot

That you too tasted
the lazy fruit,
got caught
But save us
from indulgence

You understood
that at least seven of us
stayed too content.
It helped.

III

TO THE SHE-BEAR

Sprawled,

on the bottom

Spread-eagled

Mere skin,

all fours

Come up!

"o Black, o dirtied, o

covered

o Naked, o wild, o

thighed

o Loose, o corrupted, o

lain on

o Bearer,

who has suffered

chagrin

(o Hair, o Silk

o Pleasurer

o Cedar-Box, o Wronged!)

"o Round, o flesh, o

Deliverer

o Theorist,

who would charm,

to save

o Seeker, o Imaginer

of passion

o Caught

in your own

snare

      (o Descender, so rankly

      imprisoned,

        give the Judges back

        stare for stare!)

"o Prostitute, o Goddess, o Light

  o Mate, o Equal, o Grace

  o Dunged in this Cave, throw off

all Crawlers

      (The Cow

      and the Patriarch

      are done, the Stable

      and the Son

The Presumers,

the Forgivers,

blind them all,

Breast–Brilliant!)

o Lady down there, o

Hatcher, of men

o Sister–Maker,

o Reminder: hail

Mimosa!

The

1st   To the She-Bear

Song

Sprawled,
on the bottom

Spread–eagled

Mere skin,
all fours

Come up!

Black. Dirtied.
Covered—three

of you. o Naked o wild o
thighed

o Loose, o corrupted, o
to be lain on. Hair,

Silk,
Pleasurer: o

Cedar-Box: to,
wrong you!

o Theorist,
who would charm

o Imaginer,
of passion

o Caught
in your own snare

       (Descender. If rankly
       imprisoned, give us back

       stare for stare, we
       Lookers, who are greedy

for the sight of you,
stripped

of all that gew-ga

o Prostitute Goddess Light
Mate Equal Grace (Ruth, whatever

precise number of names you go by:
Pink Woman, Negro; wonderful shoulders

in nightdresses; we'll bang down the doors
to get in, if you don't leave

the key for us: we are several, all yours!

o Dunged,
in the Cave,
throw off
the Crawlers!

o Lady Below, o Hatcher
o Reminder

o Breast–Brilliant,
blind them all!

We'll trick you,
to get back at you, but

o Wife, bung
their eyes, o

Shaped

(Sister-Maker, hail

Mimosa!

Diaries of Death

1938:   at 5 in the morning I vomited on the grass in front of my house

during the same crisis, 2 days later, I slept, at noon, against a fence
somewhere in Cambridge, in the sun

somehow I awoke free

1942:   from 3 in the afternoon until 5:30 of a Manhattan spring day,
when I was ill in bed for the second month Pearl Harbor thereafter,
one of four men who had mattered in 1938 sat and talked to me

that night, in a cheap hotel in Philadelphia, he took his life

1948:   again, spring, and I am asked to contribute money for lectures on the drama
which are to be a memorial to a second of the four, who has died,
age 42

Now, 1950, April 1st, I am called and told the man
       (who, more than any other, was, in 1938, the cause, the cause
       has thrown himself from a hotel window, unwound
       like a clock's spring, run out
       and not yet fifty years of age

    O ground of death, o factory of wills for wheels, o killer-place!

    o Inheritor of wrongs! of values which are useless, o falsenesses!

    o fourth (and fifth) who live, be not tempted to partake! Give over
New England, murder, suicide!

    There is cause, cause for effect, miseries unnecessary for a man

    who is, at best, his structures, fragile: go off, go off, go free

    from places where the strictures are too much, too much

    for you and me to bear!

"friday, Good Friday . . ."

               friday, Good Friday, which
always reminds me of Walter Strong, who grew up with me
on the Cut in Gloucester, and was such an inbred
he and his sister both drooled as long as we were kids,
and they had to wear bibs. Anyhow, Walter
grew up to be the sharpest gambler in the city

(he was so recognized last year when he got a suspended sentence
for booking the horses). Well, some years ago, one Good Friday,
we were all down to the gas station, sitting around chewing the fat,
when Walter says, "What about a little game, boys." Sez the others,
"Why, Walter! Don't you know? This is Good Friday!"
And Walter, who always sort of drawled after he grew up, answers,
"Whhhat's   goooood   aboooout   it?   Allll   Iiii   can
sssay   isss,   IIiiii   hoooope   it'll   be   gooooood
for   meeeee!"

Cinos

I

Down, throw down his like who eat
who enter and who take away outside
experience, who begin—and after—
from themselves, the feeders

Cinos are feeders, ladies,
have naught to do with Cinos, who
have naught to do with more than this:
with image more than person, more
syllable than image, more sound
than any other hother-pother
                              Thus
their furies

2

Cinos are rogues and elephants, innocents
of the impossible, do double
trouble as it is, make grounds
you cannot stand on, sweep
the table-cloth away

                              Yet mean not so, not one jot
what they seem or what they do or do not
do

This is their ambiguity: their eye
and foot are on a road much travelled
with a difference, which you travel,
and a rue their own:: the road
they see before they walk it, from that road
they wave back on themselves after
they've gone around your bend

3

This is a warning: do not
expect them back
even though the season is
extravagant, though blood
is to be let, and pods
are filling, though ladies,
despairing, take up in packs
and cults of their own
making, go off
to highways, joints, jousts, bouts
of wilding::
                    no Cinos there
Cinos
are more intimate animals, more
players

of queens with darts, differently
troublesome,
                    they
leave you with a line, cry
(as they go off)
what Cinos think
important, pass you,
for your blood,

songs, songs, songs!

Bigmans

arouse yrself, Bigmans,
arouse

cities, things
crumples
of tin, And dead men
in

Bigmans, start
moving, start
the next heave, leave
your mother's fire: your brothers
have had enough derisions
despitous, of many filths
though fructuous

Take to the streets, Bigmans,
to the streets, go
to the whore, begin:
she is sib, wrong boy

daintiness
of limbs or fingers, of hair
of hunger for the fruits of gods, of lair
of twisting paths, of proper movement, hers
hath shrunk to kill, to fear, she sits
by property defiled, by stories rifled
of initiation, she
who is ground, who is a well, who is night
who is made nothing of
now, eyeless
though powered

Bigmans, yr place
is out, out from inside, you've slept
enough the self, got fat
b'exceptionality, your own
and generally. Let go, hulk, pull out
from her house, dispose
your strength where others are, where they lie
as things do, as cities, waiting
to be waked

Bigmans, this
is an asking, is
a demand, we
ask you

                                    (draft of invocation)

148

Bigmans II

He who saw everything, of him learn, o my land, learn

of him who sought out to know what lands are for, & people, to turn

to fruitfulness after the wastings and the idlenesses, the ways

to use what is called strength after its misuse, he who had tidings

of times when deltas were of use as deltas and not floodings

of excrement

        learn of him who went a long journey to cut down

the dirty tree, the tree of false issue, the tree whose roots

make filth of the waters, cause to come down, where streams

appear to be, nothing but clottings, siltings to the bloods, the confusings

of lands and of my people, their bewilderments

and perturbations

        learn of him, o my delta, who was willing to tell

his story, who understood that to spell out is not at all to end,

that to tell is only to begin to unravel what no man can complete,

that one tale no matter how severely it is told depends

on tales once told and tales to be told when his is added

to the changeful narrative, to the head

as many-haired as there are men with courage to take up

their lives as story, as sign the ambiguity of which

no single man is master of

so, learn of this one, people

who did build a wall, who saw his job as civilizer, took on

a proposition: where waters have thrown up new land, that land

is meant to be a place where men and women can, because that land

has come up out of water after crimes of kin and blood

have been committed, where people can, my people, clean

themselves of postulations gone awry, of runners crusted, shelled

with gurry, so no sea-way, of arms turned from first purpose

of one thing only, protection of the land, of instruments

so sharp they only cut the air and, turned to human cause,

just kill, kill, kill

he built a wall around what ground

was new enough to wipe out wrongs: behold

the brightness of his wall, which shines like flesh,

yes, and look as well on that wall's inner wall

(which none can equal yet), its threshold

standing out as teeth do in free face, and white

as stone gets from the wear of feet: climb,

any of you, up on this new wall, walk on it, look out from it

with confidence and pleasure, inspect

(if you need one least speck of sureness for yourself)

the underwork, examine every brick and timber, note

the vaulting, ask yourself if you can recognize this arch, be sure

the bricks are honestly burnt, the wood carved careful, underside

and all, and then consider whether seven others did not aid him

in its raising

you'll also want to know his name, this man of us:

Bigmans, they called him, even the children stopping him, bringing

new kids to his door to show him off, saying, in their questioning way,

"Giant, this new boy wouldn't believe. We told him, you are a giant.

You are, aren't you?"

and he diffident, though fish swam in the currents of his blood,

that boys and girls had awe, not of him, of course,

but of his sleeping outer shell, he awed too that they,

these boys and girls, retained the willingness to wonder

at brightness he had only started from, so long slept through, the cubits

of his bones, the spans required to cross his chest, the octaves

of his head and of those parts which had, before his brother came,

before he left his mother's fire, made bull trouble among his folk,

he was so rampant, wild, and unacknowledged to himself

It took some doing, to bring this Bigmans in, for him

to find out what is force, how far it comes from, where

it starts, where he himself took up, what times and beats

men in their struggle are beholden to, what it is that places energies

in orders, who

is boss

With him it started from the wronged. If, in the end, he too

did do his part, in its beginning he did not hear,

it might be said he even tried, yet when his people cried:

"He leaves no air for anyone. He crowds us on. His appetite

outrages each of us until, though he be strong and handsome,

even wise, none any more can like him, can tolerate

intrusions on their peace and flesh. We wish him off, and done for, gone

some other place, however shining is his mind, whatever builder

he may seem to be, what tenderness he offers here and there,

whatever accidental, honest rage breaks out,

it does not matter. His wildness now has gone beyond our present needs.

His muscularity offends our other lives. We wish him gone, left

to himself if none will have this furious ox, whoever

brought him into being, whoever

put him here among us, however knowing

he or they are in their showing

us how to do our work.

We grant

there's no one who's his match, none

either the equal of his given nor

how he has shaped his weapons for such use,

for our use or his own, but, o makers of men, no strength

is good enough which turns on self alone, cuts through

the underbrush of choice by muscle solely, presumes to think

that all things are dispersal only, mere particulars,

that all outside the self is multiples

which ego only can cut down,

when we know (by law we only quarter sense)

that doubles are the problem, that act is one of two

at every given instant, that binary is the law if we shall move

—as he pretends he leads us—

to end this savagery, to make this delta where our city stands

a place for men and women to be one.

                                We beg whatever force presides

to raise up now now now one other man to equal Bigmans now, to right

this glistening bull of ours whose knowing

has become so useless that he roams,

corrupted of his born sophistication, a modern monster day & night, reverts

to what is worse than what we came from, that marauding

his predecessors led us out of, led us here from, led us

—until he lost remembrance of them, of, his fathers—led us

to such skills to live with pleasure and with mind

               there was no snake, no scorpion
               no wild dog or wolf,
                               in those days
               East was place of plenty, just decrees,
               the South was honey-tongued, the princes' eyes
               were lapis-lazuli, looked out even, the North
               had all what's needful for a human life, the West
               rested in security, all of us
               in one tongue gave our praise

we had things of our hands, the lions of desire had end, we were

as men and women bound

in daily, nightly round

of private point as well as of each other's use, each man

a stem, from pride in his own wildness put to use, each woman

each new time of love a maiden going in, the earth & sun right after, each

each time renewed, renewing, each time neither lesser than the other, each

returning in spring as thing and thing, halve to halve, not sure

by self, by self exaggeration, simply going on, replenished, taking

permission from what's gone before, what's larger than, what it is

that makes us want to keep on going, to find

not what we are but what it is we offer that may be

of use,

      of use as are the things our hands have made.

These things, these old offsettings of infected bats, of poisoning bugs,

of moles and flying things we know we also are true elements of,

this man, who once we took to be a leader, who seemed to have the clues

to keep us to ourselves, this son of other human kings who did,

who gave us cities where the river made an air at night so fresh

that we could put aside the day's fatigue and take on love's delight,

this Bigmans now has thrown his wisdom out,

and made his own life's cravings law.

          We ask, whoever made him, make

his equal, make a man of such impetuous heart, the two of them

will struggle with each other,

and give the rest of us some rest."

           (end, draft, part II)

In Cold Hell, in Thicket

In cold hell, in thicket, how
abstract (as high mind, as not lust, as love is) how
strong (as strut or wing, as polytope, as things are
constellated) how
strung, how cold
can a man stay (can men) confronted
thus?

All things are made bitter, words even
are made to taste like paper, wars get tossed up
like lead soldiers used to be
(in a child's attic) lined up
to be knocked down, as I am,
by firings from a spit-hardened fort, fronted
as we are, here, from where we must go

God, that man, as his acts must, as there is always
a thing he can do, he can raise himself, he raises
on a reed he raises his

Or, if it is me, what
he has to say

I

What has he to say?
In hell it is not easy
to know the traceries, the markings
(the canals, the pits, the mountings by which space
declares herself, arched, as she is, the sister,
awkward stars drawn for teats to pleasure him, the brother
who lies in stasis under her, at ease as any monarch or
a happy man

How shall he who is not happy, who has been so made unclear,
who is no longer privileged to be at ease, who, in this brush, stands
reluctant, imageless, unpleasured, caught in a sort of hell, how
shall he convert this underbrush, how turn this unbidden place
how trace and arch again
the necessary goddess?

2

The branches made against the sky are not of use, are
already done, like snow-flakes, do not, cannot service
him who has to raise   (Who puts this on, this damning of his flesh?)
he can, but how far, how sufficiently far can he raise the thickets of
this wilderness?

> How can he change, his question is
> these black and silvered knivings, these
> awkwardnesses?
>
> How can he make these blood-points into panels, into sides
> for a king's, for his own
> for a wagon, for a sleigh, for the beak of, the running sides of
> a vessel fit for
> moving?
>
> How can he make out, he asks,
> of this low eye-view,
> size?
>
> And archings traced and picked enough to hold
> to stay, as she does, as he, the brother, when,
> here where the mud is, he is frozen, not daring
> where the grass grows, to move his feet from fear
> he'll trespass on his own dissolving bones, here
> where there is altogether too much remembrance?

3

The question, the fear he raises up himself against
(against the same each act is proffered, under the eyes
each fix, the town of the earth over, is managed) is: Who
am I?

Who am I but by a fix, and another,
a particle, and the congery of particles carefully picked one by another,

       as in this thicket, each
       smallest branch, plant, fern, root
       —roots lie, on the surface, as nerves are laid open—
       must now (the bitterness of the taste of her) be
       isolated, observed, picked over, measured, raised
       as though a word, an accuracy were a pincer!
                            this

           is the abstract, this
           is the cold doing, this
           is the almost impossible

So shall you blame those
who give it up, those who say
it isn't worth the struggle?

                    (Prayer
Or a death as going over to—shot by yr own forces—to
a greener place?

                Neither
any longer
usable)

       By fixes only (not even any more by shamans)
       can the traceries
       be brought out

II

ya, selva oscura, but hell now
is not exterior, is not to be got out of, is
the coat of your own self, the beasts
emblazoned on you   And who
can turn this total thing, invert
and let the ragged sleeves be seen
by any bitch or common character?   Who
can endure it where it is, where the beasts are met,
where yourself is, your beloved is, where she
who is separate from you, is not separate, is not
goddess, is, as your core is,
the making of one hell

>   where she moves off, where she is
>   no longer arch

    (this is why he of whom we speak does not move, why
    he stands so awkward where he is, why
    his feet are held, like some ragged crane's
    off the nearest next ground, even from
    the beauty of the rotting fern his eye
    knows, as he looks down, as,
    in utmost pain if cold can be so called,
    he looks around this battlefield, this
    rotted place where men did die, where boys
    and immigrants have fallen, where nature
    (the years that she's took over)
    does not matter, where

>   that men killed, do kill, that woman kills
>   is part, too, of his question

2

That it is simple, what the difference is—
that a man, men, are now their own wood

and thus their own hell and paradise
that they are, in hell or in happiness, merely
something to be wrought, to be shaped, to be carved, for use, for
others

does not in the least lessen his, this unhappy man's
obscurities, his
confrontations

He shall step, he
will shape, he
is already also
moving off

       into the soil, on to his own bones

he will cross

      (there is always a field,
      for the strong there is always
      an alternative)

           But a field
      is not a choice, is
      as dangerous as a prayer, as a death, as any
      misleading, lady

He will cross

      And is bound to enter (as she is)
      a later wilderness.
              Yet
      what he does here, what he raises up
      (he must, the stakes are such

                  this at least
      is a certainty, this
      is a law, is not one of the questions, this
      is what was talked of as
      —what was it called, demand?)

He will do what he now does, as she will, do
carefully, do
without wavering,
without
        as even the branches,
        even in this dark place, the twigs
                              how
        even the brow
of what was once to him a beautiful face

as even the snow-flakes waver in the light's eye

        as even forever wavers (gutters
        in the wind of loss)

        even as he will forever waver

        precise as hell is, precise
        as any words, or wagon,
        can be made

For Sappho, Back

I

With a dry eye, she
saw things out of the corner of,
with a bold
she looked on any man,
with a shy eye

With a cold eye, with her eye she looked on, she looked out, she
who was not so different as you might imagine from,
who had, as nature hath, an eye to look upon her makings, to,
in her womb, know
how red, and because it is red, how
handsome blood is, how, because it is unseen, how
because it goes about its business as she does,
as nature's things have that way of doing, as
in the delight of her eye she
creates constants
    And, in the thickness of her blood, some
variants

II

As blood is, as flesh can be
is she, self-housed, and moving
moving in impeccability to be
clear, clear! to be
as, what is rhythm but
her limpidity?
     She
who is as certain as the morning is
when it arises, when it is spring, when, from wetness comes its brightness
as fresh as this beloved's fingers, lips
each new time she new turns herself to
tendernesses, she
turns her most objective, scrupulous attention, her own
self-causing
    each time it is,
    as is the morning, is
    the morning night and revelation of her
    nakednesses, new
    forever new, as fresh as is the scruple of her eye, the accurate
    kiss

III

If you would know what woman is, what
strength the reed of man unknows, forever
cannot know, look, look! in these eyes, look
as she passes, on this moving thing, which moves
as grass blade by grass blade moves, as
syllable does throw light on fellow syllable, as,
in this rare creature, each hidden, each moving thing
is light to its known, unknown brother,
as objects stand one by one by another, so
is this universe, this flow, this woman, these eyes
are sign

IV

The intimate, the intricate, what shall perplex, forever
is a matter, is it not, not of confusions to be studied and made literal,
but of a dry dance by which, as shoots one day make leaves, as
the earth's crust, when ice draws back, wrings mountains
from itself, makes valleys in whose palms
root-eating fisher folk spring up—
by such a dance, in which the dancer contradicts
the waste and easy gesture, contains
the heave within,
within, because the human is so light a structure, within
a finger, say, or there
within the gentlest swaying of
                          (of your true hips)

In such containment
                And in search for that which is the shoot, the thrust
of what you are
            (of what you were so delicately born)
                                 of what fruits
of your own making you are
                the hidden constance of which all the rest
is awkward variation

this! this
is what gives beauty to her eye, inhabitation
to her tender-taken bones, is what illumines
all her skin with satin glow
when love blows over, turning
as the leaf turns in the wind
and, with that shock of recognition, shows
its other side, the joy, the sort of terror of

a dancer going off

"Help Me, Venus, You Who Led Me On"

If you would guess, fond man, the secret,
propose to say why your beloved's foot still flashes,
in your face still flashes, still
is fire upon your force, still
doth stir the root

If on this course, as she is, as she runs, as she too looks for love,
as she, a daughter, seeks a lover,
forever seeks the lover worthy to undo the obdurate father

If, as she leads you, as she outruns you in this racing,
as you pursue both her and some more stubborn, abstract tracing,
you who go as tortoise and as hare do,
as you, slow, in search for source, and then so quickly furious

If you and she both race uncertain,
palpably uncertain, as the issue is, as,

because you both are, not as nature is, as
man and woman forever is—

Then, man, can you allow
your own bold eye to fall
the least point off, in this full running, off
this silver girl

Can you, who makes this race, or loses
who, must follow after or
be lost, resist
the inward tender of
these flying feet?

Can you, or you,
when man runs, when woman runs, when both of you are racing
as man and woman forever is,
                              with what differences,
                                             And love

the only likeness?

Other Than

cold
    cold
        on the bold

shore, as the rock
falleth the water
stands: beware

of permanence, you who would run in, who, in yr thin shallops, think
to make the land

the season
            is forever
                    cold,
and the reason the rock

(if you can call the mind

Or is it from water

that images

come?

And the boldness
never to be ice, never
to stand, never to go other than does
the slow & antient
heart: to change

is the expectation

                we previous immigrants
                tell you

Quatrain

Do not, at this high time, desert
(from pain, distraction, of the mind, of the senses, of
believing
            the raising up—we are all, we are all, forever
lone-ing
            that raising up which is, forever is, the will
of our own self-ing
desert not, here at the Bloody Angle, where even death may be,
the Cause, the Cause, it is
the cause!

Day Song

Beside her, she a limpid brook, I took
what nature salted in, delight

what she so certainly at her mixed table meant
we might, so quickly, when she gives
when she enables one of her spring instruments to give

what I, or any man or woman, must
so surely and so lightly seize

The gross, against which now is only claritas,
was wimpled off, as, on that grass, her skin

which I had known to fall by winter pain to scale

was grace

      And her fine running
      a rune-ing
      of such songs

      my stones

      are groundings
      for

If on this afternoon of spring the air
was gently confident,
                  And she
extraordinarily clear

if, here, outside,
my lady was so sure,
so obviously tender,
             and self-resting

      If in this slow mistral, so balancing she wore
      as queen of sedge
      the fragrance
      of the grass, of hay of love,
      of oats, of barley and of pease

      if on this green, the more made green
      by rain,
           And by her own
      soft self-ing

If her own quiet
so not made rotted by too close a keeping

if by such clear-kept secret is
her head so finely rising, is
articulate her arms,
                        her legs,
their longing

        If in such silver coursing, these

                                And her hips,
        as waters press against all margins,

        weave

        And if they now wear all themselves as coronal,

                then, boy, you
                have all the joy
                of that far intimate which lies,
                not as the trinkling waters of this brook where she began,
                but flood will be where she is consummate

Day Song, the Day After

Beside herself (and me, too, so help me), & she
no brook at all, jes'
what she is, another
dame
  And I can tell you, without any necessary poetic delay,
no delight at all

    (Mixed table, sd I?
    Right-schmight, me)

And as for getting yr toe in here? for getting a hold of anything?

Let's jes' leave the whole business as
altogether too god damn poetic, eh?

And just a leetle bit gross,
as the introduction service put it, despite
the fine skin, and, what had been advertised,
the grace
    ((And on the grass I slipped,
    and all thot of songs went the hell out of my head,
    at least to her, tho not to the subject of "wetting,"
    when I landed, ker-plunk,
    in that so-called fine running,
    not at the mouth, no, not at the mouth of the
    stream))

If spring was confident, or she was, I
ain't,
  & if she was clear (o that fine birdey, claritas—up
      yr—well, yr claritas)

she don't shed any of it
on me, not on this
I-Take-A-Powder injun boy

Tenderness-schmenderness?
Self-resting-festering?
Or der Balanzink?
She may the queen of it, but me,
I'm the green of it, green
as they come, bro.

           If this is self-ing, what you call it, then flee, flee!
           my leetle runnink water!

It's altogether too much like—
what is it that they call the deep stuff?—
still waterz?

The Dry Ode

It pusheth us out before it, out, and to the side.
    Gray stalks in a green field.
    Young corn in clay. And the heart,
    a seed. And the head,
    how heavy is the yield?

The crops are grass, mainly.

We make shift to do, holding down.
    Corn is as corn was. And now
    the soil is gray, the flower
    alfalfa, green, it is, is green
    again

Rotate (like they say) the clover, the grain. Go round
    the field-stone
    (or the brick-walled center, grave, whichever
    local
    to the native
    ground

For in the shade are rocks, some mustard plant, the sun
diffuse

The movement is, generally as, as weather
comes from the west.

A B C s

The word forms
on the left: you must
stand in line. Speech
is as swift as synapse
but the acquisition of same
is as long
as I am old

rat   on the first floor landing of the three-decker
             (grey)

black   eat a peck of storage batteries 'fore
           I die

cabbage my friend Cabbage, with whom to bake potatoes up
           Fisher's Hill

rust   in the bed of Beaver Brook—from the junk in it

           And the iris ("flags," we called 'em)

           And the turtle I was surprised by

up to last night's dream, the long brown body pleased
I kissed her buttock curve

Interiors,
and their registration

Words, form
but the extension of
content

Style, est verbum

The word
is image, and the reverend reverse is
Eliot

Pound
is verse

A B C s (2)

what we do not know of ourselves
of who they are who lie
coiled or unflown
in the marrow of the bone

     one sd:

         of rhythm is image
         of image is knowing
         of knowing there is
         a construct

or to find in a night who it is dwells in that wood where shapes hide
who is this woman or this man whose face we give a name to, whose shoulder
we bite, what landscape
figures ride small horses over, what bloody stumps
these dogs have, how they tear the golden cloak

                        And the boat,

how he swerves it to avoid the yelping rocks
where the tidal river rushes

A B Cs (3—for Rimbaud)

NEWS (o the latest)
& mu-sick, mu-sick—music
worse than war, worse
than peace, & they both dead
And the people's faces
like boils

Who pleas for the heart, for the return of, into the work of,
say, the running of
a street-car?

        Or shall it be rain,
        on a tent   or grass   or birds
        on a wire (5, count 'em, now 3
        on two—or does it come to 1
        on 1? Is it
        Metechevsky?

                We call it
                trillings, cleanings,
                we who want scourings

        Or the watching of, the Passaic of
        orange peels? Cats
        win in urbe, NOT
        usura   or those queer long white (like finger bandages
        balloons? The dyes
        of realism? (Cats,
        & industry, not even
        violence

                Why not the brutal, head on?
                Fruits? beauty? to want it
                so hard? Who

can beat that life
into form, who
is so hopeful—who
has misled us?

To have what back? Is it any more than
a matter of
syllables?

Yes, mouths bit
empty air

They bit. What
do they bite,
now? what we needed most
was something the extension of
claritas: what do we have
to report?

The Story of an Olson, and Bad Thing

PART 1

Bad Thing came in the night, and, this time, ate away part of my
heart. Yet I endure, knowing no cure, because, as each is, I am
stubborn, the only difference the usual one, individual difference
(huge swedish teeth like my father's, whom god keeps, because he
was really in there, and smelled of violets, but it killed him in the
end, his stubbornness, literally it brought about his death. We are
such fools, these olson males, the way we go by, the way we live
up to, like liars, like strong-teethed men, the affections!)

I, too, waste (and this was certainly one thing I took warning from
his death, so help me god) waste out mortal strength. So I live, by
warning, in daily fear I'll not break down by the nerves, as my fellows
do, but by, as he did, the blood vessels, by the breaking of, where
the fragrance is. God damn our grace, that this is how we are fated.

And yet I don't believe I shall repeat him, if for no other reason than,
that I dare not, that I must not (the way my time is quantitative and
must, thus, be turned into space) I must not break, must, somehow,
haul myself up eighty years, god damn these reeds on which men stand.

        Right now, in front of all our eyes, a man child
(sd Bolyai Farkas, on all sides they spring up, to the need of, the
season) is being born—o!
smell the blood.

PART 2

Stamina, that's what isn't, not intelligence. It wasn't only stupidity
the creator damned the race with. It was shortness of life (what Bad
Thing feeds on, knows how to nibble at). And that which we go by
in the running, breath, breath, which can, as the flesh can, give off
the odor of, same flowers.

        The original sin was simpler: all returns,
we want all returns before one good black night is over, the doctrine
of, what my people
        (it was the people we used to call the crew)
                        prove,

the whole stink, from the corruption of, are the founders of,
that which gives the lie to, what impugns, exposes
(after christianity, thus
          the counsel of, the smell of,
          and of same, the methodology,
          the fast buck:

kill, kill! he cried,
just to get rid of, just
to avoid

borning, borning, old Bitch Goddess!
you know
the answer

It takes blood, my fellow cits., even to the breaking of
vessels!
    (Vessels!)

PART 3

The ease of (with some of a heart gone, and a little of the lower
intestine, and no one but yourself, no naked white man raised by
brown people to put his hand on, and say, I heal you) the easing of

space. And he says, It sounds easy, only it ain't, as he dressed
himself in doeskin, and went off trading among distant tribes, went
looking for a place where people are still natives, and where human
business is still the business

where, if you can find sleep, see if you can find the ease, see if I
can find you, in your life, moving, as though I were a sea-horse,
because I am, because, god damn it, an olson male is
a double

    multiple, he sd, as a man, or a woman
    is (is a woman?) is
    when they resist, when they let sleep
    that dog with the whitest, sharpest teeth

      the temptation, which didn't get into the biblums,
      that is, into them so far, that is, as I knows them,

        of the brains, which always, always wants
        what it can't have because they ain't

Answers, I mean,
which have no smell at all

PART 4

Explaining the magic (where it is, here where he is, he sez, sez time,

"The only trick, the only way you save your thing, or whatever, is
obey, obey, until you've squeezed out of, out of me, out of me who
is yr onlie true enemie . . ."

The sweetest kind of essence, violets
                              is the smell of life.
And I mean serious, like magic is, like
white or black, is
the business we're here for (not here AFTER) i mean (NOW)
the smell of
these flowers
                    And don't expect me to answer,
how come. Nor do I care, even it turns out, as it just might well,
electricals, simply the odor of, from the crackling of,
a wave   H-mu, the determinant, human.
                              Or it doesn't even matter if
they reproduce same. Nature, by way of woman, does it every day.
It is still something, the fragrance, that only those with
the nose for it can smell and
CAN GIVE OFF

                    (Or that line I palmed off on him, as he ate me:
                    "I can be precise,
                    though it is no answer"

                    And why he, after he pushed through so many tribes,
                    had eaten little more than prickly pears,
                    and sucked reeds for water,

why, when he came out—and wasn't it curious, that the point at which
he emerged should have been already called, by the natives, the place
of the heart?—he carefully took the things he had made (despite
Bad Thing, and his botherings) and instead of disposing of them in
so many ways that would occur to you, he merely set them out there
where the rest of the causes of confusion are.

This act of his
is as interesting a proof as anything you shall find, of what we
might call, thinking of the people, and their problems, the other
doctrine, the contrary one, or, what we may simply call, numbers,
numbers seeming now to have a peculiar fascination, like letters, and
other such dry things, as plastics, nipples, and machines—Doctrine
#2, viz.,

> multiple observation at the same instant that others
> make less multiple observations, is the difference

(And the which doctrine can also be used to be quite precise about
the difference of this class of worker from other classes of workers,
equally necessary, whatever clothes, or however hy-brid, or what
sort of noses they wear.)

And, as against 80, 125 years, which,
because the human animal has so shrunk away from created limits,
is no longer the given

(thus, the inadequacy of all our work,
compared to the assignment,
and to the equipment given

And why we ain't
spiritchool

And why there ain't
antsirs

And why we damn well have to go
by the nose
(what nose?)

Why the whys are, in fact
(last night, as I sd, he nipped me)
because they are facts, they are only
clues:

It is clews, clews that keep
sails taut. Drama
is out of business, tears,
tears. Ships, ships, it's
steering now that is, it is
the biz-i-ness NOW, you
who care, who can
endure, it's
"bring the head 'round, keep
the wind, citizen!

(is it not the wind we obey, are
kept by?

as good a word as any is
the SINGLE INTELLIGENCE

PART LAST

At this date of 120 years cut short, I, an olson

in the l'univers concentrationnaire the flesh
(is it not extraordinary that, when a wound
is healing, we call, what it throws off, proud
flesh?) flesh, rose flesh

must also be thrown in.

And because there is no soul (in the old sense),
because there is not (at the old stand, there, now, they sell
gold from teeth,
        & from burned bones, fertilizers)

amour propre, in the old sense,
won't do.

Now all things (in the furnace of fact, all things)

(no things in the furnace, in the weather-beaten face of

doubt)

now all things (including notions, or whatever
were once validities,
        all things now stand
(including the likes of you and me, all, all

must be born out of
        (God knows you know, Old Goddess, &
        tremendous Mother)

There is birth! there is

all over the place there is

And if I, in this smother, if I
smell out one thing sharp,
or another
(where his teeth
have been in me, there—
even you know, Enemie—
I speak as modestly as
broken grass which,
under the flood, tries
to breathe, to breathe!

Say I, one blade,
to you, or
whoever:

      it is why there is so much blood
      all over the place

      END STORY

Adamo Me . . .

Ride 'em, and, by the ride, down all night, all
apocalypse

      by the, naked, tide, by

beauty, "is most difficult"   But
for that reason is, at her tips, not, NOT

to be dum-dummed, you-me, the order of the day is
shall not spread the ends of, with too much teeth, shall
stay in there, without, without, without even

the christ, is a fish, to be caught, especially
where the waves come in, where
(like a wall, they
pour,
      and only with the hands

                    (the absolute
                        danger of losing, the tow is such, &
                        below, the drag
                        of the sands)

            can you seize

1

I looked up, and there, on the wall, as though it were on a mesa,
and we walking across (or was it others, after us) there
set in clay like a demonstration, vertebra, only vertebra, only
the spines
of what once was.

If the air is wrong, or it is not sand, their houses . . .

Water, water, always water up & over, testing, testing, time,
And the little red spot glows, And it is—look! my grandchild,
who is on

                I, merely, bridge, music
                defunctive (he who was I, or
                is it, you?)

                            "For you," she wrote, "when I am not,"
                            (coyly, almost, you might say).

2

When, still, the sea pours in (still
wall) . . . Afterwards,
they sought the sun to dry off, and,

in the hollows of a sand-hill, the flesh
tastes so good they
roll over . . .

Suddenly we stumbled, and, as I sd, I looked down,
and there before my very eyes I was

    (articulated sea-serpent, or the wood
    hewn from that tree which grew up
    where they planted with him who first died
    the seed which the angel had thrust
    into his son's hand that day,
    when the light was coming up, he
    waned
          And they all standing around, his sons & daughters,
    in what astonishment, the morning should bring
    such a new thing!

    Or as small as that extinct bird
    (it was not a bird, it had
    fingers), and though it was not sand,
    it was wind which they sieved,

3

"I can be caught too, preserved,
sd Mme. B.,
for though I am difficult, it is not, for that reason, to be allowed,

you are not to be allowed, Mister B., in the clutch it is not the time
to be called OUT

        Or, for that matter, to cry out, either.

It is too much (too much, musicians say, when, say, a stick), or a
crowd, when you have runners, when you are your own men, when you
have any of us on your hands!

The law, (in her arms we lie), the law
injunctive, hit! hit!
                    or
it doesn't matter whether they find you, or yr house, or
even a child, a grandchild, your wife, her handmaiden, or,
as they so carefully pan each shovelfull, even yr possessions,
the bones of,
across their knees,
yr dog

    Man built daringly
    by water, there stayed
    because there were always those
    who found other live beings more interesting than

    nature, that is, what city folk call nature,
    trees, fields, or
    clucking hens

    The riddle is (beside femininity, that is)
    that of which beauty is only the most interesting expression,
                                                        why
    we persist, why we remain, even in the face of,
                                        curious,
    even before the example of

    He dissolved, the second dissolved
    (after some certain punishment, the which
    increaseth, yet, that it doth, does not call for
    such crying out), I dissolve,

a like scatter of bone, or
even merely sand,
                        And not even shining
like the neighboring quartz

actually disappeared, because water
trickles, or is shaken, or even roars
over

The news of the day is: 4
were swept down, 4 clung
when the silly glistening powerful match-box of a boat
missed the free-way to the lock and went
swirling over the mill-race, the sluice,
                                and off, crack,
down the water like fish-eggs or unborn bees
                                        4
were saved, the percentage
a happy one, most
unusual

                    II

The difficulty remains.
But not that it is locked in the mind past all remonstrance,
not at all.

Though this is also true: example,
that they rolled over, that the rose of their flesh shone
where the drops still had not dried in the sun, that, together,
they made a four-legged beast, and, from its making, locked

that from that day they carried away remembrance . . .

                                        none of this, nothing
shows, when, in the sand, you come up on a
dispersed bone,
                    but this is (this bone) still (still) no reason
there is none, in this air, there is no reason for
knuckling under, for,

out of difficulty allowing for, submitting to, you, me, all

no reason for

the bribe of

            both beauty AND
            eternity

            the drama OR
            the mashing

            the celebrating OR
            the thrashing

            an easy standing OR
            a posture

            the roaring AND
            the epilogue

no reason FOR

            both beauty AND
            eternity

when, as in each case, an OUT is an OUT!

        [Conc.]

187

That it glows,
that you do,
that you are,
when the flesh is
a rose

That it shine,
that you do, that you'll make,
when the mind is
all glistening

That out of the pouring,
in which you, too, (two, or all
may drown) you, you
shall stand in, shall
in the loud roaring

    (as they lay, in that roaring, they
    took up fire from where fire came,
                            why
    in their eyes, in her eyes, in his sons' eyes
    there was such bewilderment, such
    discovery, why, it could be, the difficulty, why
    he could be put out!)

Well, still, is there anything,
is there anything you and I shall do more than,
than (the difficulty) be that rose, be
what shining monstrance that we may, be
any more than a hand, a flesh, a force
and stand there in that crashing
water?

And is there anything
(beauty notwithstanding)
more difficult?

END

188

La Torre

The tower is broken, the house
where the head was used to lift,
where awe was
And the hands

      (It is broken!
      And the sounds
      are sweet, the air
      acrid, in the night fear
      is fragrant

           The end of something has a satisfaction.
           When the structures go, light
           comes through

To begin again. Lightning
is an axe, transfer
of force subject to object is
order: destroy!

      To destroy
      is to start again, is a factor of
      sun, fire is
      when the sun is out, dowsed

                (To cause the jaws to grind
                before the nostrils flare
                to let breath in

Stand clear! Here
it comes down and with it the heart has
what was, what was
we do lament

Let him who knows not how to pray
go to sea

      Where there are no walls
      there are no laws, forms, sounds, odors
      to grab hold of

Let the tower fall!
Where space is born
man has a beach to ground on

      We have taken too little note of this:
      the sound of a hammer on a nail can be as clear as
      the blood a knife can make spurt from a round taut belly

2

In the laden air
we are no longer cold.
Birds spring up, and on the fragrant sea
rafts come toward us lashed of wreckage and young tree.
They bring the quarried stuff we need to try this new-found strength.
It will take new stone, new tufa, to finish off this rising tower.

The Cause, the Cause

It is the cause the cause, still, it is (and she, still
even though the method be
new, be

the rods and cones of, a pigeon's or, a rabbit's
eye, or be
who, man, is that woman you now dream of, who
woman, is that
man

named & featured, yet
who it is you sit beside, each of you, there, by the bubbling caldron in which
                                                                bones
and furniture are tossed (a grisly soup from which child's fingers drop, flames
spill out
on treacherous ground across which he leads you, i
lead you on, in,
a devils', angels'
dancings, the measured feet (clean, & sweet as hair is, used
to dry an ankle, toes
                    hair, wild quiet hair crushed
where cylinder & annulet compose
no dream

increasing rhein timed to come closer, closer
repeat, repeat, as regular as

                    by that fire you sit you dream, you two, you
talk about some other

2

it is the cause, yes, and the movements contain, the nightmare is
the day's ambiguous responses, her
harassments, his
flying off, his sort of looking out by cones, is it, or is it old, like bones
anyway, his
watchings
where the arc is now being pushed, can be, pushed, her
unreasonable opinions, her
subjects so baldly introduced, her rods, her

in the eye, in the eye of his will, her
multiple withholdings, her
not at all dumb dance, her measurings

3

put it this way (to make the case specific, as well as, historic: he
smothered her
because he could not free his half self from her likeness, carried (jealous)
buried, you can say, and no more mirroring her—no, not at all, in fact
a she, initiate with himself alone. another creature concealed in him—
a female male to him in his confusion—made male by one point short majority

and thus
                (no confirmation offered, proferred him by his grown unround world

                        ((his world become a rotted apple, no light
                            on why, at this queer juncture, he should find himself a
                            double

halved, in his own eye, halved, he
cried out for love of her, pressed down, pressed down, and—
crown of his no longer endurable, not sufficiently regular
pain—he
killed this other
for half love of another
Eve

4

nor is this all. nor is the story (upper case) so small
as he, and she, alone. in fact it is, there is, another half, the tragedy
repeats itself in inverse, increasing inverse (transvest) plane:

                        on this even more rotted stage, the rage—
no longer only male (the half's gone over!) repeats, repeats!

for woman, too, is joined & sundered, returned
is now (alas)—she, too—returned
to mono-beast, she too conceals a brother

And from that Cain once seen, in the light suddenly on the edge of the pot,
     jumping
from the fire up, recognized—
again,
murder, another
murder

5

To murder to be free from incubus when difference, difference only
is the cause (the cause here spoiled)

All form and essence both brought down, mixed, in this middle place, this
where there is neither one nor the other, this by man and woman dirtied, this
fouled place

But still the cause, it is the cause by which things stand
(by which all eyes are two, and in this fact the day by night
stand, all moving things are made to stay, to stay in place, are brought
together

what they are, what a dream is, a man a woman are
the hidden others of which they themselves are the face, by

a hair of difference, are
no greater difference than,
the cause, is
life from its own ending

Of Mathilde

the fragrance is
>   what cannot be put on, is raiment spun
>   of what looks like nothing, is
>   what stands strong
>   in a man's mind

is what she gives off, what love
gives off

but love, what is love but
that only those who obey
are fragrant?

and the obedience?
>   Is not dance   Is not dream   Is
>   more wrestling than (he was right) than
>   dance   And dream
>   is no more than appetite

In all this—what we cover, in the enigma, by the word love—
it is particularly true, that to repeat experience is
sensationalism
>   From which no fragrance cometh
>   And no web

>   Mathilde

is love—or better, what is at the heart of all this, a word
we better pronounce as the French do, if we will give it its
content, courage, there is no sliding in Mathilde, Mathilde is
love, she
stays in there, in
where the self cannot be pleased, where
a trouble is, obedience doth go against desire, at least
one kind of wish, that it let up

Which it will not. This
Arachne did not know, this, perhaps, Mathilde
does not know. Yet,
because she is not sentimental or so vain, she
without deformation wears
her unseen work.

The Gate Is Prouti

a fountain—from four blocks away—can look like ice.
but then, the way brown flesh can mass on bones.

flesh, too, can die away—from distance, coming in.

There Are Sounds . . .

There are sounds, but can immoralists

                             (And then there was a skirt, a
shining ass swept by a skirt so cunningly I
was all for mounting same right there,
and then and then and then

Or a voice sat squat on a pillow
over against my own, and the communication
was most direct, most (right along the floor there was, most
serious, if the intent is most serious

If it is not   (I heard, later, that one made one pass at one's
                wife, and
                one kicked one the hell out of one's
                house

serious, given such a sound, and
in the face of the overwhelming shrine, overwhelming
worship of, fear,
the loss, such quantity
is measured out so small

We are. But the name of our country is not known, the citizens
are hard to find: Boston,
or Anacostia. Or it is as much there
as it is anywhere, for where is it
but thee & me, and thee be a bit,
as am me, just that little bite, enough
to make discrimination possible texture on out, to go
to go towards,
                from among the doubles,
                             what
we are here for

Question: what
makes us want to, who what is it
saves us from confusion, and its ludicrous consequences, the ukase: DEBUNK

Answer: it is not easy
to keep the light in, to keep in
what light, has made its way through, even
this sliding present, this (along the floor, this, in this giddy room, o!
        you cleaners, you! who look so much like a new broom, who
        are better than anything but

but the very thing which must
that which must
be

Issue, Mood

                        still go funny, in the face of him
                        on money
crazy, straight   like
all-right,   people say, right in the face of
mad   (prat): not chuman not chuman not
                        hoomin

butchart   butchart   del mar   gesell
    del mar   butchart
        gesell   del mar And the Big

Shot sd (((I'd
ask the same question (face to) to-
day))
                    in an-
                                swer (wot
abt this stamp-tax, this
carrying charge you
 & yr dollar
  bill)

HE SD:
        NAIVE

O BOY, if that don't put
me *on!*
                (And the same B.S., now?
hamburg, once thru the grinder red, done in, his
so–fist–ik–kayshun!)

Who dare impugn
another's innocence?

By inversal ONLY,
the
proposition:
        NO

                                (the inversal, EP to BS, pointed
this way: white (once through the wringer),
so much else than innocence being used, being
thrust on you, IMPOSING (ex., "so that,
when you have yr hands on any BUGGAH"

                CAN HE?
"Do not,   IS HE,
    be a Senator,   ABLE
      in yr country, MR.   (I think not)
Poet-Economist

The poles are: HARD METAL vs.
            NATIONAL DEBT. Now,
I'm a newt dealer, myself, asking,
after so long is it not remarkable
that the creature (even taken out of stone)
breathes?

                    Comes
the revolution, does
this laborer lose
this labor of
his arm?   Or this Lake,

Maracaibo, its
oil?

Either way, it seems to me, he or him, both,
does it not come to, The tidy
fear chaos?

Not to woo it, but,
who's wrong, what's
society?
          and who
be thee? be thee
one of the Innocents?

You see, I take it
there are some certain other premises.
Or, better, some certain other isolated facts
(not worked for, Horatio!) quote:
                              "the art
of collecting   rising thence by a process of
& arranging,   induction to
          a mass of

          OH YES
reform
          O reform it
          altogether!
                    the habit
to look to society to make it
new.
          bah.

                              (who
                    cannot honestly make it
                    stick.)

                         Equity?
                    With the hills?

                              Hills,
                              Sirrah?

Signs

fog, and orchid sun
how easily
or cloud, and you can bear to look
at him become a most bright moon
these insubstantial things obscure
his light

as image cause
reality, they
so easily exceed
reality, close
the even hardened
eye

        (a token, swiped
        from sky: even
        in the city, look, things

are to be observed, how much
a man may be misled, then,
headed in, stop
                    CAR
STOP

ah! he!

The Moon Is the Number 18

is a monstrance,
the blue dogs bay,
and the son sits,
grieving

is a grinning god, is
the mouth of, is
the dripping moon

while in the tower the cat
preens
and all motion
is a crab

and there is nothing he can do but what they do, watch
the face of waters, and fire

      The blue dogs paw,
      lick the droppings, dew

or blood, whatever
results are. And night,
the crab, rays round
attentive as the cat to catch
human sound

The blue dogs rue,
as he does, as he would howl, confronting
the wind which rocks what was her, while prayers
striate the snow, words blow
as questions cross fast, fast
as flames, as flames form, melt
along any darkness

Birth is an instance as is a host, namely, death

The moon has no air

In the red tower
in that tower where she also sat
in that particular tower where watching & moving are,
there,
there where what triumph there is, is: there
is all substance, all creature
all there is against the dirty moon, against
number, image, sortilege—

alone with cat & crab,
and sound is, is, his
conjecture

Abstract #1, Yucatan

the fish is speech, or see
what, cut
in stone, starts, for

when the sea breaks, watch
watch: it is the
tongue, and

he who introduces the words (the
interlocutor) the
beginner of the word, he

you will find, he
has scales, he
gives off motion as

in the sun the wind the light, a fish
moves

This

mexico)   could not
have guessed: wood, a
bowl of gray wood, of

an afternoon, already
shadowed (4
pm: very fast, high, sharp
rockets, a crazy trumpet
of a band, few
people, sloppy
cowboys picadors matadors bulls

> *but out there, on that dirt, in front, directly*
> *before your eyes, more, yr existence:*

death, the
possibility of same, the certitude
right there in front of yr
eyes, god damn yr
eyes
this bull and this man (these men) can
kill
one another

What one knows
put out, & quietly out, put out right exactly I mean OUT
in front of all eyes, including
>   *the bull's, who runs out so*
>   *lightly, with such*
>   *declarations of*
>   *his presence*

>   *the man, so*
>   *careful, such*
>   *preparations (the bull only about to find out), the man*
>   *so clothed, such tools, and*
>   *running back to*

>   *so ludicrously the*
>   *barricade, the bull, too, smelling*
>   *the wood, where an opening is, how*
>   *to get out of*

                        Whoever
conceived this action, this
thing, this
instant declaration of that which you know is all
that constitutes both what you are and what is going on at all time
as of you or anyone since and as long as whatever
it is that it is, is

        this
        bullfight:

the bull so much not
animal (as the word
is) his
experience so very clear, there, his
bewilderment, tries, angers (no
fear, mere increasing sense from confrontation that
he is
involved

the men (the man) so much more
animal, so
aware, their
courage (fear) so
very clear, so very much the reason why
we too are
involved, why
we, here,

            ((the man, down in that dirt, so much
                a scampering, so much (advancing) a
                sort of picked bantam))

those horns

that voice repeating "to-ro" "to-ro" "to-ro"

those words, wooing

that head, the plain danger of

you

have been

asked

He, Who, in His Abandoned Infancy, Spoke of Jesus, Caesar, Those Who Beg, and Hell

Crossed-over dreams, or infertile
crusades, made such
by the filth and lumber
of the present leadership, o!
may they be sucked up
by their own orange cloud, their own
displaced sea, they
who can teach nothing of vice
or of a death without regrets, nothing
of a life so lived

This one, awake
(ending his life in a sort of continuing dream)

spoke of strange things sweetly
(as he had made verse sweet in his time)
with a voice which would have raised me
had my own heart not been squeezed
this narrow

Knowing All Ways,
Including the Transposition of
Continents

I have seen enough: ugliness
in the streets,
and in the flesh I love

I have gone as far as I will go: justice
is not distributable, outside
or in

I have had all I intend
of cause or man: the unselected
(my own) is enough
to be bothered with. Today
I serve beauty of selection alone
—and without enormous reference to stones
or to the tramp of worms
in the veins. Image
can be exact to fact, or
how is this art twin to what is,

what was,
what goes on?

America, Europe, Asia,
I have no further use for you: your clamor
divides me from love,
and from new noises.

Concerning Exaggeration, or
How, Properly, to Heap Up

I

About blood, he said, be
more circumspect, for that matter,
these days, about anything
has been cried in the streets. We are called on
to correct all
economies

I am not my parts. I am one system,
affect all others, act, and express myself as such, wild
or indifferent

2

Or birth. ("He with the squint cried aloud.") She
came up out of a wave caused by the fall of her father's parts

neatly sickled off by a brother as handsome as she. Another
was hid in his father's thigh, was hid from a jealous wife,
before his natural mother bore him. A third
was an egg, was born of an egg because his mother was too old,
and built a city in a night, protected only
by a cap of bread

No wonders: the sun
crawls down the tree's branches and through the roots into the earth
each night, and there are tigers there
which eat it

      a man
who had mastered all languages but Arabic
broke a friend's skull with a shovel just
for some silver plate, though he excused himself
saying, the friend had been familiar
with his wife

      Or he
who was as fleet as the herds he'd run his life with,
had to be taught by a courtesan human speech
in order that he might enter the city
and put an end to the Leader's lusts

              or that one
who came back from the war to find his double
was in his house and bed and even had a mole
in the right place, the man was so confused
he wondered who he was

3

The head, too. I look around me, and I find two, only two
who are as he was who wore a hawk on the back of his neck, the wings
curved round the sides of the head to frame the brilliant

human face, the muteness arguing, the muteness of both,
that this one at least, this leader,
was informed, was recognizing other force
than that which one might call
his own

    As it was for me in a dream
    when I was a horse on both sides of a river
    and a lady of flowers, and another, laid hands on me,
    each on each side

        Or that night my friend the dramatist
    arranged us all in a charade so that two of us
    passed through the door a centaur while a huge murderess
    fed water-lilies gently to crocodiles

            And I twist,
            in the early morning, asking
            where
            does it stop

4

All, is of the matter. Dignity
is not to be confused with realism, is not found
(he was canny enough to say)
in the straight-on

        however much it does lie
in particulars—as distorted as an instant is, is
content. And its form? How shall you find it
if you are not, in like degree, allowable, are not
as it is, at least, in preparation for
an equal act?

And, if this is true,
how can you avoid the conclusion, how
can you be otherwise than
a metaphor

       than as fabulous as to move
except as your own fingers duplicate
a long-nailed god, your eye
to be so trained by night
it goes as slow as weights
(as slow as Shiva's turning toe), as fast—how run
except as he did (as tern flies), how gauge yourself
except as also Cenozoic beast (as she is afterwards,
no more than tired animal, who speaks
as how else can you too speak
except as she listened who hunched
over those craters and caked pools drunk
from the earth's gases, and said
he has put tortoises
under twelve gold covers
on twelve gold plates

             To speak of blood
             is so very willful,
             or self-incising. In any case,
             he who is presented with her answer is
             that answer: the mephitic
             is only confirmatory. Yet
             the vapor of those instants
             —blood, breath, head, what—
             require like
             circumspection

                     (was what he said,
                     at that point of
                     his time)

To Gerhardt, There, Among Europe's Things of Which He Has Written Us in His "Brief an Creeley und Olson"

so pawed,
by this long last Bear-son

    with no crockery broken,
    but no smile in my mouth

        June 28th, '51, on this horst
        on the Heat Equator, a mediterranean sea
        to the east, and north
        what saves America from desert, waters
        and thus rain-bearing winds,
        by subsidence, salt-waters
           (by which they came,
           the whelps, looking
           for youth

Which they found.
        And have continuously sought
                    to kill

        (o Old Man,
in winter, when before me, cross my path

in summer, when behind me, cross my path

If you want to shut yourself in, shut yourself in
If you do not want to shut yourself in, come out

        A zoo
        is what he's come to, the old

Beginner, the old
Winner

Who took all,
for awhile

(My grandfather, my grandmother,
why have you died?
Did a hand to hand struggle come?
Did a war, the size of a man's fist come?)

I

The proposition, Gerhardt
is to get it straight, right
from the start.

Help raise the bones
of the great man.

Meat and bones we won't throw away.
We pile it up in a lonely place.

We do not throw on the ground.
Your meat and bones without purpose.
We take bones and meat.

O Grandfather,
you went to war

The first duty is
to knock out his teeth, saying
"These are the teeth with which you devour all animals."

I offer you no proper names
either from great cities
on the other side of civilization

which have only to be visited
to be got the hell out of, by bus
or motorcycle, simply because place
as a force is a lie.
or at most a small truth,
now that man has no oar to screw down into the earth, and say
here i'll plant, does not know
why he should cease
staying on the prowl

You climbed up the tree after some foul berry
and fell down and died
You ate berries, fell from the rock
and died
You ate sorb berries
and died
You ate raspberries,
drowned in the swamp and died

Or from the other side of time, from a time on the other side of yourself
from which you have so lightly borrowed men, naming them as though,
like your litany of Europe's places, you could take up
their power: magic, my light-fingered faust,
is not so easily sympathetic. Nor are the ladies
worn so decoratively.

The top of the spring plant
noisily chewing

The top of the summer plant
noisily chewing

On a summer day walk before and behind me
on a winter day

2

Nor can I talk of method, in the face of your letter,
in verse or otherwise,
as though it were a dance
of rains, or schmerz, of words as signs worn
like a toupee on the head of a Poe cast
in plaster, any method otherwise than
he practised it who gave it up,
after a summer in his mother's barn,
because the place smelled so, because time
his time, precisely this now
And with no back references, no
floating over Asia arrogating
how a raiding party moves in advance of a nation thereby
eventually
giving a language the international power
poets take advantage of. As they also,
with much less reason, from too much economics speak
of the dream
in a peasant's bent shoulders, as though it were true
they cared a damn
for his conversation

        On a mountain with dry stalks, walk
        with a resounding tread

        On a mountain with meadow-sweet
        walk with a resounding tread

        On the way to your fathers,
        join them

3

Nor of a film, or of strange birds,
or of ordinary ones. Nor with the power of American vocables

would I arm you in Kansas, when you come,
or there, if you have to stay, where you feel so strongly
the dead center of the top of time

              I am giving you a present

              I am giving you a present

For you forget (forgetting
is much more your problem
than you know, right-handed one
who so beautifully reminds me
that the birds stand
in the middle of the air
and that always, in that apsed place
in which so many have kneeled
as I do not have the soul to kneel, the fields
are forever harvested, and happy heaven
leans over backwards
to pour its blessings by downfall
on to black earth

Admitting that among the ruins
        with a like schmerz in every vessel of his throat,
        he repeated, "Among the ruins, among them
        the finest memory in the Orient"
one will go about picking up old pieces
        bric-a-brac, he snorted, who did not know whereof he spoke,
        he had so allowed himself to be removed, to back-trail
or put it immediately out of the mind, as some can,
stuff the construction hole quickly with a skyscraper

but you will remember that even Caesar comes to this, certainly you
who has written of Hamlet's death, who is able to handle such large counters
as the classic poet handled bank-notes in our time, before prizes
were his lot, and I am envious, who can do neither

that the point of the rotting of man in his place is also
(beside the long-lived earth of good farmers, its manuring,
what Duncan pointed out America and Russia are very careless with)
what blows about and blocks a hole where the wind was used to go

        (While walking on the earth with stalks
        you received a present

        While walking on the earth with the stalks of plants
        your head was crushed

        You could not see, your eyes got small,
        you could not defecate, you were small
        you could not,
        therefore you died

It is a rod of mountain ash I give you, Rainer Maria Gerhardt,
instead of any other thing, in order that you may also be
left-handed, as he was, your Grandfather,
whom you have all forgotten, have even lost the song of, how
he was to be addressed:

        "Great man,
         in climbing up the tree,
         broke his leg."

I am urging you from here
where nothing is brutal,
not even the old economics
    (I do not dare to breathe
    for what I know the new
    will do) and only the kids kill
frigate-birds, because they have to
to develop a throwing arm

        (as your people knew, if I can lead you
        to go back far enough,
        which is not one step from where you are

"His ear is the earth.
Let you be careful"

that he must be hunted, that to eat
you shall bring him down

"Your head
is the size of a ladle

Your soul
is of the size of a thread

Do not enter my soul by day,
do not enter my dreams by night

that woman—who is, with more resistance
than you seem to have allowed, named—
lends herself to him as concubine

what you forget is, you

are their son! You are not

Telemachus. And that you come back

under your own

steam

There are no broken stones, no statues, no images, phrases, composition
otherwise than
what Creeley and I also have,
and without reference to
what reigned in the house
and is now well dismissed

Let you pray to him, we say
who are without such fatherhood:

"Show your house in spring.

Show a mound of snow in your house in winter.

In summer go in back of and in front of
the children.

Think not badly of the man, go right."

4

Or come here
where we will welcome you
with nothing but what is, with
no useful allusions, with no birds
but those we stone, nothing to eat
but ourselves, no end and no beginning, I assure you, yet
not at all primitive, living as we do in a space we do not need to contrive

And with the predecessors who, though they are not our nouns, the verbs
are like!

So we are possessed of what you cry over, time
and magic numbers

Language,
my enemie,
is no such system:

"Hey, old man, the war arrived.

Be still, old man.

219

Your mouth is shut,

your door is shut,"

As I said, I am giving you a present.
To all false dimensions,
including his superb one
who refused to allow the social question in,
to all such fathers and false girls
(one of his, I notice, you take, seriously)
why not say what, somewhere, you must hear the echo of?

"One eye
sees heaven,
another eye
sees earth

For the problem is one of focus, of the field as well as the point of
vision: you will solve your problem best
without displacement

"One ear
hears heaven,
another ear
hears earth."

In such simplicities I would have you address me,
another time

5

The old man, my grandfather, died.
The old woman, my grandmother, died.
And now my father visits me, clothed
in a face he never wore, with an odor
I do not know as his, as his was meadow-sweet.

He sits, grieving, that she should have worried,
and I look up at him as he sits there
and if I am his son, this man
is from as far a place and time
as yours is, carries with him
the strangeness you and I will carry
for our sons, and for like reason,
that we are such that can be pawed

"We are no murderers," they used so carefully to say.

"We have put in order the bones of him
  whom others kill."

You see, we are experienced of what you speak of: silence
with no covering of ashes, geraniums also
and loaded with aphis

of all but war,

but war, too, is dead as the lotus is dead

And our hardness

has been exaggerated. You see,
we see nothing downward: we walk, as your grandfather walked,
without looking at his feet

"And because of meeting the great man,
  a feast is held

Warm yourself,
  over the fire of grandfather

This is an offering to the guests, a holiday
of the great man

He will feel satisfied

He will not take revenge

The stick is a reminder, Gerhardt. And the song? what seems
to have been forgotten?

Here it is (as we say here, in our anti-cultural speech, made up
of particulars only, which we don't, somehow, confuse with gossip:

"To his resting place in spring,

to his house in autumn,

I shall go

With autumn plant, arouse the mountain

With spring plant, arouse the mountain

In summer, walk in the background,
do not frighten the children,
do not sniff, neither here
nor there."

The Fathers

To wed good blood to bad blood to alleviate
the bad: he did this, how consciously who
knows. For, for him, the black moods
did not pass, each year he was more caught

in the vise of his father, that nervousness
he might fall down into what his brother
reached or his own old defense of his sister
from the implicit vice, he would take it,
in the family's past. He fought
on this line: that fatherness
could reconstitute itself, he
could be father as he did not think others
were (only one was, he surmised—a surmise
was, in the nature of his case, a fear—a
swaggering unplanning delightful one
of the oldest patriarchal dispensation, one of those
in the living present—the bodies and anti-bodies
in the larger blood—who keep the game
by which men did once know the business,
the major business was in good hands, in
the Maker's able paws). But he, this nervous
jumpy swift uncomfortably lacerating
lacerated man, had only one such sanction, the poor
one: his particular maker (as most of us have
who do not have the Other, our own
father) So
he watched his wife and every instant of event
of all the happenings of his mood-ridden fellows
so subtly and so carefully he was boss
of each new situation, surprisingly
the ablest and the swiftest to close up, to cover
such lesions in front of all our eyes
as his own rough long history of blood
—the inside front—had taught him—
and he, he thought, had come out victor of
by mixing him with her patent
good.

        Against him set this other.
Actor—and made such to remove himself
from self and family. Bloodless,

but lucid to behaviors
of troubled souls, of those there are so many of, they
who want a father as a mother to rub and hold
their hands—those fainting hands—and he
by acting (from the viscera, he'd claim,
yet truth is, his ableness
was in his likeness to all these
as it is always so of mechanism that
it cannot disengage itself that far
that it is cold, so cold it's hot—
hot as blood is hot when blood
does not slow in delta
of its own fertile mud).

He knew one thing from make-up
and from proper costume, that
a face is shining afterwards
by law patriarchy deprives these of: the dropping
into any of several of the wells of other waters we
are capable of, those
pools, mineral, reflective, hot,
emerald, he'd not push his patients in, he'd pass
not into their or his own roles (could he do this
he'd be a father each of them might use);
but it was in to any other's moods he'd go
(as actors do, that dirtiness) the passive
sensuality all hand-holding calls for, the uncleanness of
dependence (that state which one of you is out of,
now independence is so slightly known?)

What this man does by disengagement from
his father, mother, brother, place
is of our matter as the other—that all of us
who live too late for the old thing
live too early for the new: the world
and us as one, no division
of labor, property and grace, no Shoulder
like His on which to throw

any important matter, these obscurities
the man of blood will deal with to his end, the bloodless man
will push off on to others he will envy, the social things
as actor and administrator he'll
stay competent in, but lose
his soul

      as who of you shall not lose if you fail
      to be the inside-out the inside and the out now are
      because the Father, the old tumbler, has
      tumbled down?

Applause

(for Nick Cernovich)

I

Out, all the way, without
family, without
an immediate object of your love, so god
what's looked for, or,
to be more accurate, what
is prayed to, cold dancer
in the sun

It does not matter
some think the heart
is of the matter, the old heart, the heavy one

the enlarged sheep heart, the heart
of the sacrificed animals—
                    that this is first,
is what we depart from, that that one was right to ask
that he offer his son's, like any sheep's,
and thus his, own, his own wolf's heart

Or that the lesions instants give way to, how suddenly
the fabric is not there, and is as quickly there again as, how holes
in the blood are not known, that this disturbance
can be enlarged
can support any other man than he who first finds it
can be made to mock
the universe, thus wear the mask of
a judge

If these are part of your causes,
and I do not know that a man who kneels knows cause, or cares
the need ahead is so very much greater—
it does not matter; each of us
has to clear himself of his own materials, to resist
an overfondness for his source, for title
drawn by any other court of deed than he himself

It comes to this, to the simplest: are the appearances not
what it is, is it not exactly what it looks like?
                                Who are any of us
to be so sure that pain
or the refused tears which force words to blubber in the mouth
are not all of it, despite
how little either has to do with bones and flesh, how
they get capable to do
what you now have here done?

2

A deal of life you have undone, unknowingly
disposed of

unknowingly, perhaps—though that it matters
I am not at all aware of. For consciousness
is art and myth and you who dance,
who dance so, is borner
for all men on the four seas (are) burdened,
confused by discourse, her
false clarities, the same
of the sensual heart
                    as you perhaps are too,
when you are not in motion, are not
in the sun

          There is a myth a man can not be self
          until he's wandered his self-world over, found
          his blood to be a rock on which he might have broken,
          his liver was a shining pool, his kidney
          is a lady who whores, his head
          is the lightest part—is a dandelion, his leg
          is a fish

               brothers
                    (that it is not true
               we are not   )

3

You have wandered in a place of kindness in which a cat must die
it so resembled human beings, assuming (as you have)
that there are ultimates
in conversation with some birds—or that man's monologue

can have end put to it if a saint can manage,
by virtue of those very empty instant intervals
(which are not insane) to engage
the god himself

But what I see is no such thing, no sacred ring achieved, no mixing
with any other thing, nor man, fish, god or beast,
not even with a place upon the ground to dance on, no intrusion
even upon the ground of yourself, no prayer
except as prayer is solely as we speak to one another and are heard,
as he listens who is clean of slaughter and of pantomime:

                                                                    description

is what you here lay low, and by distinctions
—in this levitican world—we may
with no least loading say, the beauty here
is methodological

4

Your knowing
is of an order of the blood permitting
breath to blow back any feathers of a bird without worrying
how he speaks, the wading man to note without identification
the consensual fish which swims in the shallow waters like his feet,
to kneel to pick raspberries in the difficult place that woods are, to look
at what was grey so long turn green remembering
how it was gold before it was green because it came from him
who is such, or is red, depending on his hour

                                           who, by his action,
of which your practice is the finest duplication, does
at the same time that the rocks stop melting make
such flesh as on your bones now moves

5

A saint
does not dance
here in the sun: your mother,
and your brother, are not absent
                                        though you have not made all your round
of the Seven Lakes, have not walked into
all the Eleven Woods, have not found all the parts, all
that man or saint or god has to do with
                                        yet
by going, as you go now before my eyes, by feet alone, by throw
of what works under, the bobbing
of your exact head, the droppage
of an arm as hinge, you show a heart the old heart stays as,
                    is glutton, pusher, feeder, to be offered
                    to any diorite knife of priest or fool
                    until it knows how young it is, how strong

                    what has been long unknown, what god, what half god
                    of a kingly system

Issues from the Hand of God

I am too fucking innocent to be gay, he roared. Let there be born
a new Banquet, let there be a wild bed, let you
get the hell aside from me with
your too easy advances, your
too easy attacks

I'll not mix my goods with Neo-Classicists,
those from the capitals, or who talk about
small town folk. Go by me, Recitalists, all
arguers, even those who are a little bit right

      It is too early to be so wise, so bright,
        to still stay, or to jump ahead, you, Performers!

Let my lazy brilliant cats do their leaping, their yawning, even shit
in front of us in the circus Ring, without you making any of your quick
back or forward interpretations of, my animals: let all you simplicimusses
shut your pusses, let me be wholly vulgar when fineness is dullness, bright-
                                    ness
                                      es

come a penny apiece, are an arcade, when all you are are peep shows,
through the littlest hole, ass or eye

      You of the Theatre, Inigo Jones murdered
      against a brick wall, still know nothing, with
      your babble of—ah, movement

        You of the People, yes,
        likewise, and not my great beasts

Swing, sway, bounce—bah, where they belong is
where they are, in the trees, or with the children or, the balls are
walk the dog, see my pretty dance!

        And curb same, I say, from me,
        the next Passerby

          And the truckdriver is more psychotic than you are,
          Mayor of Highway America

Both of you, he spat, do a little fucking in public a little thinking
in private, if sway swing bounce grind protest and the
                                        latest McCarran bill
are either art or action—do be homosexual or as frenchy as
Madelein Le Seur, anything, to clean out, your eye and
your arse. Or, give me my money back

        If this is all you offer to
        what proceeds from,
        and towards my beasts

coital coital coital, she kept repeating, with her faced turned
to the wall
        "Make it clear, both of you, if you can't
make use of it."
And some ate slowly peanut crackers, and the others rushed off into the rain.

A Round
&
A Canon

1   As, certainly, it is not you who sway
    (Black-eyed Susan) but it is the wind
    has this affection for you

        that this child of mine
               hangs
   where the arc does not yet know which

(the swing does not) the moment
over or back, innocent or wise

in mid-air

about to fall either way is such
a lovely bird of a wild human motion

2   A bird
knows too much, or it strikes me he knows enough
to awake to a day to sing a day down

              And when he falls—o
all saints & recitalists, consider
what a very high heart, what a high heat

                        such nerves
I cannot keep him alive, holding
him in my hand, winged or pawed, he fell
from his own world, his own careful context, those
balances

        Even a spoon
of the finest honey, or a splint, or,
tried down his throat like his father,
the finest worm

              Won't do. He dies, his eyes
close upward, the film first, the milky way
of his dying
              (as the Two who shyly rule
off the north in the night settle, distractedly,
in the sea

              He ceases to fly or to sing. And no reference
to the twisting of the neck of
the spitting black goose

                              he dies
as the instant dies, as I die
for an instant listening
to the slightest
error

Letter for Melville 1951

written to be read AWAY FROM the Melville Society's "One Hundredth Birthday
Party" for MOBY-DICK at Williams College, Labor Day Weekend, Sept. 2–4, 1951

MY DEAR—:

I do thank you, that we hear from you, but the
Melville Society invitation came in the same mail with your news of
this thing, and do you for a moment think, who have known me 17
years, that I would come near, that I would have anything to do with
their business other than to expose it for the promotion it is, than to
do my best to make clear who these creatures are who take on them-
selves to celebrate a spotless book a wicked man once made?

that I find anywhere in my being any excuse for
this abomination, for the false & dirty thing which it is—nothing
more than a bunch of commercial travellers from the several colleges?
Note this incredible copy: "Those who are planning to take part in
the English Institute of Columbia University on September 5–8 will
find it convenient to attend both conferences"! Can anything be
clearer, as to how Melville is being used? And all the other vulgarities
of ease and come-on: how pretty the trees are this time of year, how
nice of Williams College to take our fifteen bucks, how you won't
run over anyone, the conference is so planned—o no let's not run
over anyone but him, and just exactly here in the Berkshire hills

where he outwrote himself, just where he—when we go together in the sight-seeing bus—where—the house will be open, it has been arranged—he was very clean with his knife, the arrowhead of his attention having struck, there we'll be able to forget he fell in a rut in that very road and had, thereafter, a most bad crick in his back

o these things we can—we must—not speak of, we must avoid *all* of the traffic except the meals, the sessions, the other points, of interest

for there are most important things to be taken care of: you see, each of us has families (maybe we have as many children as he did) and if we don't or we have only a wife because we really prefer boys, in any case, no matter what the circumstances which we will not mention in the speeches (you know that sort of thing we can only talk about in the halls, outside the meetings, or, at table, out of the corners of our mouths—you might say, out of a crack in the grave where a certain sort of barbed ivy has broken in over the years it has lain and multiplied flat on the rather silly stone others took some care in placing over the remains—we cannot forget, even for this instant, that, in order, too, that we can think that we ourselves are of some present importance, we *have* to—I know, we really would prefer to be free, *but*—we do have to have an income, so, you see, you must excuse us if we scratch each other's backs with a dead man's hand

for after all, who but us, who but us has had the niceness to organize ourselves in his name, who, outside us, is remembering that this man a year ago one hundred years ago (you see, we *are* very accurate about our celebrations, know such things as dates) was, just where we are gathering just ahead of labor day (walked coldly in a cold & narrow hall by one window of that hall to the north, into a room, a very small room also with one window to the same white north) to avoid the traffic who is, but us, provided with dormitories and catering services?

234

Timed in such a way to avoid him, to see
he gets a lot of lip (who hung in a huge jaw)
and no service at all (none of this chicken, he
who is beyond that sort of recall, beyond
any modern highway (which would have saved him
from sciatica? well, that
we cannot do for him but we can
we now know so much, we can make clear
how he erred, how, in other ways
—we have made such studies and
we permit ourselves to think—they
allow us to tell each other how wise
he was

He was. Few flying fish
no dolphins and in that glassy sea
two very silly whales throwing
that spout of theirs you might call sibylline
it disappears so fast, why
this year a hundred years ago he
had moved on, was offering
to such as these
a rural bowl of milk, subtitled
the ambiguities

    July
above Sigsbee deep,
the *Lucero del Alba,*
500 tons, 200,000 board feet
of mahogany, the Captain
25, part Negro, part American Indian and perhaps
a little of a certain Cereno, by name
Orestes Camargo
     Herman Melville
looked up again at the weather, noted
that landlessness   And it was not so much truth

as he had thought, even though the ratlines
could still take his weight (185, eyes
blue, hair auburn, a muscular man knowing
that knowledge
is only what makes a ship shape, takes care
of the precision of the crossed sign, the feather
and the anchor, the thing
which is not the head but is
where they cross, the edge
the moving edge of force, the wedding
of sea and sky (or land & sky), the Egyptian
the American backwards

> (The stern, at evening,
> a place for conversation, to drop paper boats, to ask
> why clouds are painters' business, why now he
> would not write *Moby-Dick*)

Was writing
Pierre: the world
had moved on, in that hallway, moved
north north east, had moved him

> O such fools
> neither of virtue nor of truth
> to associate with
> > to sit to table by
> as once before you, and Harry, and I
> the same table the same Broadhall saw
> water raised by another such to tell us
> this beast hauled up out of great water was
> society!
> > this Harvard and this Yale
> as Ossa on Pelion (or,
> as one less than he but
> by that lessness still
> a very great man, said
> of another—who never learned a thing

from Melville—worth
"five Oxfords on ten thousand Cambridges"!

o that these fellow diners of yours might know
that poets move very fast, that it is true
it is very wise to stay the hell out of
such traffic, of such labor
which knows no weekend

Please to carry my damnations to each of them
as they sit upon their arse-bones variously
however differently padded, or switching

                        to say please, to them
(whom I would not please any more than he will: he is flying
for the weekend, from Pensacola, where,
any moment, he will dock

please say some very simple things, ask them
to be accurate:
ask one to tell you
what it was like to be a Congregational minister's son Midwest
how hard it was for a boy who liked to read to have to pitch, instead,
hay; and how, now that he has published books, now that he has done that
(even though his edition of this here celebrated man's verse
whom we thought we came here to talk about
has so many carelessnesses in it that, as of this date,
it is quite necessary to do it over)
let him tell you, that no matter how difficult it is
to work in an apartment in a bedroom in a very big city
because the kids are bothersome and have to be locked out, and the wife
is only too good, yet, he did republish enough of this other man
to now have a different professional title, a better salary
and though he wishes he were at Harvard or a Whale,
he is, isn't he, if he is quite accurate, much more liked
by his president?

There'll be main speeches, and one
will do the same thing that other did that other time, tell you
(as he did then who has, since, lost a son in war, society
is such a shambles, such a beast, and altogether not
that white whale), this new one, this new book-maker
will talk about democracy, has such a nose
is so imbued with progress he will classify
the various modes of same (what,
because it was the '30s, and hope was larger, that other
gave us in a broader view) but press him, ask him
is it not true you have, instead, made all this make your way
into several little magazines however old they are?

                              (How much light
                    the black & white man threw—Orestes!—on
                    democracy!)

                    as, if you were on the floor that night, you could see
                    just what are the differences of the hidden rears
                    of each of your fellow celebrators

Myself, I'd like to extricate you who have the blood of him, and another
who loves him as a doctor knows
a family doctor, how
his mother stayed inside him, how
the compact came out hate, and what
this kept him from, despite
how far he travelled

                    (The match-box, with a match for mast,
                    goes backward gaily, bumping
                    along the wake)

What they'll forget—they'll smother you—is
there is only one society, there is no other than
how many we do not know, where

and why they read a book, and that
the reading of a book can save a life, they
do not come to banquets, and Nathaniel Hawthorne
whom Herman Melville loved
will not come, nor Raymond Weaver
who loved them both because they loved each other.

You have the right to be there
because you loved an old man's walk
and took a little attic box, and books.
And there is he, the doctor, whom I love
and by his presence side by side with you
will speak for Melville and myself, he
who was himself saved, who
because, in the middle of the Atlantic,
an appendectomy was called for, read
a sea story once, and since
has gone by the pole-star, a scalpel overside
for rudder, has moved on from Calypso, huge
in the despatch of
the quick-silver god

Yet I wish so very much that neither of you mixed
(as Leyda hasn't) in this middle place, in such salad
as these caterers will serve!

For you will have to hear one very bright man speak, so bright
he'll sound so good that every one of you will think
he knows whereof he speaks, he'll say such forward things, he'll tag
the deific principle in nature, the heroic
principle in man, he'll spell
what you who do not have such time to read as he
such definitions so denotatively clear you'll think you'll understand
(discourse is such a lie) that Herman Melville
was no professional, could not accomplish
such mentality and so, as amateur (as this clear neuter will make clear)
was anguished all his life in struggle, not with himself, he'll say,

no, not with when
shall i eat my lunch Elizabeth has set outside the door so quiet
it was not even a mouse, my prose today
is likewise, the cows, what a damned nuisance they also are, why
do i continue to extend my language horizontally when
i damn well know what is
a water-spout

No, he'll skillfully confuse you, he knows such words
as mythic, such adjectives that fall so easily you'll think it's true
Melville was a risky but creative mingling
                    (how they put words on, that this lad was so
who stowed himself with roaches and a blue-shining corpse at age 16: "Hey!
Jackson!"

                    the diced bones—now his too, he
                    who is also of the one society
                    who likewise lifted altars
                    too high (a typewriter
                    in a tree) and spilled himself
                    into the honey-head, died
                    the blond ant
                    so pleasantly

                            as though he did not want to woo
                            to chance a Bronx grave, preferred
                            to choose his own headland

All these that you will sit with—"a mingling," he will drone on,
"of the fortunate and the injurious"

                    And only you, and Harry (who knows)
                    will not be envious, will know
                    that he knows not one thing
                    this brightest of these mischievous men
                    who does not know that it is not the point
                    either of the hook or the plume which lies

240

cut on this brave man's grave
—on all of us—
but that where they cross is motion,
where they constantly moving cross anew, cut
this new instant open—as he is who
is this weekend in his old place
presume on

                              I tell you,

he'll look on you all with an eye you have the color of.

He'll not say a word because he need not, he said so many.

"pitcher, how . . ."

pitcher, how
exactly is
the feeling of the threads
what it is—that is,
the drama we know about,
the g(love)

or how is bush league bush
(man) made major, made
to bear in, to bear
down? in what sense is
to hit long before the ball
reaches
whoever?

where does giddiness
where is it
ceased—how can you say how
you can be said to be
cool, can throw it
exactly as how the ball is, how
you be sd to hurl?

(again): the whirl
is very much exaggerated, the
crowd, the afternoon, and, even,
the exhilaration of the home
run, though the centerfield wall
—to point at it—is exactly
a like term, is also
as you pitch

that is, as of a day, a
double day, say, as this, when
there is a crowd, how would you say
how far back you are reaching from,
say, big train, from, the dirt, in what way
do you obey
the given, the
taken—how much grip
do your fingers have
on those threads, or,
for that matter,
the hide, eh?

The Ring of

it was the west wind caught her up, as
she rose
from the genital
wave, and bore her from the delicate
foam, home
to her isle

and those lovers
of the difficult, the hours
of the golden day welcomed her, clad her, were
as though they had made her, were wild
to bring this new thing born
of the ring of the sea pink
& naked, this girl, brought her
to the face of the gods, violets
in her hair

Beauty, and she
said no to zeus & them all, all were not or
was it she chose the ugliest
to bed with, or was it straight
and to expiate the nature of beauty, was it?

knowing hours, anyway,
she did not stay long, or the lame
was only one part, & the handsome
mars had her   And the child
had that name, the arrow of
as the flight of, the move of
his mother who adorneth

with myrtle the dolphin and words
they rise, they do who
are born of like
elements

For Cy Twombly Faced
with His First Chicago & N.Y. Shows

Ashurbanipal. Or the stern-view
of a whaler, (Male, who conserves
she who generates). Wrought iron
turns black stone, pours
as the cement of the earth's rocks
stilled, when the cooling came,
the hottest hugest cooling

Paint heats, or is caused to flow
in his hands, causes
what is, which is who
he is, how dwelleth
where the two forever are
who in their meeting make
what is, and so, what was

form,
    &,
        what the A hides, the abstract of
what each of us bends
                the eye around

An Ode on Nativity

I

All cries rise, & the three of us
observe how fast Orion
marks midnight
at the climax
of the sky
     while the boat of the moon settles
as red in the southwest
as the orb of her was, for this boy, once,
the first time he saw her whole halloween face northeast
across the skating pond as he came down to the ice, December
his seventh year.
       Winter, in this zone,
is an off & on thing, where the air
is sometimes as shining as ice is
when the sky's lights . . . When the ducks
are the only skaters
     And a crèche
is a commerciality

   (The same year, a ball of fire
    the same place—exactly through
    the same trees
    was fire:
        the Sawyer lumber company yard
        was a moon of pain, at the end of itself,
        and the death of horses I saw burning,
        fallen through the floors
        into the buried Blackstone River the city
        had hidden under itself, had grown over

  At any time, & this time
  a city
jangles

             Man's splendor
is a question of which
birth

II

The cries rise, & one of us
has not even eyes to see the night's sky
burning, or the hollows
made coves of mist & frost, the barns
covered over, and nothing in the night but two of us
following the blind highway to catch all glimpses
of the settling, rocking moon

             December, in this year
is a new thing, where I whisper
bye-low, and the pond
is full to its shores again, so full
I read the moon where grass would not reveal it
a month ago, and the ducks make noises
like my daughter does, stir
in the crèche of things

                  (His mother, 80, and we
                  ate oysters after the burial: we had knelt
                  with his sister, now Mary Josephine,
                  in the prayery of the convent of the church
                  where my mother & father had been married

                  And she told us tales of my family
                  I had not heard, how my grandfather
                  rolled wild in the green grass
                  on the banks of that same now underground river
                  to cool himself from the steel mill's fires
                  stripped down to his red underwear

she was that gay, to have seen her daughter
and that the two of us had had that car
to take the Sisters downtown and drop them
where they had to go

                              I had watched them
swirl off in their black habits
before I started the car again
in the snow of that street, the same street
my father had taken me to, to buy my first cap

     At any time, & now, again, in this new year
     the place of your birth, even a city, rings

in & out of
tune

     What shall be
my daughter's second
birth?

III

All things now rise, and the cries of men to be born
in ways afresh, aside from all old narratives, away
from intervals too wide to mark the grasses

               (not those on which cattle feed, or single stars
               which show the way to buy bad goods
               in green & red lit stores, no symbols

the grasses in the ice, or Orion's sweep, or
the closeness of turning snows, these
can tell the tale of any one of us stormed or quieted
by our own things, what belong, tenaciously,
to our own selves

Any season, in this fresh time
is off & on to that degree that any of us miss
the vision, lose the instant and decision, the close
which can be nothing more and no thing else
than that which unborn form you are the content of, which you
alone can make to shine, throw that like light
even where the mud was and now there is a surface
ducks, at least, can walk on. And I
have company
in the night

In this year, in this time
when spirits do not walk abroad, when men alone walk

when to walk is so difficult

when the divine tempter also walks
renewing his offer—that choice

(to turn
from the gross fire, to hide
as that boy almost did, to bury himself
from the fearful face—twice!—that winter

to roll like a dog or his grandfather
in the snowbank on the edge of the pond's ice

to find comfort somewhere, to avoid
the burning—To go to grass
as his daughter now suckles. Some way! he cries out
not to see those horses' agonies:

Is light, is there any light, any
to pay the price of
fire?

IV

The question stays
in the city out of tune, the skies
not seen, now, again, in
a bare winter time:

              is there any birth
any other splendor than
the brilliance of the going on, the loneliness
whence all our cries arise?

"At midnight, after hours of love . . ."

At midnight, after hours of love, I ate

and drank wine, sitting on the edge of the bed.

The whole time, I thought of Ovid

at Tomi. It could have been because I was wrapped

in a blanket.

The Clouds

Out the same picture window the pine bow
Then, it was rain gleaming from its needles, now
it is pale light of morning come, and she

who has just cried (I, too, then, cause)
from tears arising with lightness commands me, notice
the quarter moon, how it punctures its own clouds

For a Lady of Whom I Speak

who walks on white feet turned
as her hand touches what is also turned
in this straightening man,

                         Artemis
had to be so shod, and Cybele's hands
differently invoke,
                   but she of whom I speak
has the night, and the moon, when it is full,
makes each night's darkness
different

To the Algae

Never to say no to the algae suddenly
pink coral spine

The Civil War

Or Captain Philip Sheridan,
quartermaster, getting siege guns
to New Madrid

Or that the average age
of the 100,000 soldiers at Shiloh
must have been 18–19

That maybe Sidney Johnston
purposely let himself bleed to death,
he had made such a mess of Donelson

That one has to upset things,
to get at them, that you do have to turn
the ground under.

Or up, is it?

That faces were once unique,
each one looked like itself, it was not
Bell Telephone executives, all up

from the ranks. That a face
ought to fit
who wears it, not belong

to the company (Selig Smith,
4th Indiana, died
with a locket

      and the other man
cut off some of Booth's hair,
so that it was Booth

his mother
might say. The way even proof
was particular

      One has this difficulty,
nowadays, that the faces are obvious
even when they're open. It's as though

an idea was lost: that you can't do
any more than you are. And therefore
you are. It's as though you really had

secrets. One secret. That you go in there
on the assumption the other guy
is the one who's going to get it

And you find out,
you did. You look
at yourself in the mirror

The mirror
is a civil war

The Connection

The trouble is there's
too many people: one-fourth
of all the human beings who ever lived
are alive right now WOW nothing
can be left alone, the smallest
idea in the world will be swallowed
up and processed by half a million
idiots before it has a chance
to find out what's in it YOU
likewise. It's rough. And where
did it come from?
                  Better
find out.
       Try
the winter of 1861–62, the place
the Tennessee and the Cumberland
rivers, specifically the headquarters
of one Sam Grant
at Savannah, a few miles down
from Crump's Landing and Pittsburgh
Landing
               Even the names
keep the weight
of the goods
that were then,
still,
so much forage, corn, cloth, guns,
horses, rifled
180 pound
batteries,
pay,
to be unloaded.

Intelligence,
was the one part of the operation which,
says the commentator (mathematician,
Indiana University) Grant,
in forming for the first time the duties
of staff officers adequate to 100,000
men, did not cover—or maybe he
did, that is, there was a Colonel Webster

The point is, one can see suddenly
—and, like I say, the *weight* of the goods
not yet diminished because the old was
what was going to have to change,
yet all that was was holding its
content, that it had been, up to then,
small enough, even if large, to have another
time to it. And weight. And men
could go about it with connection
to it

There, suddenly, in "enemy" country
more men than had previously
needed more things than obviously,
in a short time, any number of men
had ever required to do a job
so much
            And there were no rules.

If the method, which now gobbles up
both the connection and the substance,
turns the latter into gloss-

and the former you will spin
out of yourself as the poet says

                    that a stasis
from a chrysalis

254

has stretched its wings,

you will have nothing to show,

you will do what it occurs to you

you have to do, and it will shake

nobody
                    except a like one

and it will take some time

for that one

to find out

if so, it's all right, it's
only a hundred years ago
that the method—and it didn't,
then, lose the goods—had to
come into being

                         mind you,
Sam Grant didn't
intend
any harm

          It's those, today,
who have lost the hands to make a balance
to weigh
the goods—who have no gloves on their face—

who don't look at you,

whom you cannot look at,

whom you cannot

abide

     And you must

because there is a connection.

The Friend

He was a man made a bank
of the present
          It's crazy,
how it was,

that you didn't know it
but you was being racked up

for da future! You was bills,
for an account

And of course it didn't occur to you then
that that was why you didn't think you had any
value!

Now what happens, at this end?
You discover all this. But,
where are you? where's he?
what about the bank?

It's simply—compound
interest and all that. Only

you ain't there, you weren't
denominations.

And he? He's got

Confederate money

on his hands—for cereal ad

prizes!

He wasn't there,
in the first place

And who does he know you as?

His own small change. The interest

is all his

War on the Mind in a Time of Love

quartermasters and filibusterers
was the beginning
of the new

and all those who heark back
to a better time
ought to get out, they'll never

make it

Now this doesn't mean
one has to put up with
the present, clearly

the successors
of the quartermasters and the filibusters

ain't anything, they're

worse, they're

out the other side, gone

beyond. They make nothing,

and much of it. They sell

what you quickly

can't make use of (a lady

       naked on a horse,

                    a child

                    making connections,

                    a tree

                    stripped of leaves

will overcome

the attention,   leisure

can't be filled

                    with art

Traffic managers

have no desire

A Discrete Gloss

The tide, the number 9 and creation
whatever sits outside you is
by what difference what
you also are: this church
or this slaughter house behind it, both
under palms alongside the mud-flats the sea leaves
in front of this three-time city

In what sense is
what happens before the eye
so very different from
what actually goes on within: this man
letting a fat whore hug him in the bus
as it goes counter to the eastering earth,
and I stare, until both of us turn away
as the bus stops and she goes behind it to piss

Your eye, the wanderer, sees more.
Or do you know what it focuses on, what happens
somewhere else: where, say, the sea
is more sea, and men
do not take Saturday Sunday off, arguing
they need to clean the gurry, a boat
takes that much drying, that much
sun

When the field of focus
is not as admitted as the point is,
what loss!   Who loves
without an object, who dreams
without an incubus, who fears
without cause?   Or dies
without all animalness, the disgorging
of breath blood bowels so tenderly
who can say the affections
are not the conquerors?

That what we do with what we are
is what ends all distraction.
As fiercely as the eye
is fierce.   Or death
is fierce.   Who cares
that they have taught us otherwise,
that they still noise it about

there are abstract things, human birds
with wings which only once
(in Giotto's hands) made
black and orange sense?

You who can seize
as the sun seizes.   Who drinks
by a stem as brilliant as that stopless eater of flowers. Who acts
as swiftly as a plant turns light to green. Or this chameleon's throat
wops red red red and why
I do not know, but that he does, that you do
that you can take some human thigh bone you've picked up
and with a stone tool carve such likeness on it
as much conjecture as the man you draw
was Quetzalcoatl more a sea-horse than himself—
such as you makes gorging nature at her blackest root
a silly starer too.

The day of man returns in your precisions, kin
(ahau, katun), the force
of force where force forever is
and man forgets: what is the world
that he can separate himself so simply from it,
or their soul, that I can locate it, or your act
that you can say its cause?

Man is no creature of his own discourse:
here on this beach made by the tide which passed
and dragged away old guts (or the birds
had it before the fish fed) and he turned, I turned
away, where nine madereros left a politician cut and stoned for dead
(where she pissed), it can be seen
that these boats dry in colors only he
had an eye for. And it says, it says here
in the face of everything it says
this, is the more exact

Kin

(for Hazel Larsen)

Measure by your footsteps, sd the voice, the days
will follow after.
                He compared his. He sd: counted
is the end of the earth, look, twelve
footsteps. Plus one
where I stand.
             And the sky and the land leaned
over.

In the air
there is no death.
             Man
is thirteen.
        In the cloud–mist
of himself.

Thirteen added, Seven added, One. At 20,
he raised his voice: its basis,
the sun asked. And got no answer, for the hollows
were still buried, the dawn
had not yet come
             Anger
came after man. And the ability
to count.
       So there were days, there were
suns.

This is the count of them.

The Thing Was Moving

It's so beautiful, life, goddamn death
that we have to die, only the mind knows
what lies next the heart or a five-petaled flower
restores the fringed gentians I used to so love
I'd lie amongst them in the meadow near the house
which was later covered by a dump to make an athletic field
and the brook was gone to which we tried to speed our sleds
from the hill the house stood on and which the dump
was meant to join, the loss punctuated by the shooting
my father taught me with the rifle he gave me from the back porch
of the three-decker, the rats living among the cans and peat
as the dump came closer, and I hated
all of it (the same porch the chameleon he had bought me
escaped from, from the cage I'd made it
of old screen when we brought it home from the circus

the smoke from the dump-fires all the time the thing was moving
toward us, covering the meadow, coming from the hill
(where we had had the single cable swing had broke
that day i was alone there and i had flown
out over all that space, and my glasses
beyond me, and my back to this day . . . and i groping
not to tell my parents, and to find the glasses
to find my way back. The fire-engines
in the evening dousing—and no flames but the littlest, all
smoke turning into steam there, but the excitement . . .

the concrete sections, when the dump began to reach
the brook, to put it under, like hoops we could not roll
in which—they were so high—we lost ourselves
like tunnels, or took it we were five-figured forms
fit to fill a circle and be acrobats, our heads
wedged but no movement of those sections even

when we pried them and were unknowingly in such danger
as when we built the club-house of railroad ties
on the edge of another flat, the swamp where the man
and his horse and team went down in the quicksand, and we
did not know until after the cops had broken down the structure
and even later when the auto showrooms covered it, and piles
had to be driven . . . the hunting, of each other, before the brook
was let in and only way above, or below at Chandler Street
was it any more where I had sunk in, where the irises were,
where I had seen my first turtle, or further up, where
girls had swum naked that day I had tittupped
from the piano lesson, seeking my friends, and suddenly,
coming on the pool, had heard the voices first, and slowed
so that I saw them from the bushes (the older woman
turning me back . . . the invasion

or the ford (below Dick Marsden's house) horses crossed
and we sailed boats, or made dams, the wonder
of the way the hill sloped up there, the gradual way
before it became a suburb and was still the West
(the trench we were sure had been emplacements
of King Phillip's Wars ended before the ford, before
the whole brook system got transverse to what it was below
near where I lived, Hill's Farm getting its fields
from the change of the direction of its flow,
and the topography
                    the flowers (as well as the ball field)
were located, in my space, by this curving
from west to south, the farm marking the change
and running against the foot of my house, the brick wall
on which all the wood stood which shook
when the wind bellied down that valley and struck
the broad back of the house and I used to think
why the whipping of the house on that third-floor
didn't throw it down, and only that the storm
was not like marching men on a bridge, was out of step
was irregular as men are, and as multiple, the times we are
and our materials are so much more numerous

than any such thing as the heart's flow
or the sun's coming up, why
man is man's delight, and there is no backward
except his, how far it goes, as far
as any thing he's made, dug up or lighted
by a flare in some such cave as I never knew
except as that concrete hid my brook and I was as large
(before they put the pieces in below ground) inside any one hoop
as any pentamerous thing, this figwort
which provokes me
and I study
bract thallus involucre whorl
of all my life, of torus I am, holding
all I shall be, hungry
that it should never end, that my throat
which has no longer thymus and all that went with it
might speak forever the glory of
what it is to live, so bashful as man is
bare

"He / in the dark stall . . ."

He
in the dark stall, no day now for him, to paw
only, to bellow—and all done
to keep him from harming himself, my bull
blinded—pink-eye, they said, but now
they ask if he was born to become this way, to be
useless, all that force
                              (my
heart)

Neither accident nor necessity
as mars my bull, puts out
these men's eye, that light, however much it is what we all do
that does cause that white filming puts them out
of action (how it is the eye dies
right before your own, as you watch, after you feel
the falling—the sickness
(which is what it is even though it is not
by nature, nor by accident

                (how
when it happens—as it did, then, last night, me, randy,
and left, in the end, with young men, only they, out of youth,
having kept in, my contemporaries having gone off, carrying
their darkness into darkness
                he
who had said, "10 years I have been mobile,
and I want some stability" and whose dilemma
had been made so clear to him that just his mobility
was why he was (to the degree he is) open

                      how more dies
than eye, than more than his sickness darkens him, how
each of us present die, our head, heart, cock, feet fall
that little which is the world when force in another
dies: this
is the loss, the too little noticed loss
the little loss whereby light, the hammer, is denied
and dimension—what we are here for
                  (that beauty
the identity of mind and feeling, act:
                last night, a second man
walked up again to his fond point, and broke, said: "Such mechanics
is all that I am capable of, too"—that lie
that in one mite particular of force we are allowed to see ourselves
as repetitions of another, that new stupidity
(to which each one of us is open as our skin is

to some mean mosquito of a germ who bores like staphylococcus
and makes boils which can—they told me, some weeks later,
it could have killed me, that lump, under my right arm)
that we are common in our likenesses when men have known
who had the will to know that only differences, the
irregularities we are custodians of, are
where we are alive—and where we give life to
each other

What loss of premise leaves all these, my fellows,
as my bull, so stalled? What simpleness of stance,
of courage, of simplicity have they been robbed of,
they let themselves lose instants of the day

                                        or such a roaring instant as last night
when four of us were—for that instant before two let go the force—
such bulls?
            Why are they now, this happy murmurous day, stumbling
as my poor bull is, up there where I cannot hear his calling?

Man's commons are awry, his eye is elsewhere than in his head, and so
his shots upon the target are as wide and failing as is darkness when darkness
is the day put out, the day he was meant to work and live in (the night
the only proper darkness, when he sleeps

Man is no longer archer, he
who once could bring a mastodon down that instant that he fed
by shot of arrow into that one place such hide of strength is not, the eye
into which he had the muscle so to drive his arrow (eye to drive it from his bow)
he could feed all about him days upon that fibrous flesh
marbled with fat and built from that huge animal's feeding
on fir cones, larch and pine, sedges, mosses, wild thyme,
Alpine poppy, buttercup, and grass

I mean no ancientness or primitivism as equal of what we ourselves here have:
I mean only, where were those two men's eyes last night that they

could lose, for any instant, their own strength, their contribution
back to force where each of us is propelled from, that bow
of which we are the arrows as well as we are users of the same:

the target, surely, is ourselves, from outside. And from in
there, too, the circles, and the bull's eye, that
is clear, if we leave it—clear. And shoot for it, do
first things first—have it, straight.

Black Mt. College Has a Few Words for a Visitor

Name names, Paul Goodman
                        or else your own
will be the Everyman of sugar sweet, the ginger cookie
to scare the Witch with you, poor boy—if we must have such classes
as "equals," the young, your lads, the fearful lasses

                                    ((these rimes
Huss too would make, as of so good a man as you here pose
yourself to be, dear you, dear true, dear clear, your poor
dear doom, your going away not rightly used. He'd send you
what I send you too, a little reedy Cross pulling feed
out a bottle filled with what now rimes with sis (poor Sis
who don't get half a chance by contrast to the boys because
her tender ender's such a portcullis it's good
for nothing more than making those fond ones you'd—what do you say?
lay bare? o Paul

who has a rougher thought, who knew he could corrupt an army
were it not he had his friends he owed a something to, a rose
perhaps or rose inopportunely on a cop, and there! right on the street
or in the middle of Grand Central Palace, look! he showed
what he did not admit he meant

Look: us equals, that is, also sons of witches, are covered now with cookies
dipped in same from your fell poem. It fell, all right, four footed
with one foot short where five were called for—five, sd the Sphinx,
confronted with senescence and with you, still running running running
from her hot breath who bore you, Hansel Paul, to bore us—all.

Merce of Egypt

1   I sing the tree is a heron
    I praise long grass.
    I wear the lion skin
    over the long skirt
    to the ankle. The ankle
    is a heron

    I look straightly backward. Or I bend to the side straightly
    to raise the sheaf
    up the stick of the leg
    as the bittern's leg, raised
    as slow as
    his neck grows
    as the wheat. The presentation,
    the representation,
    is flat

I am followed by women and a small boy in white carrying a duck,
all have flat feet and, foot before foot, the women with black wigs
And I intent
upon idlers,
and flowers

2   the sedge
    as tall as I am, the rushes
    as I am

      as far as I am animal, antelope
    with such's attendant carnivores

                            and rows of beaters
    drive the game to the hunter, or into nets,
    where it is thick-wooded or there are open spaces
    with low shrubs

3   I speak downfall, the ball of my foot
    on the neck of the earth, the hardsong
    of the rise of all trees, the jay
    who uses the air. I am the recovered sickle
    with the grass-stains still on the flint of its teeth.
    I am the six-rowed barley
    they cut down.

    I am tree. The boy of the back of my legs
    is roots. I am water fowl
    when motion is the season of my river, and the wild boar
    casts me. But my time
    is hawkweed,

4   I hold what the wind blows, and silt.
    I hide in the swamps of the valley to escape civil war,

and marauding soldiers. In the new procession
I am first, and carry wine
made of dandelions. The new rites
are my bones

I built my first settlement
in groves

5   as they would flail crops
when the spring comes, and flood, the tassels
rise, as my head

A Toss, for John Cage

The young dog runs and leaps,
the old dog dislikes his likes
(or is this another of those either-or's,
neither of which applies?)

The young dog, say, is, like they say, the way it was,
or it might yet be. And the old dog—
is he asking to be new, or asking us to be? If he is,
surely you'll not counter with that dodge about the sort
you can't teach such tricks to. For how is this giggling
at the end of the rope, or how shadows
on the wall—what's
serious?

Take it another way, take water
(or be classical—fire, air, earth, too) ask him
about vessel, ask this old dog to ask his 64 numbers,
the 16 trigrams, a question, have him throw his 3 pennies
(the old Three, dat old number) to find you out in what way his 20 Minutes
despite all the new wine therein (I'll believe his discoveries)
is not a bottle, is
so blown, doth
intervene, hath
beginning. And ends
like an hexameter.

At the same time allowing that demonism she spoke of (and who cannot
who can look into that cherry eye, delight
in that orange head and jaw, hear
those three lemons go "Hm"—I'm allowing, for one,
because the bars, the jackpot, I haven't yet heard come up, but
that's what I'm always playing for), the demonism,
as she said, of the order of order, the mathematics of it
that all is everything, that it is not nothing. She knew
that there are three worlds, that everything is—that order is—the Creator is
a grin. But allowing that it is, isn't the moment of it,
in this case, that what grins
is a man?

Or put it a third way, his way, and without his daot or dawg: A,
all city noises, B, country noises, C, electronic, D,
music's, and speech, E, arbitrary sounds, and F—fur, say,
or the finger drawn across a surface, any of the small cries
which need amplification for us to hear, those, say, cats
hear, or bats, or—to jump—the ducks
Ted Williams . . . this library
for our ears, this new Biblioteque, in it
is there yet recorded that other thing which is a duration,
hath frequency, overtone, attack, is serial—
have you got that in, have you caught it,
that which I catch
in your hm?

We come to it: is it any more than something
we don't need analogy for, or anecdote, no quote
not even on magnetic tape, no matter how we need
all the means that any of us, in fact just such tricks
as you have taught us, so long as not one last of us forgets
—so long as you don't leave out—that you, too, have in mind
you taught yourself the tricks, old dog (having in mind,
as you so surely did, how very boring how very quickly
a young dog is

The Leader

They slew him, the women
for the second time he
was meat, the red–headed
man: they served him
to their maws

      (He walked straight into the canyon,
      looked back, looked at them
      and in that glance, by it

They ate him, they did, again, as,
secretly, they seem to have, before
when he was eucharistically present, the boy
was spitted for their wills gone
all teeth

      (He kept ahead, he moved large
      —small in the look of his size

beneath the sandstone walls—he started up
the river bed, leaving his back open to

Why they are, and he not loving anything but
his own life, that generousness, that he give
with no expectation of anything back—he,
up to then, often, in the glaring sun had sat
singing out his love, nor found
tranquillity to ease his yearning, always
sleepless cares within his soul wore him
the while he looked for woman's rosy countenance. Instead,
such as these crowded around
and in foul odor and with loud whetted axes

       He moved up, out of the shadows
       of the lower river, past the white sand,
       up ten miles where the water had cut the most
       down through the rock, and bottom land,
       ten feet off the stream bed, grew peach trees
       which glowed from the sun which fell down the sides
       of the pinnacle—there, he sang such songs women,
       in whose cheeks men's risks raised color,
       listened

         while back where he had been his fellows
       branded those others that they, disfigured,
       would never forget their deed
       of hate

"The winds / which blew my daughter . . ."

The winds
which blew my daughter
in, the 4
directions: Hines,
born in Cork, brought up in
Galway; Reynolds,
Longford, and come here
not from that particular lord's slavery
but from his fellows'
who pinched all the peasantry
so that even his had to go
one by one to the States, South
Dakota first. Wilcock, wool,
from the east riding of
Yorkshire; Olsons, gardeners
Nöricke, iron workers
Örebru

Feathers
in her blood

From the Inca

The mighty man and the mother-egg

leg over leg over leg

Dramatis
Personae

live's on it
love's on it
: honor
on top of
the hill. Until vertigo

seized him. Fell from it, into
the sea. Was last reported
as lost. Last seen,
disappeared
into the element. Penduto

from heights, head
down. Or that one
answered
an ad. Was chosen,
and since
has been charming
the wood pulp, talks
at an increasing
sugar, walks
like the Mayflower
Doughnut Company,
shows the white collar
at the crucial
occasion. Is
Caucasian, will not falter
at the meeting when presented
to a hostess with uncovered breasts,
crosses his hands gently
when the lady bowed before him
in her gold and white sari.

Has been known
to cross oceans
on missions
without erring
on arriving. Sits under awnings
where others
would put on
all sail, would even shove
around capes with moon and stuns'l
up. Is stud
apud
nada, has not sheathe
upon nether, has not parts
for carrying. Carries caps
on foreteeth, hath smile
for beginning. Doth call "my"
to his dog, speaks nicely
on television, has fat rump
for charcoal, is perishing
by chicken, sells selves
on Wednesday, does not cross
Sunday, eats buns
on Monday. Was unanimously elected President
by all odds while wood-lots
stood by themselves
and cow-birds
laid eggs
in other birds'
nests. The chestnut-throated warbler
warbled. Does not make any
missteps. Was put down
by standing by
when friend's friend
was being kicked
in head
by two strangers. Did not move
fast enough
for door to car

to be sprung
from said hinges. Was last seen
in all places
had hitherto
been, is not known
to have shown
any effect. Will swell by absorption
of all nearness, will not pray for the dead
on All Souls' Day, will not be seen
where the fellow was who fell out of
the sky

      was at the knees
      of the sun's face
      as he came. And landed
      just over our heads
      as we passed through
      the entrance
      to the building

      And the eyes in his head
      were as ours

The Collected Poems Of

like lines of verse REDBURN
is composed: London
is the queer house Harry Bolton and he, Liverpool
is the woman and child those steps down from the street, Lancelot
Hey, the ship

is the shanghaid corpse which burns in the forepeak as Spiritus
Sancti, Jackson
is the blood he coughs on the stays'l before he pitches
and dies

and THE TOWN-HO the hardness a Rimbaud
or a Melville
make boats by
which lurch
or are Pequods

That Clarel,
or The Pleasure Party,
are not so written, are not
from that base, is no reason
to neglect what's in them, what failed
in the lines
                though (equally true) the success
                is also no excuse
                to exaggerate the verse as proper proof of

                in the face of that face (the Town-ho!
                that boy, Red-burn

                        And neither any of this of the moment of
THE BOAT, let me call it, for a change, the hollowed out thing, the bower
in the Arcasides: what came at the maker,
the riddle of that
femininity

        what we are dealing with here,

Not hard as youth (that softness
the sentimentality made
the Renaissance, so explored the world only
to boss it)

            another hardness
could take the son of a gentleman
as an angle, the shame
to have to have sold
hats!

        why not let's talk about Shakespeare, pose
Steelkilt over against his Hamlet or his Lear, and say flatly how
feminine Shakespeare is, how his triumph
and Dostoevsky's is, that they opposed violence
by that means, by that accumulated
experience. They did offset adolescence,
were bored
by the frontier

As Melville was, but his difference
        methodologically it is true, he was feminine,
        but an altogether different feminine, more that genetic one
        of a child—tho here one must be very precise,
        for a child is so quickly gendered, is conspicuous
        so early—as baby—in those drives we call male
        and female, those
        importances
his differences is the hardness
as are things when things are properly constituted, are
proportions more than urban ones, are enough to fall in with the course of
nature and each other—
                a matter of ends, not
                methodology

                        In Shakespeare and Dostoevsky, a
                        disposition, the one onlie veritie of
                        the psychological act (and no use in it
                        after them

Termini, what determines
Melville. And why, at a certain point, this point,

he has to be talked of in respect to only one other,
Omeros
        (euripides
        the other hard one
these three
              Plus possibly rimbaud, though
              rimbaud may only seem so now, simply
              that he is the most "modern"
              and made such decisions as
              to enlist and fight in Indonesia,
              did go trading among the Harrar,
              was made a member of the Institut Geographie,
              had books sent to find out more about meteorology

              And Euripides that different
              that he did not need to bear down so hard on ends,
              pillars, openings: his hardness
              was the one methodology of the lot, and my guess is because
              he inherited
                      as Herodotus did
                              the oral
        the old
        narrative, what, now
                      (this long after S, & D, & M)
        is so very much back in business: that the play of a fowl
        or the mind of a fox is worth more than an Aesop, is
        as big as, and a better gimmick for, to present
        Gyges
              or the ladies tear up Creon, crying
              "Ai-yee!
              Iach-
              oi!"

Not Homer nor Melville, neither Caloopso nor that she
who as a mower a blade of grass in the field. . . .

And so you'll find out, you'll find
that the area and the devices of, the virtues

of verse and prose and drama not at all in anything but
Redburn, or behind Clarel, in Vine, say, or that "Indian"
—what's his name?—from Baltimore?

or a phrase

Or those lines, what Anarch jest
what Cosmic blunder split
—I, we—
the human integral
asunder!

and shied
—let you know!—
the fractions
through the gate, those multiples
—her—
jaws

Common Place

The full moon, as she tipped the hill, rising
had trees on her face
               And when I came in, I sd to Libby, Come
to the window, and see (she having hoped
it would be the night of the full moon she'd have her baby, having heard
that it is true, mothers do, like the earth, get pulled—or is it the moon
is pulled?

Then I asked her, had she had a great strength
that day, had she wanted to clean house, or at least sweep
the floor?

Con had sd, when we first saw it, how fast
it rises. And I, to be irritable, had corrected, you mean
the earth is surprising how it
turns. To which she protested, I'd rather
be old-fashioned, that it is the moon
is rising

As, shortly thereafter, when we had reached the pond, and the moon
was as I said it would be, on the waters already, that high, Con sd,
think of the Indian eyes have seen
this same thing, and I, not so contrary but still wanting to differ,
any words, in a sense, being an irritation, saying, yes,
to get back to that ignorance of how hills come
into existence, to be so straight a moon is a moon, and yet
not to lose what we do know, in other words that durance
of man, that anything he knows does not take away,
there is so much he does not know; or at least for Lib
or for us, what happened or was to happen was itself
so itself nothing we knew or said was
any more than more (which is what all
means, doesn't it?

And meant to Indians too,
along this hill?

"It's got to this . . ."

It's got to this, that anything
against the sky is big, a bantam's
tail even, seen so, is as noble as
any hero's
casque—or the ventilator
on the hen house   so much like such
a warrior's
looking about him

And I
am the more impressed
by the two be-bops walking the rails
That one saying, the trouble is these steps
are too far apart, but the other having it,
It ain't that, it's
the bannisters
are so low

"my poor dumb body . . ."

my poor dumb body
which must also be obeyed to,
indeed, which, first and last,
has my obedience willy-nilly

yet my poor dumb body
is not easy to come to obey,
it goes so much its own way,
and I go about mine, taking it
I am master

which my poor dumb body
has to take, it would even let me
waste it, beat out of it its will,
except that in its blindness,
its plain dumbness

my poor body knows
what I do not know
and whose, then,
is the mastery?

"my poor dumb body . . ."

my poor dumb body
which must also be obeyed to,
indeed, which, first and last,
has my obedience,
willy-nilly, yet
is so hard to come to obey,
it goes its own way
as I would mine, taking it
I am its master,

which of course I am, except
that in its blindness, its
plain dumbness it knows
what I also have to know
to be
mastered

Well

I can see in the night
no matter how close you are

But in the day, in the light
I see too many things to see this one

well

The Mast

I had to unship the mast or we would have been over, & in, to
the depth just there, the American Channel, the dark blue

as against the brilliance of the lighter color from the sands
of the shallow water closer in to the banks
                                        I had made the mast,
and it was too big for the boat, too high
& heavy. It wasn't the area
of the sail.
Or anything the matter with the rigging.

                              Without power, & only a poor oar,
I worked in, over the shallows, to a thing of an island was for birds.
And that day it was no thing more than that—a place to ground,
& figure out how to cross that channel, and get back. When we did,
I was a lather, and lost the pleasure of the evening.

But now, this day, that day jumps
another way: that island
is what I read, or saw—or it is Fisher's Hill
where Cabbage and I . . . it leaps on me
like a man caught boys, & kept them there,
in cinder caves (the harshness,
and the holes, the rottenness
of corals

        I am flooded
with a boy's time
                    with that going off
to a place of my own
                        where Cabbage and I went, where,
patently,
I still am

        And waters and islands

                        (but not the boat,
at least not that boat)

                    are not Island #9, are not American
Channel

                    Or are such
                    as I

                        are not any chart, any such place
as I then was, almost swamping her, & pulling out (to be cool),
& sweating, to bring her in

That now the island (the grit
that it was—a guano, or a piece of sand a good storm . . .)
should bulk as all my secret self
                              even to this (beside the man)
                              that I am Theda Bara beaten
                              with a poker
                              by a step-mother. Even this trace
                              is one of the edges which scrapes
                              as I am suddenly grounded

                              (as my leg was torn
                              so I still have the scars
                              the day I slipped and it got wedged
                              in that split rock the barnacles
                              had covered both faces of)

all that world
            is not at all
                        gone

Yet, like the island, or Fisher's Hill (now one mass of semi-detached
                              houses, the dreariness
                              of yards

I am this master would, today, not take that boat to sea
or enjoy, as he did, that boy, such
revery, yet does all these things,

on new matters, as clumsily, as
happily, as
surely

And am that advantage that
I have all of it,
as he did not have

             (Or what did he have less
than I, now, have?

             or I, then, Cayo Hueso?

                         What, if I am more, am I?

I am. That would be the insistence, or there is nothing here
but memory—that thing makes the new streets on the edge of a city, & new houses
a scene wind and boys and roofing papers are the only life of

that channel
would be bluer,
would be more seen were I there today. As that mast
would be right, would be cut and shaped, would not be shipped
no matter how many days . . . (or, in better matters, the years

That this is the difference, for the boy, too, that the fantasy
does not retract, it only
comes home: he knows
who the man is, I know
the wicked step-mother, I go off
without escaping, Cabbage
is me

    And the mast

For a Man Gone to Stuttgart Who Left an Automobile Behind Him

the callacanthus
out again (the golden fury seen
thru those red candles

not at all a dead car, curiously,
even though it hasn't moved as what pushes out buds
has

not deadhead (as Grady's
two were, all winter

Beyond, the grove of little dogwood (today's
entry

    But, by the heady red flowers (their smell
will be heavy), the large dogwood (the single bush,
back of the stone steps,
glares

2

and it came out this way (just after you had left,
a year ago

suddenly the spring field is blue, of figwort
and the callacanthus smell is intercepted by that color
as the dogwood was by the green of my pleasure
that I slept under it, for an hour, and woke,
as they have, to the rising of
the forces

"The sea / is an archeology . . ."

The sea
is an archeology: eight fathom down, on Dogger Bank, the bones
fishermen curse from the trawls snapped and the nets torn
are woolly rhinoceros and giant deer, a catch proves
the mouth of a river debouched just here where
one fisherman and another want
simpler things

Proensa

for Creeley and Blackburn

here, a Sunday, when light
is fall's
whiteness
            when no smallness
(of even a bed) contains
the affairs of men (when not even Salonika
one can be count of, or marry
Constantine's niece, in Cyprus, and sport
imperial arms)

and yet one does know
an air to suck, and where,
in six inches, shafts
of the sun have fallen

in such manner they
stay as the straight body they
sang, because we,
by usage and by nature, also
have known
                what they were as clear in as
(Peking,
had less important
things

If love was
(when fighting was, when the heart
was eaten
to correct
national abuses,

if love was
so clearly sung, and sirventes
did serve
to stir things up

And now they don't

Ladies
are not to be abandoned,
are forever
abandoned,
                    the clothes
we wrap love in,
we are to be hunted, until
we, too, are brought to our mistress's
bed, to be laughed over
for the clothes we wear

    And to be cured
(by her and her husband)

as our tongue
was also once cut,

and healed enough, meanwhile,
for us to sing with

Jas Jargon

Like a man on a stick on a sidewalk being peddled by a low pitchman

Or lines on oneself as a pissed off William Blake, the wryness
of aeternitas

what socialism
has come to!

        O the dream
busted!

        O

shit

    as though we were as aged, or as young, as

—either way—dried

sticks. A bundle. What fardels

the gifted and the utterly giftedless

Princes

have become—o

Becoming!

       Poor

man, that they should weep for them-

selves. Or be jejune

that he will hop/

step/

one/

day!

       O the grave

of the plastered

hope

        O soap

to wash the Stalinist

pigs—oh people, o

Toronto

         O catch-

on!

Maya Against Itzas

O Sun! With your eye of a great bird,
look down on us pleading
before your throne

O rolling Sun,
who ripens us.
And our crops:

we are crushed
as by a great stone

The Boat

I

Sacred sycamore and the odor of cedar wood (the odor of the buried boat

Trying to keep up with the day, the sun going as fast as it does

Linen gear. Three-decker. Celestial food-stuffs. How to voyage
through the night

         "O marvelous Necessity, who with supreme reason
constrainest all effects"

II

The irretrievable, passing

The objective immortality of the past

88 pieces of limestone for a sky

III

I was slung between stone and wood

Rather, the red bird buffing two lead figures to give to another figure

Or the tiller gone in the mouth of the crocodile

Actually, the water: not anything buried in anything not in the night

                                          not in the sand

                                          not in the fishes' mouths

Solely the Diorite coming up through the sea

IV

The past is to be sealed for after the feast-day

Or to be looked over by those who have the nose for

It is not pictures

V

The night, very fast

The Soul

artists and writers:

not good enough,

she sd

                    He speaks

                  in apothegms, another

                  sd

While the red auto
with the tires askew
keeps following
each move I make, adheres
to me,
backing down the avenue
to lure the woman in it
to the secret place

and when she gets out
she is a fat girl
with a squeak for a voice
asking her mother
permission to go to
the store

Da Boyg

It ain't a woman
he looks like

from behind.
Or a lion

coming on.
Nor does he have

anything,
round about

—not even
sand.

"Meself,"
he sez

and any man,
crying his

helplessness,
asking her

to unclasp
her knees

beats the boyg

But the Boyg?

He's got

big ears,

small eyes,

a hide

and a

tail—

on the front of him

Love

(down,
to my soul:

        assume your nature as yourself,
        for the love of God

                    not even good enough

Stories
       only
          the possibility
                of discrete
                    men

There is no intelligence
the equal of
the situation

There are only
          two ways:
          create the situation
                    (and this is love)
          or avoid it.
              This also can be
Love.

The Motion

the motion
not verbal
        the newt
        less active
                than I: the fire pink
                not me
                        (the words
                        not me

not my nature
I
        Not even honor
        anything
                but that my freshness
                not be opened
                    (as my mail must not be,
                        before I do.

No doctrine
        even that the flower flames
                if I don't. No capture
if the captive,
        even the instant,
            is not I.

Thus thou.

The Pavement

the pavement
I take so long
to go along by

        the walk
        from the house
        to the store

              I can't jump over

The obduracy
of spirit, the doubt
of person, the locus
only the place
I was not conceived in

Only where I was named

because I was known

for the first time

                    to be there. And I

                    unknown

And

who am I

        any more than

                who knows

the lines

        I break my father's spine,

                the cracks

I break my mother's back

        are so wide,

                they are not so easily

Used.

A Story

It was a place
of fountains.

I had gotten there
driving a fast car
down a difficult road
with a maimed man
in the back seat
by using a flashlight
to see my way

I had made a right turn
slewing, from the speed,
and the sharpness
of the angle.

I had stopped
at these springs
for a drink of water,
from a bubbler.
A woman
in another car,
with a man beside her,

asked me

for a glass of water.

I brought it

to her. And she said,

don't you know

there is also

hot water

here?

Peograms

life is funny:
it shoots around
like a crazy bullet

when a young man hit her,
it was like an orange crate
hit by an axe the way
she slewed

Lessless Headless
made poetness
his subjectless

For Lessless Headless
had no poetness
in his natureless

So Lessless Headless
wrote essays
in every magazineless

And said less
than any
livingless

The Real

The neck of
the cone
       she
on the left,
       he
all for me, protesting

on the right

Did you kiss me there,
pointing

I have a bruise

You've been funny
all day

      Picasso
called it a wound,
not I

      And when I got my car out of the mud
it followed me,
      adhering

I Believe in You . . .

      you & Rimbaud,
you are right to love the Great Mother

And to despair in a time when Kore only
(when Demeter has to be looked for

when only the Maiden (when woman
does not know she is also who hunts
for herself
      Instead of finding half herself
in every ad.

There is no hell when hell is
toothpaste. And Demeter

Oh, Woman:
lay about you!
        Slay!
            That you may have cause again
to seek yourself, to go out among flowers crying
"Kore! Kore!", knowing

the King of Hell
also has you

Red Mallows

           (for WCW)

red mallows, the language blooming
like those flowers, August,
in my garden this morning, he
said, the first time this year

     as flowers do

declaring the accidence
not by the law, not by nature
(admitting her regularity,
and the need for relations)
but by what troubles discourse:

     that it is I
     who speaks

Beauty—what others love in us—
is not responsible to us, she
said, and thereby, also,
raised the question:

       form
       descends

And the inhabitation
—the eyes, and the ears,
responsible agents, the places
they have to nose into, nose
about—it is they

       who also
       come up

The Death of Europe

(a funeral poem for Rainer M. Gerhardt)

Rainer,
the man who was about to celebrate his 52nd birthday
the day I learned of your death at 28, said:
"I lie out on Dionysius' tongue"!

the sort of language you talked, and I did,
correctingly—
        as I heard this other German wrongly,

from his accent, and because I was thinking of you,
talking of how much you gave us all hearing
in Germany (as I watch a salamander on the end of a dead pine branch
snagging flies), what I heard this man almost twice your age say was,
"I lie out on a dinosaur's tongue"!

for my sense, still, is that,
despite your sophistication
and your immense labors . . .

It will take some telling. It has to do with what WCW
(of all that you published in *fragmente,* to see Bill's
R R BUMS in futura!

                              it has to do with how far back are

Americans
as well as,
Germans

                    "walk on spongey feet
                    if you would cross

                    carry purslane
                    if you get into her bed

                    guard the changes
                    when you scratch your ear

    I

It is this business
that you should die!
Who shot up,
out of the ruins,
and hung there,
in the sky,
the first of Europe
I could have words with:

as Hölderlin on Patmos you
trying to hold bay leaves
on a cinder block!

> Now I can only console you,
> sing of willows,
> and dead branches,
> worry the meanness
> that you do not live,
> wear the ashes
> of loss

> Neither of us
> carrying a stick
> any more

Creeley told me
how you lived

II

I have urged anyone
back (as Williams asked
that Sam Houston
be recognized
              as I said,
Rainer, plant
your ash

> "I drive a stake into the ground, isn't it silly,"
I said out loud in the night, "to drive a stake into the ground?"

How primitive
does one have to get? Or,

as you and I were both open
to the charge: how large

can a quote

get, he

said, eyeing me

with a blue

eye

                  Were your eyes

                  brown, Rainer?

                  Rainer,

                  who is in the ground,

                  what did you look like?

                  Did you die of your head bursting

                  like a land-mine?

                  Did you walk

                  on your own unplanted self?

III

It is not hell you came into,
or came out of. It is not moly
any of us are given. It is merely
that we are possessed of
the irascible. We are blind
not from the darkness
but by creation we are

moles. We are let out
sightless, and thus miss
what we are given, what woman
is, what your two sons
looking out of a picture at me,
sitting on some small hillside—

they have brown eyes, surely.

> Rainer, the thyrsus
> is down
>
> I can no longer
> put anything
> into your hands
>
> It does no good
> for me to wish
> to arm you
>
> I can only carry laurel,
> and some red flowers,
> mere memorials, not cut
> with my own knife an oar
> for you, last poet
> of a civilization
>
> You are nowhere
> but in the ground

IV

What breaks my heart
is that your grandfather
did not do better, that our grandmothers
(I think we agreed)

did not tell us
the proper tales

so that we are as raw
as our inventions, have not the teeth
to bite off Grandfather's
paws

(O, Rainer,
you should have ridden your bike
across the Atlantic instead of your mind,
that bothered itself too much
with how we were hanging on
to the horse's tail, fared, fared
we who had Sam Houston, not
Ulysses

         I can only cry: Those
         who gave you not enough
         caused you to settle for
         too little

               The ground
         is now the sky

V

But even Bill
is not protected,
no swift messenger
puts pussley
even in his hand,
open,

as it is, no one says how
to eat
at the hairy table

                        (as your scalp
also lifted,
                        as your ears
did not stay

silk

                              O my collapsed brother,
                              the body
                              does bring us
                              down
                                    The images
                              have to be
                              contradicted
                                        The metamorphoses
                              are to be
                              undone

                              The stick,
                              and the ear

                              are to be no more than

                              they are: the cedar

                              and the lebanon

                              of this impossible

                              life.

                              I give you no visit

                              to your mother.

What you have left us

is what you did

It is enough

It is what we

praise

I take back

the stick.

I open my hand

to throw dirt

into your grave

I praise you

who watched the riding

on the horse's back

It was your glory to know

that we must mount

O that the Earth

had to be given to you

this way!

O Rainer, rest

in the false

peace

Let us who live

try

Going from Battle to Battle

The earth lay golden green
in the summer sunlight

The ancient mountains
spilled the afternoon
as firmly as they've flattened
all the valleys

And life is new
the generous day

Small Birds, to Agree with the Leaves, Come in the Fall

as   in the amusement park   they have these streams of water
go straight up in the air, the red ball bobbing

unable to get out   yet vivid   the bobbing
of the forms, the veil

so strong no thing once caught
has but this mist, is but in this maid's

loving arms held so to glisten
in what colors you or I may show

> the water loves so much
> because of all things it loves
> it loves itself so little

the language is touch and from this slightness what tosses
stays in the air, do not think down or out

that you or it, that the park
or the store-window, or your girl

> it is water keeps you up, the
>
> evanescence

I, Mencius, Pupil of the Master . . .

the dross of verse. Rhyme!
when iron (steel)
has expelled Confucius
from China. Pittsburgh!
beware: the Master
bewrays his vertu.
To clank like you do
he brings coolie verse
to teach you equity,
who layed down such rails!

Who doesn't know a whorehouse
from a palace (who doesn't know the Bowery
is still the Bowery, even if it is winos
who look like a cold wind, put out their hands
to keep up their pants

    that the willow or the peach blossom
    . . . Whistler, be with America
    at this hour

    open galleries. And sell
    Chinese prints, at the opening,
    even let the old ladies in—

    let decoration thrive, when
    clank is let back
    into your song

      when voluntarism
    abandons
    poetic means

Noise! that Confucius himself
should try to alter it, he
who taught us all
that no line must sleep,
that as the line goes so goes
the Nation! that the Master
should now be embraced by the demon
he drove off!   O Ruler

      in the time of chow,
      that the Soldier
      should lose the Battle!

      that what the eye sees,
      that in the East the sun untangles itself
      from among branches,
      should be made to sound as though there were still roads
      on which men hustled
      to get to paradise, to get to
      Bremerton
      shipyards!

II

that the great 'ear
can no longer 'hear!

      o Whitman,
      let us keep our trade with you when
      the Distributor
      who couldn't go beyond wood,
      apparently,
      has gone out of business

      let us not wear shoddy
      mashed out of

even the Master's
old clothes, let us bite off Father's
where the wool's
got too long (o Solomon Levi

in your store on Salem Street,
we'll go there to buy our ulsterettes,
and everything else that's neat

III

We'll to these woods
no more, where we were used
to get so much, (Old Bones
do not try to dance

go still
now that your legs

the Charleston
is still for us

You can watch
It is too late
to try to teach us

we are the process

and our feet

We do not march

We still look
And see

what we see

We do not see
ballads
other than our own.

O'Ryan

O'Ryan 1

Overall, mover of the unnumbered

————————

who did twelve labors, rose
at 4 AM. And when I complained
that I could not do as much,
she turned it on me this way,
that if he went to bed at 2
and rose at 4, you
rise at 2
and go to bed at 4. I thinking,
how neat. And necessary, we
who don't have God to encourage us,
at least that aim
in the business. Or think women
as much as those did who had God
We love em, we do not do without em
our necks are bent, we do see
the reflection, we do know
who's who, how what we ride
rides us, how there are twelve houses
to be got through: what one are you at,
fellow fellow? My purpose

is to invoke you, not at all any
muse.   Or at least none
that you are beholden
to, that you know
by taking sight, by merely

looking up. No zodiac
neither the one which comes after
pleasure, nor that one
after labors. The cincture now,
the emblem of the championship,
is care—by your mother's fire.
And sleep—sometime sodden sleep.

I don't read your face. Or you mine.
By looking up or down. Neither
the light nor the dark do we brawn
by. We do it all, I take it, my
fellow.
               Will you join me
in one on the house?

               Shall we drink
to the ladies?

O'Ryan 2

Tell me something, tell me
how you got that way

how'dya lose your
what stuck you in the pants

why did they ask you
to take on so much

Tell me something, tell me
what made you do it

why did you buy
so much shit

how come you got so far off
the rail

tell me, where are you
nowadays, what makes you

look so warm in the eye, who
told you your flesh is

as rosy as your
baby's, as rosy as

Rosy, as, your
moth-er's, as who got you up

in the morning
in the morning

Tell me: how'dya
get up? how did you

stand up after all
that lying down

what took
that look off

your face, how come you
shine, no shine

at all, all white
and looking all over

hey, bruiser: tell me

something

O'Ryan 3

I heard they got you
on a rape charge

Or was it mugging
Or just minding

your own business, that you looked too much
like your fellow men?

was it they burned you
on the yellow tree?

O'Ryan 4

The story starts. It's
cinema
        Mah

Or chuck, chuck, I'll
play with your rosy

Kate's the girl for a
sail–
           or for a

bosun, a gunner, a-
merican (heave me a

sigh, he said, I lost
her, I lost her

by saying too much
by opening my mouth

And who comes along
but a sly guy, a guy

who doesn't do anything but
sigh—and of course

she was his, of course

We couldn't love you
if we didn't love you

with our mouth shut

O'Ryan 5

In other words
there ain't no villain
in this piece,
none at all.

There isn't any,
anyway.   You find me one.

who isn't some stinking
sonofabitch of a man

O'Ryan 6

Your mother's. Your
mother's like they say

in a Chinese novel, to be as straight about it
as a sign can

As a sign in a can

We begin,
that way.

Virgin.
        OK.

And let her rest, let her
if you can give it to her

if you can give it to her soul, if you can find out
what you owe her, what peace

a woman is, how you are all there
or you ain't, you haven't

slaked her thirst, you haven't
What a man has to do, he has to

meet his mother in hell

O'Ryan 7

Woman is a man's
all cause

A man don't have
no other

He can look, he's got
plenty, it's a short

he's got all the sky
to get up into, to get off his

But a woman is a man's
   yes
      yes
         yes

O'Ryan 8

He was all lit up
like a pinball machine

a son of the working
classes

He came down on her
in the middle of the road

he belted her, he pinned his shoulders
to her

And he scowled
right through his back

O'Ryan 9

It's that way that's all
whether you like it or not

even if you can get it
all prettied up

Or you're that damned fool literate
you buy store bought clothes

Don't fool yourself
Underneath all them poems

it's night

you got a hard on

and it's

to be made

O'Ryan 10

He loved a girl
And her name was Woods.

He wooed her in the Maytime,
he wooed her in the fall

He wooed her after all the others,
he wooed her in his shoes,
he wooed her in the creases
between his rotten toes

He wooed her even though
she threw the book at him
he ran as fast as he could run
to keep his first look at her bum

She knew her business like the smartest
one, a female as the poems say
she got him and she slew him, he was that far gone
he couldn't leave off, she was so much his poison
so much his dish, he'd turn on a dime
to give her her wish

But the thing they didn't know
who didn't know him, was he knew how
she looked when she looked at him

And now you can see, there's a moral here.
It happened in Crete. Or if you're discreet,

I can tell you
more: it's no different, just down the street

O'Ryan 11–15

11

Letsuzstayawayfromparades

12

I can't tell a thing.
Why I let them go!

If you'll lend me your ear
I'll send you back a pea

It's somewhere here,
but I'll bite my arse

how one does slip
on the fucking grass

There's a way thru rime,
there's a way ain't verse

but o, poor fellows:
would you try to pass

what isn't anywhere
back up your mother's

or hers, or whose, or
even your own?—parse

that one

13

They were so realistic
shooting the King of Babylon
after Tamurlaine made him
his Asia fool

that they killed a pregnant woman
who was there to see
what the play was all about,
a real live bullet

just went astray

13

There was Ericson's Isle
off the Vineyard shore
had a 3-ton boulder
was supposed to say
the Norski's had been here
900 years before

—only a Captain Brandt
in 1903
with a cook and some kittens
had wintered there

And they had much time on their hands

As well, of course, that they both knew

Norwegian

14

a clowder of cats
in a city backyard

fed by the neighbors
in the block about

on dout

and on destruction

15

Joe Ball
got too tall
too quick
like Wallace corn

—and now the American left
is shorn,
one raises eggs,
the other sub-si-dies

And all you union men,
don't you snicker
at these millionaires,
you got so many
irons in your refrigerators
you better not sneeze

you better get down on your knees
and ask forgiveness for your

corn

And your Sim-mons-beds

True Numbers

one face, two face, three

one face, two face, three

down with the unitary

down with the unitary

up psychology, it's

for women, it's

terrific, there's

no question—but

one face, two face, three,

at least, it's—me!

New Poem

I have a foolishness here which is lamp-like.
Thus the words came, between the two pines
by the old house, an issue of the mind

as deliberate as a dream is suddenly
in the mouth.

I do not know what it means, and question,
therefore, any right I have to offer it,
question whether any statement
which is not immediately clear and first-rate
is pertinent to another man

Or that it stand up by form alone, this
is the other possibility, never
the creation of an emotional
situation. Words are not love.

The love of words can be a betrayal.
Yet I persist. I have a foolishness here
This part of it
is acceptable. A man can use this. Love
is a foolishness. It requires foolishness.
It goes against sense. It is lamp–like.

Anecdotes of the Late War

I

the lethargic vs violence as alternatives of each other for los americanos
     & U S Grant (at Shiloh, as ex.) had the gall to stay
     inside a lethargy until it let him down into either
     vice (Galena, or, as president) or

a virtue of such a movement as, example,
Vicksburg

say that he struck, going down, either
morass or
rock—and when it was rock, he was

—this wld seem to be the power in the principle—

able to comprehend the movement of mass of men, the
transposition of the
Mississippi   (Or
continents, example,
somebody else than:
grant

        better, that is, that a man stay lethargic than
blow somebody's face off—off,
the face of, blow
the earth

2

that (like the man sd) Booth
killing Lincoln is the melodrama right with
the drama: Mister Christ and
Broadway
        Or going out to Bull Run looking for
Waterloo. the
diorama. And having to get the fastidious hell home
that afternoon
as fast as the carriage horses
can't make it (Lee Highway
littered with broken
elegances

                    Reverse of
sic transit gloria, the
Latin American whom the cab driver told me
he picked up at Union Station had
one word of english—link-
cone. And drove him
straight to the monument, the man
went up the stairs and fell down on his knees
where he could see the statue and stayed there
in the attitude of prayer

3

whoop,
went the bird
in the tree the day
the fellow
fell down
in the thicket

whoop, was the bird's
lay as the fellow lay

and I picked up a minie ball
(the way
it can be
again
of an afternoon,

or with the French girl Brandy Station
was
thick grass
and the gray house and back of it

yes   mam   the   movement
of horses, as
—I repeat—
the bird.

4

West Point it wasn't. Nor New England. Nor
those cavalry
flauntlets

    As the Mexican War was
    filibusterers
    in the West,
    and cadets
    before Chapultepec: the elevator

    goink down
    from waterloo,
    the Civil War

was the basement. Only nobody
except butternut
and his fellow on the other side
wanted to believe it, they all wanted

what Jay Gould got

(and Joe Blow got swap
in the side of the head

5

Now you take this Forrest, Nathan Bedford Forrest. He stalks the Western
theater of operations as something the English, to this day, think Lee
wouldn't have surpassed had anybody dared to give this Memphis slave-
trader the width of men and field to command which he only had as
first Grand Wizard of the Ku Klux Klan. And didn't use, Forrest
could already avoid the temptation of the Filibusterer, he had applied
first principles in the War.

What I'd wanted to say was,
that he's a man so locked in the act of himself

(right up to after Davis had been taken
and no last movie scene to the way he was still
cutting tracks behind U.S. Army units, a very

exact and busy man.

I also have to voice this impression of him to give, if it
does, the sense of how he was:

     he's like a man his tongue was cut out,
     before even Shiloh showed him
     an extraordinary executive
     of men horses and goods

6

Two things still aren't brought in to give context to the War: (1), that
you don't get Grant except as you find what he was that Geo Washington
also comes alive at only if you realize he was to real estate—

               and I mean land
when land was as oil steel and what, now?

Managing men, wasn't it, when men suddenly what was Grant's

because of the industrial revolution

were what the guys who died then were

             For the first time,
like that, the sprawled fellow Devil's Glen, natural
resource.

    The other half of it—(2)—that each one of them,

Butternut,

and Yankee Doodle,

weren't as different as North and South, farmer and factory etc.

They were—for the first time—enough of them.

                                        Plus railroad tracks
                                        to be moved around as
utility

        The leaders,   Grant Sherman Forrest not
                            Jeb Stuart
        and themselves

        the birth of

        the recent   And Lincoln

        likewise   (after Christ

        Link-cone

7

You take it
from there

8

What he said was, in that instance
I got there first
with the most men

Grant didn't hurry.
He just had the most.

More of the latter died.

The Bride

The bride leaves her father's house
traditio
She is expelled
by the house's gods
sparagma

She crosses a space of two and a half feet
ambitus
She is carried in a crown
She is kept white or neutral
It is a herald guides her.
That the people sing
oi 'umen, oi 'umenaie,
to escort her
to carry her across
to a new house,
has to do with the space (Hymen
does) she is left in, between
her father's gods,
and her husband's. Between them
there is a carefully left indefeasible
band of soil no plow

may touch. She belongs,
as she is carried,
to pomp.

At the new terminus
'oroi, Theoi 'orioi
she is stopped: "This
is my field," cries
the husband's god,
"the man or ox
who touch me, his house
shall disappear, his race
shall be extinguished,
his land shall rot, the dogstar
will destroy his harvest, he himself
will be covered with ulcers.
Stay off!"
She cannot go into her new house.
Her husband must take her. She must cry out.
The women who accompany her
must try to defend her. He must seize her. He must carry her
across the sill. Her feet must not touch. *Talassie!*
O talassie!

In her new home
is *telos*. She is sprinkled
with water, she touches
the fire. She has new gods,
and if he or she would part,
spiteful, frightful
shall be the act:
phrikode, allokota, skithropa

The Picture

what a traffick amongst limbs and loins,
wombs, we and our children are, tupping
the white lamb, legs flying, grasping
in the air the hips, locking
about the intruder, the fucking
we are the topside bottoms–up agents
of. The picture, so drawn

"He treads on edges of being . . ."

He treads on edges of being where the drop
is abyss. He hangs. He has no fear
of taking his own life in his hands. He says he is lucky
to be alive. The pay–off
is otherwise, he takes life
in his hands. This
is what the abyss
beckons. And who does not know why not
go down, get up, find what is there,
not throw any bridge across the fetid
air?

Sut Lovingood

papa eats bread
mama eats danderlions
and the worm
am the end of it
all

King's Mountain

I

Major Patrick Ferguson,
the night before,
wrote his friend Timpany
(the letter recently turned up addressed
"Major Tenpenny, Saluda,"
that he was the King of King's
Mountain:
      you can see him,
dreaming of the morrow,
as he says himself,
on one hill and General Sumpter
(I suppose his only fit opponent)
on the other—

"like the two kings of Brentford,"
he writes, "we shall salute
each other," the poor cultured man,
36 years old, who had been to a play,
when laid up in London, George Villers'
Rehearsal . . .

Against which came,
on the morrow,
950
hard men,
over–mountain men

And Ferguson also
identifies them as well
to his friend Timpany,
that he is expecting them:

"an inundation of
Barbarians"

> hear it,
> if you would hear
> what happened, hear
> the two things:
>
> Ferguson,
> who had slaughtered all
> in a house in New Jersey,
> stuffing em with bayonets, he
> who had invented a new rifle,
> and could kill six
> to the minute, yet
> used the knife

he placed himself atop
King's Mountain like
a squirrel

and the Barbarians
(it's true, they read
Swift
and likewise killing
in their case, Indians, had named a river
Lulgelub)
it was rifles,
Deckard rifles,
they did their work with
October 7th, 1780

Ferguson
had six bullets in him,
any one of which . . . and his white horse
sprang wildly down the mountainside

          (Sumter,
          wasn't even heard of

II

One can't even bring
these Barbarians
alive: they are still
too new, 1950

          Campbell
in a white shirt   (like fish-buyers
                    the Boston market,   the O'Haras

          Shelby maybe   (sweating, like a grocery store manager
                    getting in stock

          Sevier   (Judah Benjamin, and today
                    the intelligence of
                    Frankfurter—or
                    Purefoy, that sort of
                    opportunism

                    Williams,
    clearer: after the immediate
    return (like Moses Shelby) greedy

    for now, wanting it all, at 36,

    without waiting   grab it,
                                           while you can—and getting

    well, Moses Shelby didn't get what Isaac Shelby got (got to be Governor of Kentucky &
            the dreary error

    of 1823, trying to establish that Campbell

    was a coward because he, Isaac, having even been Governor

    hadn't got a jeweled sword from the state of North Carolina

    as Campbell had, from Virginia, & Jefferson

    and Williams, well,

    he got a mortal wound that day, *after* the British showed the white flag!
                                   Some Tory—or there are those who say

    it was a fellow South Carolinian—had had enough

    of that Colonel

                                           enough
                                           of that
                                           bravado Barbarians
                                           are loaded with

III

You can't get em
that easily—fringed shirts,
corn pone
and squirrel guns:
Boones

> You can't get em,
> now, buggering
> the universe

> > You can only
> > get that they win.

IV

Pat. sat
on his mountain.
In the afternoon
of the next day
he was dead.

Watauga,
had done him in

> They had come over the mountains. He had asked
for it. He had even come up as far as Old Fort. They had Cherokees
on one side. And Ferguson on the other. It was a time question,
a neat one: could they turn him away before the Cherokee turned
on them? And the fact of the matter seems to be that they got back
just in time, 1000 Cherokee were on the march, having heard that
one-half the population west of the Alleghenies was over the ridge,
at King's Mountain.

347

They were back in less than three weeks. They left
Sycamore Flats September 25th. They came through the west wall at
the Bald Place of Roan Mountain. They passed through the east wall at Gillespie's
Gap in the Blue Ridge. Some went the long way down, through Turkey Cove. The others
got to Burke County Courthouse by way of North Cove.
At Gilbert Town Ferguson was gone. At Cowpens they found out he
was east. From Cowpens 950 of them went all night after him.
It was a way they hunted anyhow. It took till afternoon. They got
him, where he'd holed up.

Nobody to this day can say why he chose King's
Mountain. It's one of those contradictions. It's just what Bar-
barians don't involve themselves in. Their reflex is more literal.
Or they are less encumbered, is it?

It isn't just Indians who taught these settlers
how to fight Redcoats. They were different beforehand. They had
new careers to lead them on. They didn't care for what Ferguson
cared for—even his two mistresses, passing as cooks, Virginia Sal
who died that day, the redhead, and Virginia Paul, who went back to some
other English camp. They didn't even have that to divert them, the
classy sort of dame. (They tell a story of a Mrs Lytle, four miles
southwest of Old Fort. Her husband was a Whig. And away. So when she
heard that Ferguson was coming to search out her husband, she dolled
herself up in her best. Which turned out to be a beaver hat her hus-
band had bought her and in Crooked Creek Cove she had little chance
to show off. So up she put it on, and when Ferguson rode to her door,
she did him a courtesy like he hadn't seen since he'd left Charleston
—and a beaver hat he probably never had seen perched on such a lady,
she comes off, in the story, about like one of those tourist Indians
of Peru. Well anyway, her husband wasn't home, and Ferguson rode on.
But one of his soldiers—one of those Crackers, Tory crackers

—it is important to note that of the 1125 "British" at
King's Mountain only a hundred were Regulars and the rest
were the same breed of Scotch-Irish English Dutch as the
mountain men, the same coves and creeks, it was civil
war—

as the column turned, swept off Mrs Lytle's hat, replacing it with
his own beat-up felt, saying "I cannot leave so handsome a lady without having
something to remember you by.")

Ferguson wasn't all bad. Indeed, it was Lord Germaine
who ordered the killing, hanging and stealing had aroused the
western men. Cornwallis, was only carrying out orders when he
made Ferguson Inspector General of militia. The crazy thing is,
the British were no worse than their Indian allies.
Or for that matter the settlers' neighbors!

We'll come to that. The battle of King's Mountain
has an aftermath. And in its light—in the light of the pine torches
of the hangings at Bickerstaff's—a side of Shelby,
Sevier, Campbell is revealed which is the complement of the efficiency
they showed in the fight itself, the answer to what is worth getting
at about this small engagement of the Revolution, no inundation of
Barbarians, no actor sitting on one of two hills, but the nature
of cruelty now—for which read man against himself. Or after

what had changed
that Ferguson
comes out a warm-hearted
dandy?

and Shelby, Sevier, Campbell
what we have known too much of?

Yet we have no choice:

what the latter are   (even Eisenhower)

V

DePeyster put it
clearly: "The rifleman placed himself where bayonets alone
could be used. And then only against trees."

349

There is the story of the boy at King's Mountain who shot
his gun *after* a grenadier had pinned him to the ground
through both his right hand and his right thigh. And the
pain when his friend had to kick his hand to dislodge the
bayonet was the first pain he knew. And only when he tried his
gun again did he find it empty and realize the grenadier was
dead on top of him from his own shot.

It was more like killing bears, at the last moment, tumbling into
the rhododendron thicket just as the claws were raking you.

Of the 31 American dead, 17 were officers—a measure, of who
was standing up. Shelby himself had the hair on his temple
burned off.

And Ferguson
was full of bullets.

VI

It's not a melee.
Or a story of
heroisms.
It's not even errors.

It's a Saturday afternoon,
a persistent rain,
one hour and five minutes
of a severe fight
up and on a mountain.

The bulk of each force
are neighbors,
generally from the Piedmont
of Virginia and the Carolinas.
The Americans
figure to go home, the Loyalists

not so, until the British
rule again the southern
colonies.

The Americans do go home,
in fact run like hell back
to the mountains,
not so much to take on the Cherokee
as from certainty Tarleton
will be after them,
not even knowing
what they have done—that Tarleton, in fact,
and Cornwallis—
are running as fast away from them,
those days after the battle,
as they are running, themselves

In these details
King's Mountain
is no more nor less

And interests me
no more nor less

Its interest is the crazy thing a man two days ago sat in my car and
said to me his grandfather justified the hangings of the ten men
he said were hung, in these words:

(mind you, the man who talked to me had learned in school that those
hangings after King's Mountain were not according to the rules
of warfare, and had come home to ask his grandfather why his father and
his uncles had been a part of it)

And the grandfather said

"There was no government. We had killed all we could. What were we
going to do with prisoners? These were men who had burned our houses,

killed people, who would, if we turned them loose, do the same thing
the next day. So we hung them, from the same tree."

The man said, in a thousand years, where would you find . . . and I said,
but wait, do you know Fort Pillow? And of course he did, and instant-
ly recognized

VII

It isn't even the passion of civil war here clear which gives
King's Mountain its dimension. Like I said, the fact that Campbell
and Shelby held a kangaroo court and did find 30 prisoners
guilty and allowed the execution of nine three by three until
the tenth, and probably the worst of the Tories, was slobbered over
by his son while the son cut his thongs and he bounded away through
the soldiers four-deep on each side of the Hanging Oak . . . this es-
cape broke the concentration, and Shelby and Campbell ordered the exe-
cutions stopped.

It's the edge here which, as in the whole American thing right up
to at least 1945, is where the life is. It isn't in the persons, like,
for example, it *is* in Ferguson, you can feel the man, recognize him as
flesh and blood, see him write his letter to his friend, watch him die
—even see Shelby etc. most in the light of all of them pressing up,
after the battle, to see Ferguson laid out: the English Major, the one
they were hunting, the catch.

It's the other measure: what glistens in the first days' sun after
September 25th as they ride along Grassy Creek of the North Toe River;
or as Campbell's white shirt stuck out all the hour and five minutes
of the fight itself

or how, from October 2nd on, in the rain, the men even swathed their
guns and powder inside their hunting shirts and rode cold and naked
as Indians away from the Catawba

the whole thing is

the Catawba, Watauga, Crooked Creek
that the Deckard rifle was manufactured in Lancaster, Pa
by a person of that name,
a gun of remarkable precision for a long shot,
spiral grooved, with a barrel some thirty inches long,
and with its stock some three and a half or four feet,
carrying bullets varying from thirty to seventy to the pound of lead

or that they carried no more than a blanket, a cup, and a wallet
of parched corn meal mixed with maple sugar, the horse
to pick his own living, hoppled out, of nights, to keep him
from straying away, and a few beeves, for the first two days,
driven along in the rear until they slowed the horsemen up too much
and were slaughtered the whole morning of Wednesday, the 29th,
at their resting place of the night before, at Shelving Rock,
about a mile beyond the Crab Orchard, alongside Big Doe River.
Here a man named Miller resided, who shod several of the horses
of the party.

You can't go further
to oppose Ferguson
than this.

Or you couldn't,
up to 1945.

Put it this way:
before October 7, 1780
—or, say, until men had broken over the Blue Ridge to the forks of
Holston, or the Watauga, or were still trying to get past Swannanoa
Gap—
you couldn't have said positively that Ferguson
was done.

But that day he was.
And since.

Now?

The Post Virginal

(for John Wieners)

$F = ci^2$ Keats: the intensity of object   The trouble

with symbol,

it does not trouble. One is the product of one TIMES

one. And that a new object . . . that the blue eyes

can't see their own face

don't mean they don't look. In fact

the law of times is, that a discrimination

is only restored by the multiplication

of each discrimination by another, no matter

how many it takes. Even if it is one,

it is multiplied by itself. This is known

as discontent.

That all things recur

is not the equal of the fact that they occur (God

is interesting in three ways:

that he invented so much, that he invented so little
and that so much of so little occurs anew

Waste, limit & mortality

These are the powers.

There are two classes.

354

There are those who have by having what there is to have.

These are they who suffer. Suffering is a medium

which doesn't have the relief

of talent. Desire without form begets

Form is not life. Form is creation. It changes the condition

of men. It does not disturb nature. Nature, like god,

is not so interesting. Man

is interesting

"As I went in and out I heard pieces . . ."

As I went in and out I heard pieces
of the conversation
    The psychopath
took her to a bootlegger. The boot-
legger took them to Marion, and won
$1000 in a poker game. Louie—

    He loves her,
but he don't dare. They irritate
each other like skin. At 8 o'clock

in the morning he went back. She
wasn't there. At 5 o'clock, in the

evening, he wired her brother. At 12

she showed up: the bootlegger had

got rid of the psychopath but

he also made a nuisance of him-

self, he wanted his pay. She has

had bad days ever since, and Louie—

Said this one, electrons

                    sd that one, stars

Tensors—

          now Louie

          And Eloise

o how one remembers how all one's associates
did likewise, did likewise, from Danvers
to Greenpoint, from Danvers

                    And Louie

is from Louisiana, the marshes

of men and women—which turn out to be slots

one can put the memories in and out

But Eloise

can't

OH, I don't want to hear any more

pieces

De Los Cantares

(Set over Orontes.
And there fell against
Kati (the Catti)
in 1 2 88
An inscription.
No words spoken.

And was stood off
by the barbarians,
had to marry
one of their daughters

When the person doesn't know,
the person has to find out.

By one nine one three this way,
the precepts were dead, the Eggwyptes

weren't passing on any-
thing, we howled

But to live in the same house? Better,
you should have a red truck. The motor was frozen
and it burned as I sat there full of glee, only then
noticing that I had her in first gear when what I needed
was to back up, which I then tried, and it didn't move
any more than the right rear tire slipped around and,
equally gaily, I thought I must throw some gravel,
or maybe there was some behind me

And of course there wasn't. There isn't. There isn't even any crystal
ahead. We begin in alluvium, or we dash down as those drivers (Wyoming)
go around curves, make it
to Kadesh. We have the powers of new machines. We cut down.
We set olibanum also aside. We smell wildly
what comes out under the hood on the winter day. The incense now
is the earth offered
to the sun. We sacrifice
hugely (as, indeed, we look out differently
than those who lost their beloveds in the first war.
We lost ours by gaining them. Our faces
are pressed against walls. We see
thattaway.

We pick up potsherds
where they got no

decision. And the potsherds become the triumphs
of our numismatics.

We read 'um
backwards,

we do

Evil

Evil—1

for a man to come out of the sea, they
asked for it

And it came out, only
it was stone

And it overshadowed
everything, it would not stop

growing, it was going
to blot out

the sun, it was green,
and dark,

and immense, its shoulders
were more than the land

until somebody
dove down

and found it was the easiest thing in the world
to turn over, it wasn't

attached to anything, it wasn't even buried
in the slime

of the bottom.

Evil—2

He said, he feeds
on the energy of others

And it wasn't quite
what my skin told me

I said, he creates
the stones he eats

He can only eat
what he can create

There is creation
which is stone

Evil—3

Nothing is more boring
than stone

But their fear
that he would shadow

the sun is real. Monotony
is a factor

of chaos, a cause.

          Hear
the stone cry:

          I am empty.
Hear!

And fear

Evil—4

"I am empty. I will be
fill"

     "I will fill me
of you"

        "I will. You
are who I say

you are." "You are mine,"
said the stone,

the immaculate
stone

The Seven Songs

Man knows his day, it has,
except for the sun, no regularity.
Or it has on a scale which his death is,
season. A day is a unit of nature,
pushing—so many trees to fill out rings
or bees to fill out bees or hives, or beasts
for market, crops for beasts. Or men. The wind
has no order, nor snow, rain is only, and soil,
intention. And driven on a path
a man cannot complete. A man can watch the sun
do what he cannot do, establish
day. But a day, finally, is a man's
death day.

     Night! night, love and precision
hang over us—and not the moon's, the moon's
a night's sun which repeats at night the season
the day is (as indeed the sun, for which we thank it,
does more than give us life, it asserts in daytime
the order the night is totally composed of

              o order of night, Orion
glaring in his action at man staring
                 Charles' Wain
goes upside down in hours, decants
And yet the next night is back in like position
to attempt again
to break the trace or the tropism holds it turning
on the North Star

         or the whole sky moves in halves
and an alley goes down the middle man walks

Venus is gone for weeks
or she returns in symmetry-asymmetry to fix any of us
as the North Star doesn't because it doesn't budge—it's
only valuable for ships

The motions of the night, o Memory
who is the mother and forgetfulness the forgotten father,
let man retake the night. The day has dispersed us, thrown us
as bodies into the process, and the night, man throws up cities
to prevent him from, while he goes, as he does, double
as he is, and the night and the day hold out to him
the two he is, as he has two to do, he has to order
and to intend. O History, o Urania, o

seven songs

A Newly Discovered 'Homeric' Hymn

(for Jane Harrison, if she were alive)

Hail and beware the dead who will talk life until you are blue
in the face. And you will not understand what is wrong,
they will not be blue, they will have tears in their eyes,
they will seem to you so much more full of life
than the rest of us, and they will ask so much, not of you no
but of life, they will cry, isn't it this way, if it isn't
I don't care for it, and you will feel the blackmail, you will not know
what to answer, it will all have become one mass

Hail and beware them, for they come from where you have not been,
they come from where you cannot have come, they come into life
by a different gate. They come from a place which is not easily known,
it is known only to those who have died. They carry seeds
you must not touch, you must not touch the pot they taste of,
no one must touch the pot, no one must, in their season.

Hail and beware them, in their season. Take care. Prepare
to receive them, they carry what the living cannot do without,
but take the proper precautions, do the prescribed things, let
down the thread from the right shoulder. And from the forehead.
And listen to what they say, listen to the talk, hear
every word of it—they are drunk from the pot, they speak
like no living man may speak, they have the seeds in their mouth—
listen, and beware

Hail them solely that they have the seeds in their mouth, they
are drunk, you cannot do without a drunkenness, seeds can't,
they must be soaked in the contents of the pot, they must be all one mass.
But you who live cannot know what else the seeds must be. Hail
and beware the earth, where the dead come from. Life
is not of the earth. The dead are of the earth. Hail and beware
the earth, where the pot is buried.

Greet the dead in the dead man's time. He is drunk of the pot.
He speaks like spring does. He will deceive you. You are meant
to be deceived. You must observe the drunkenness. You are not to
drink. But you must hear, and see. You must beware.

Hail them, and fall off. Fall off! The drink is not yours,
it is not yours! You do not come
from the same place, you do not suffer as the dead do,
they do not suffer, they need, because they have drunk of the pot,
they need. Do not drink of the pot, do not touch it. Do not touch
them.

    Beware the dead. And hail them. They teach you drunkenness.
You have your own place to drink. Hail and beware them, when they come.

The Whole World

—for Steve

Even culture
ought to
enjoy itself, hang
with pleasure
over the pink pond-lily
in the Garden of Epicurus

or the business man be burly
from his goods

only the poet
should have the right of his own stories

I

To imagine that classes
requires that professions

have something to do. The illusion
of energy

is what pleasure there is
as much after you might lift a stone

as anything: five minutes. Thereafter,
it's somebody else's

The vision of man
is cool, there is no need to fuss it
or believe, to have a Golgotha

or a change, to expect least of all
what was—what was,
we put away, we do not go on dieing
unnecessary dreams

            We look into the pool
and damn well see Echo lying
at the bottom: the surface

does not defract
anything, it is limpid, we pick the water up
in the cup of our hands, it is a pleasure to drink
as the flower is a pink ice, or, if the water's a shaft, the tit
is a fish's eye,

            in the garden of Epicurus

2

Or the stars are
in the night
rosy. You walk out
with your head walking
along them, you do have the possibility, the wealth's
where it ever was.

                    That anybody owes anybody anything
                    is true now as
                    as much as a stone
                    or a Rothschild
                    will sing. You will sing
                    with a big voice
                    out into the afternoon:

                    it is as somebody strolling
                    in somebody's formalized deer park
                    no matter what some other time

The pond-lily we speak of no doubt
is a lotus.
No doubt.

And the fish idle pleasantly, you can see them,
without doctrine,
at the roots

and the mud is,
and not the lovely lady's body,
neither the surface which one pushes back,
nor the very bottom—who goes there
where no one
need help us?

      Where it is cool
      if the fish

      and the flower

      and the stone

      and the face

      :it's crazy
      what a garden
      the vertical
      is. Five minutes.
      Or less. You will notice
      anything.

3

That anything lasts
is what keeps any of us lingering
from the pool

        I would cut a stripe from it for you

367

Quail

When my soul was raging, a flock of birds which whir up
struck from the dead leaves and drummed
across the air—I seized on them, in the winter sun,
to do likewise, to let the chastisings
be such noise I rose on it and whirred
as quail do

"Cry pain, & the dogs of yrself devour . . ."

Cry pain, & the dogs of yrself devour
you. The long trace
will outrun
yr nakedness. Catch
where you caught
on the rock, and the rock
will hold you
until the next sun
can take you off,
take care of you, your misery
your own, the rest of us
also borne, the sun
covering

The Alba

Love requires
talk of itself

Its own ebullience
runs
to its own inquiry

Love is love
because it's endless
Once it has begun
it is at once
everywhere
It is an empiry.

Love is no object
Love is form because love
is its own subject,
love is the only subject, the rest
requires form.

This is why it has been called volatile.
It is not. It is simply that it is very difficult
to believe
that there should be only one subject
in all the universe

Love I

For that it is love and covers us
        out of all the ports.
For that it is not easily seen, apparently,
and is known only to those who know it.
For that it is excessive.
For that it does not yield
        to anything else.
For that it keeps us
        clean.

For that the hair on the head
        is part of it,
for that desire knows only one end.
For that love is restless in all its other
        proceedings,
however much those proceedings make possible
        the end of desire
For that the beloved is ever
        in one's thought.
For that this is the grace
        which falls from love

For that we are clothed by it,
        for that we are strengthened.
For that the feet return to be child's
        feet, that is,
        as hands are
For how it tears rampant
        at all ports
For that it is transparent.
For that it makes each of us
        lucid

For that it heightens.
For that it lightens
For that it makes a society of its own
that is only that membership,
that all others are to be wept for,
        to be so bereft

For that to celebrate it
is to make it sound too easy
For it is not hornpipes, it glanceth
and so it throws its colors over anything.

For that it is not easily taken.
For that it takes.
For that what you give, you get everything
        back
For that it is abundant
        as nothing else is
For that it changes
        the core
For that one does not live
        except in its obedience
For that where it is,
        life is,
        and without it
        there is retraction

For that the voice of love
        is in the voice,
for that the eyes of love
        are the eyes.
For that it does not hide,
it is in all things.
For the pity of love
is that there are those who do not love.

For all those who want it,
        there is want.
For all those who will not,
        there is will.
For all those who fail it,
        there is failure
For all those,
        love goes to them and says
        love

For that all may love,
        love is.
For that it has this periphery.
For that its center
        is so available,
for that its center
        is what all wants

For that love may be more known.

"The chain of memory is resurrection . . ."

The chain of memory is resurrection   I am a vain man

I am interested in the size of the brain-case

of CroMagnon man and that his descendants are Guanches

right now in the Canary Islands, and that my father & mother

lie buried beside each other in the Swedish cemetery

in Worcester, Massachusetts. And my grandmother too.
Even if the Hineses are in St John's cemetery. Those stones
speak to me, my ear is their sea-shell as in Marin County
the big trees as well as the eucalyptus hold sounds
of Asia and Indians the myrtle, comes from Australia

The vector of space is resurrection. We walk on the earth
under which they lie who also matter to us, as well as those
who are distant, from whom we have got separated (as we are
separated from those we have not yet known: the loveliness
of man, that he shoots up men suddenly on the horizon
there is a new person who speaks as Ed Marshall does

and all the back country, the roads I have ridden
without headlights the moon was so bright on the houses
and I was coming from a love in Lawrence, and Georgetown
Rowley Ipswich lay out in the night, not blank at all as
now that Marshall has spoken, all the faces
and the stones
and Concord Avenue
rise into being: the onslaught,
he calls it,
resurrection

The being of man is resurrection, the genetic flow
of each life which has given life, the tenderness
none of us

is without. Let it come back. Let it be
where it is:

> "My soul is Chichester and my origin
>
> is a womb whether one likes it or not."

My ugliness,
said Juan Belmonte—to every Spaniard
I was part of himself:

> the bull (or whether he's a lion
>
> or a horse or the great snake)
>
> hammers us, mine beat me against
>
> the brick wall until I thought
>
> this is it, and it was only a redheaded boy
>
> diverted him

Direction—a directed magnitude—is
resurrection

> All that has been
>
> suddenly is: time

is the face
of recognition, Rhoda Straw; or my son
is a Magyar. The luminousness
of my daughter
to her mother
by a stream:

> apocatastasis

how it occurs, that in this instant I seek to speak

as though the species were a weed-seed a grass a barley corn

in the cup of my palm. And I was trying

to hear what it said, I was putting my heart down

to catch the pain

Resurrection

is. It is the avowal. It is the admission. The renewal

is the restoration: the man in the dark with the animal

fat lamp

is my father. Or my grandfather. And the fat lady

who was weak from a heart attack and her granddaughter

I used to see courtin the boy on the motorcycle,

is my mother. Or my grandmother. The Venus

of Willendorf. We move

between two horns, the gate

of horn. And the animal or snake who warns us

propels: we must woo the thing

to get its feet together so that its shoulder blades

are open, so that the aorta

One of the horns

is resurrection, the other horn

is any one of us: a river

is my sword, the Annisquam is my metal

you will have yours (a meadow his was, gone,

boy, in the dance and another

had a tree or there was a third

had a bicycle seat, and the face of all women,

he said,

they sat on. Bless the powers

that be

          This is a poem of celebration of the powers that be.

The large theme

is the smallest (the thumbtack

in the way of the inkbottle, the incident

which does not change the course even if the surface

of the day is changed because a hand followed a diaper

into the wringer up to the elbow, the smallest content

is a grit of occasion, the irrelevant

is only known

like the shape of the soul

to the person involved, the absolutes

sit in the palm of the hand which can't close

from the pain. I do not know

what you know at the same time that I do. My vanity

is only the exercise

of my privilege as yours, conceivably,

might be as hers, the peahen, is

also brilliant when she takes it up: Willendorf,

the stone, breathes back

into life. The resurrection
at the farthest point, and

        out of the green poison
        now the death of spring the jungle
        is in the gulley the growth
        has gone to the tropics small spring
        is over

        small spring
          while where my river flows
        spring is long. Here where the ice
        and the jungle once were identical
        spring is small

        the blossoms
        are already gone green green
        the worst green
        like paint floods
        the sky
        is like a bedroom wall
        in a motel

        the horrors
        of season too fast.
        Without resurrection
        all is too fast. The trees

crawl over everything like facts

like the fascination of irrelevant

events: to hew

o the dirty summer too early

for a man to catch up with

spring is dead! spring the horn

is dead. I Adonis

Lift me, life of being

I lift

the shape of my soul. In the face of spring

gone

into the growth

as the body was burned

on the sticks and went up

as smoke into the pale sky

o father

o mother

put into the ground

(o the beloved ones

they must dance

the thick green

which covers us, the appetite of nature

we stand off, the loss

of loss

In the chain of being

we arise, we make sparse

the virid covering, we lay bare

the dead, the winter ground, the snow

which makes the forsythia first

the first blossom

and in the two weeks of spring:

damn the green growth gone

to green bloom, the resurrection

is sparse   Desire

is spare   The confusion

of physical enjoyment

and desire   Desire

is resurrection

The soul

is an onslaught

"Anubis will stare . . ."

Anubis will stare.

        Be sure.

           And the splendor,

madam, (which you forfeit

           A man is right,

Or he is nothing. He is right down the middle (down

from the crown. And to the foundation. Or he isn't.

And he knows it.

        You needn't worry. It isn't you

who'll stare, or seven bald men

lined up in hell

to look your naked sister over:

                the burlesk show

                of Pandora, the curious bitch,

                who dragged after

But shall we blame her

who was only curious,

and not the pious one,

                the man, the culture-hero,

                the First righteousness,

                who took it he could keep us

from sin?

And in a fennel-stalk

enabled men to make metal

the better to kill himself with?

In other words,

death does get in,

no matter.

Plenty of matter, that you, too, you

shall die. And without an eye. You'll be without your peeled

eye, you switch. You make yourself a rule (it was rattan in school,

and what it was my grandfather whaled my uncle with was so stiff

it ridged the walnut bed I slept in after I found him dead that morning,

with his nightcap on, and the liver spots, and cold the lovely flesh was

hiked up in the featherbed as he was used to sleep and I was used

to waken him.

You, who duck around a car, or sit in it

with eyes

averted

You were not given that jewel

to look adjectives out of it.

She stares at you.

It is context you stink of, any of us, until Anubis

is returned to where she comes out of (where your poor sister

took such a beating from an equally righteous ruler—

where the bald–headed men

will make a stripper

out of you,

you will lose

one of seven garments

at each of hell's seven doors

Until you do smell by nature.

The dogface

is there for good reasons.

There are nephilim.

Nature mismates

as well as she creates.

But I call for cases,

as I call you: the word

is doctrinal. The daughters

of men deserve

the sons

of god. It is not from such featherbeds

that the things which crawl

and try to blot out the peach blossoms

which won't blot out—

the germs,

and crooked bodied eyed and purposed flying things—

the box

was not opened; she *sat*

on it. And he did steal

fire

He did not. He was merely a man. He didn't steal anything. He merely
opposed himself. He probably talked. And talked so well there were those
who said he talked too much. Including Mister zoose, the governing
gander, the envious one (who couldn't stay away from
the daughters of men.

O Anubis! Guard 'em. Teach 'em
to be women. Tell 'em.
to get out of hell.

Open up there. It's the law. Get out of
your car. And we'll see if you can walk steady down
the white line, in the middle of, the highway.

(How good are your eyes?
I'm asking.

Give over the wheel,
if you ain't drivin'
the buggy.
Anubis
don't go for anything
but Porsches.

She's the dog-face one,

the jackal.

Beware of her.

The Lordly and Isolate Satyrs

The lordly and isolate Satyrs—look at them come in
on the left side of the beach
like a motorcycle club! And the handsomest of them,
the one who has a woman, driving that snazzy
convertible
                    Wow, did you ever see even in a museum
such a collection of boddisatvahs, the way
they come up to their stop, each of them
as though it was a rudder
the way they have to sit above it
and come to a stop on it, the monumental solidity
of themselves, the Easter Island
they make of the beach, the Red-headed Men

                    These are the Androgynes,
the Fathers behind the father, the Great Halves

Or as that one was, inside his pants, the Yiddish poet
a vegetarian. Or another—all in his mouth—a snarl
of the Sources. Or the one I loved most, who once,
once only, let go the pain, the night he got drunk,
and I put him to bed, and he said, Bad blood.

Or the one who cracks and doesn't know
that what he thinks are a thousand questions are suddenly
a thousand lumps thrown up where the cloaca
again has burst: one looks into the face and exactly as suddenly
it isn't the large eyes and nose but the ridiculously small mouth
which you are looking down as one end of

                                —as the Snarled Man
is a monocyte.

          Hail the ambiguous Fathers, and look closely
at them, they are the unadmitted, the club of Themselves,
weary riders, but who sit upon the landscape as the Great
Stones. And only have fun among themselves. They are
the lonely ones

          Hail them, and watch out. The rest of us,
on the beach as we had previously known it, did not know
there was this left side. As they came riding in from the sea
—we did not notice them until they were already creating
the beach we had not known was there—but we assume
they came in from the sea. We assume that. We don't know.

          In any case the whole sea was now a hemisphere,
and our eyes like half a fly's, we saw twice as much. Every-
thing opened, even if the newcomers just sat, didn't,
for an instant, pay us any attention. We were as we had been,
in that respect. We were as usual, the children were being fed pop
and potato chips, and everyone was sprawled as people are
on a beach. Something had happened but the change
wasn't at all evident. A few drops of rain
would have made more of a disturbance.

          There we were. They, in occupation of the whole view
in front of us and off to the left where we were not used to look.
And we, watching them pant from their exertions, and talk to each other,
the one in the convertible the only one who seemed to be circulating.
And he was dressed in magnificent clothes, and the woman with him

a dazzling blond, the new dye making her hair a delicious
streaked ash. She was as distant as the others. She sat in her flesh too.

These are our counterparts, the unknown ones.
They are here. We do not look upon them as invaders. Dimensionally
they are larger than we—all but the woman. But we are not suddenly
small. We are as we are. We don't even move, on the beach.

It is a stasis. Across nothing at all we stare at them.
We can see what they are. They don't notice us. They have merely
and suddenly moved in. They occupy our view. They are between us
and the ocean. And they have given us a whole new half of beach.

As of this moment, there is nothing else to report.
It is Easter Island transplanted to us. With the sun, and a warm
summer day, and sails out on the harbor they're here, the Con-
temporaries. They have come in.

Except for the stirring of the leader, they are still
catching their breath. They are almost like scooters the way
they sit there, up a little, on their thing. It is as though
the extra effort of it tired them the most. Yet that just there
was where their weight and separateness—their immensities—
lay. Why they seem like boddisatvahs. The only thing one noticed
is the way their face breaks when they call across to each other.
Or actually speak quite quietly, not wasting breath. But the face
loses all containment, they are fifteen year old boys at the moment
they speak to each other. They are not gods. They are not even stone.
They are doubles. They are only Source. When they act like us
they go to pieces. One notices then that their skin
is only creased like red-neck farmers. And that they are all
freckled. The red-headed people have the hardest time
to possess themselves. Is it because they were over-
fired? Or why—even to their beautiful women—do the red ones
have only that half of the weight?

We look at them, and begin to know. We begin to see
who they are. We see why they are satyrs, and why one half
of the beach was unknown to us. And now that it is known,
now that the beach goes all the way to the headland we thought
we were huddling ourselves up against, it turns out it is the
same. It is beach. The Visitors—Resters—who, by being there,
made manifest what we had not known—that the beach fronted wholly
to the sea—have only done that, completed the beach.

The difference is
we are more on it. The beauty of the white of the sun's light, the
blue the water is, and the sky, the movement on the painted lands-
cape, the boy-town the scene was, is now pierced with angels and
with fire. And winter's ice shall be as brilliant in its time as
life truly is, as Nature is only the offerer, and it is we
who look to see what the beauty is.

These visitors, now stirring
to advance, to go on wherever they do go restlessly never completing
their tour, going off on their motorcycles, each alone except for
the handsome one, isolate huge creatures wearing down nothing as
they go, their huge third leg like carborundum, only the vault
of their being taking rest, the awkward boddhas

We stay. And watch them
gather themselves up. We have no feeling except love. They are not
ours. They are of another name. These are what the gods are. They
look like us. They are only in all parts larger. But the size is
only different. The difference is, they are not here, they are not
on this beach in this sun which, tomorrow, when we come to swim,
will be another summer day. They can't talk to us. We have no desire
to stop them any more than, as they made their camp, only possibly
the woman in the convertible one might have wanted to be familiar
with. The Leader was too much as they.

They go. And the day

As the Dead Prey Upon Us

As the dead prey upon us,
they are the dead in ourselves,
awake, my sleeping ones, I cry out to you,
disentangle the nets of being!

I pushed my car, it had been sitting so long unused.
I thought the tires looked as though they only needed air.
But suddenly the huge underbody was above me, and the rear tires
were masses of rubber and thread variously clinging together

as were the dead souls in the living room, gathered
about my mother, some of them taking care to pass
beneath the beam of the movie projector, some record
playing on the victrola, and all of them
desperate with the tawdriness of their life in hell

I turned to the young man on my right and asked, "How is it,
there?" And he begged me protestingly don't ask, we are poor
poor. And the whole room was suddenly posters and presentations
of brake linings and other automotive accessories, cardboard
displays, the dead roaming from one to another
as bored back in life as they are in hell, poor and doomed
to mere equipments

                       my mother, as alive as ever she was, asleep
when I entered the house as I often found her in a rocker
under the lamp, and awaking, as I came up to her, as she ever had

I found out she returns to the house once a week, and with her
the throng of the unknown young who center on her as much in death
as other like suited and dressed people did in life

O the dead!

        and the Indian woman and I
        enabled the blue deer
        to walk

        and the blue deer talked,
        in the next room,
        a Negro talk

        it was like walking a jackass,
        and its talk
        was the pressing gabber of gammers
        of old women

        and we helped walk it around the room
        because it was seeking socks
        or shoes for its hooves
        now that it was acquiring

        human possibilities

In the five hindrances men and angels
stay caught in the net, in the immense nets
which spread out across each plane of being, the multiple nets
which hamper at each step of the ladders as the angels
and the demons
and men
go up and down

        Walk the jackass
        Hear the victrola
        Let the automobile
        be tucked into a corner of the white fence
        when it is a white chair. Purity

is only an instant of being, the trammels

recur

In the five hindrances, perfection
is hidden

            I shall get
            to the place
            10 minutes late.

            It will be 20 minutes
            of 9. And I don't know,

            without the car,

            how I shall get there

O peace, my mother, I do not know
how differently I could have done
what I did or did not do.

            That you are back each week
            that you fall asleep
            with your face to the right

            that you are as present there
            when I come in as you were
            when you were alive

            that you are as solid, and your flesh
            is as I knew it, that you have the company
            I am used to your having

            but o, that you all find it
            such a cheapness!

o peace, mother, for the mammothness
of the comings and goings
of the ladders of life

The nets we are entangled in. Awake,
my soul, let the power into the last wrinkle
of being, let none of the threads and rubber of the tires
be left upon the earth. Let even your mother
go. Let there be only paradise

The desperateness is, that the instant
which is also paradise (paradise
is happiness) dissolves
into the next instant, and power
flows to meet the next occurrence

        Is it any wonder
        my mother comes back?
        Do not that throng
        rightly seek the room
        where they might expect
        happiness? They did not complain
        of life, they obviously wanted
        the movie, each other, merely to pass
        among each other there,
     where the real is, even to the display cards,
     to be out of hell

        The poverty
        of hell

O souls, in life and in death,
awake, even as you sleep, even in sleep
know what wind
even under the crankcase of the ugly automobile
lifts it away, clears the sodden weights of goods,
equipment, entertainment, the foods the Indian woman,
the filthy blue deer, the 4 by 3 foot 'Viewbook,'
the heaviness of the old house, the stuffed inner room
lifts the sodden nets

and they disappear as ghosts do,
as spider webs, nothing
before the hand of man

The vent! You must have the vent,
or you shall die. Which means
never to die, the ghastliness

of going, and forever
coming back, returning
to the instants which were not lived

O mother, this I could not have done,
I could not have lived what you didn't,
I am myself netted in my own being

I want to die. I want to make that instant, too,
perfect

O my soul, slip
the cog

II

The death in life (death itself)
is endless, eternity
is the false cause

The knot is other wise, each topological corner
presents itself, and no sword
cuts it, each knot is itself its fire

each knot of which the net is made
is for the hands to untake
the knot's making. And touch alone

can turn the knot into its own flame

        (o mother, if you had once touched me

        o mother, if I had once touched you)

The car did not burn. Its underside
was not presented to me
a grotesque corpse. The old man

merely removed it as I looked up at it,
and put it in a corner of the picket fence
like was it my mother's white dog?

or a child's chair

        The woman,
        playing on the grass,
        with her son (the woman next door)

        was angry with me whatever it was
        slipped across the playpen or whatever
        she had out there on the grass

        And I was quite flip in reply
        that anyone who used plastic
        had to expect things to skid

        and break, that I couldn't worry
        that her son might have been hurt
        by whatever it was I sent skidding

        down on them.

        It was just then I went into my house
        and to my utter astonishment
        found my mother sitting there

as she always had sat, as must she always
forever sit there her head lolling
into sleep? Awake, awake my mother

what wind will lift you too
forever from the tawdriness,
make you rich as all those souls

crave crave crave

to be rich?

They are right. We must have
what we want. We cannot afford
not to. We have only one course:

the nets which entangle us are flames

O souls, burn
alive, burn now

that you may forever
have peace, have

what you crave

O souls,
go into everything,
let not one knot pass
through your fingers

let not any they tell you
you must sleep as the net
comes through your authentic hands

What passes
is what is, what shall be, what has

been, what hell and heaven is
is earth to be rent, to shoot you
through the screen of flame which each knot
hides as all knots are a wall ready
to be shot open by you

                        the nets of being
are only eternal if you sleep as your hands
ought to be busy. Method, method

I too call on you to come
to the aid of all men, to women most
who know most, to woman to tell
men to awake. Awake, men,
awake

I ask my mother
to sleep. I ask her
to stay in the chair.
My chair
is in the corner of the fence.
She sits by the fireplace made of paving stones. The blue deer
need not trouble either of us.

And if she sits in happiness the souls
who trouble her and me
will also rest. The automobile

has been hauled away.

Variations Done for
Gerald Van De Wiele

I. Le Bonheur

dogwood flakes
what is green

the petals
from the apple
blow on the road

mourning doves
mark the sway
of the afternoon, bees
dig the plum blossoms

the morning
stands up straight, the night
is blue from the full of the April moon

iris and lilac, birds
birds, yellow flowers
white flowers, the Diesel
does not let up dragging
the plow

      as the whippoorwill,
the night's tractor, grinds
his song

      and no other birds but us
are as busy (O saisons, o chateaux!

Délires!

                    What soul
is without fault?

Nobody studies
happiness

Every time the cock crows
I salute him

I have no longer any excuse
for envy. My life

has been given its orders: the seasons
seize

the soul and the body, and make mock
of any dispersed effort. The hour of death

is the only trespass

II. The Charge

dogwood flakes
the green

the petals from the apple-trees
fall for the feet to walk on

the birds are so many they are
loud, in the afternoon

they distract, as so many bees do
suddenly all over the place

With spring one knows today to see
that in the morning each thing

is separate but by noon
they have melted into each other

and by night only crazy things
like the full moon and the whippoorwill

and us, are busy. We are busy
if we can get by that whiskered bird,

that nightjar, and get across, the moon
is our conversation, she will say

what soul
isn't in default?

can you afford not to make
the magical study

which happiness is? do you hear
the cock when he crows? do you know the charge,

that you shall have no envy, that your life
has its orders, that the seasons

seize you too, that no body and soul are one
if they are not wrought

in this retort? that otherwise efforts
are efforts? And that the hour of your flight

will be the hour of your death?

III. Spring

The dogwood
lights up the day.

The April moon
flakes the night.

Birds, suddenly,
are a multitude

The flowers are ravined
by bees, the fruit blossoms

are thrown to the ground, the wind
the rain forces everything. Noise—

even the night is drummed
by whippoorwills, and we get

as busy, we plow, we move,
we break out, we love. The secret

which got lost neither hides
nor reveals itself, it shows forth

tokens. And we rush
to catch up. The body

whips the soul. In its great desire
it demands the elixir

In the roar of spring,
transmutations. Envy

drags herself off. The fault of the body and the soul
—that they are not one—

the matutinal cock clangs
and singleness: we salute you

season of no bungling

The Perfume!

The perfume
of flowers: a plane

of air I walk into
is lime or narcissus

is as strong as lemon
on the path. And in bed

in the night the poison
of desire the elixir

pours into the season
of me.
        Arouse,
soul and body,

as one. Arise,
sleep: in one motion

are all the terms. The notion
there is anything dispersed

is heresy. The charge
does not change, the charge

is to be found out, the state
of change is the confusion,

the wobble. The force
comes through

on a direct line, a nucleus
is a cluster which seeks

to cluster. The lustre of us
is only what the poison

gives off. Virid! virid!
the green spring

is poison. The flowers
burn of it. I burn of it. The smoke

I smell occurs as quick
as that tanager just now landed

on the pine, perfume
in the air

It is a bauble
what the heart is,

the sceptre!

"The perfume / of flowers! . . ."

The perfume
of flowers! A haw

drops such odour
it stops me

in the wall
of its fall. Love

arrests

Lime-trees
saturate

the night. We walk
in it

On a path jonquils
fill

the air. Love
is a scent

"The perfume / of flowers! . . ."

The perfume
of flowers! A quince

drops such odour
it stops one

in the wall
of its fall. The beloved

arrests

Lime-trees
make a smoke
of night. The night of the beloved
is a smoke

Jonquils
are knobby flowers. They send up
in the air
their perfume. In the day the beloved
is a jonquil

403

The Encounter

Nauset Billerica   —   to get the fid in
Nauset Billerica   —   to open up
Nauset Billerica   (-*ficatio*)

So they made them a barricade,
as they usually did every night.
And on awakening, they said a prayer

The huggery occurred at Nauset.
I was there. The night
was all meat—fibroid. At midnight
a great & hideous cry.
We shot off muskets, and the noise
ceased. It was wolves,
we concluded. Later,
trying to get back to sleep,
it was thick again, we were with persons,
it was at places, we were talking
and listening,
as close as any one can be
to the thing we grasp,
to the sense we have it in our grasp. Half-awake
I felt safe,
with the logs the height of a man open
to leeward. The pine bows we were lying on—

it wasn't yet morning,
the fire was still going
in the middle of us

it's about what I mean. As it fell out,
I hadn't yet succeeded

in getting it back. I woke up saying to myself,
Billerica. Billerica.
I don't know why. I don't know
Billerica. It is another place.

After prayer, we prepared ourselves for breakfast,
and for a journey. It was the hour of the twilight
in the morning

some said it was best not to carry the armour down.
I was one of those. I clung to mine. I was encumbered,
my feet sank more than was necessary, because of it,
into the sand. I wanted to keep it, I didn't want to give up
any protection. It seemed a protection, what had happened
in the night, I felt it was worth carrying
into the day, to get at it, to stay in the mood,
not to let the day slide over, to let the prayer cover me,
cover it, cover each of us, to stay in the skein
as it had got wound, either, if one could, to open it,
otherwise, to leave it as it was, to stay in it—

I went to and from the shallop saying to myself
Billerica. The water was not high enough,
we had to lay the things down on the shore,
and come back for breakfast.

It was all gone, with the shock, when we heard the same cry
we had heard in the night, the same voices
though they varied their notes. Though it is still with me.

"Woach! Woach! Ha! Ha! Hach! Woach!" Their arrows
came flying amongst us.

                        It hadn't done me any good,
to try to keep the plate over me. I was naked
in the sand. It was only that the others
put up such a good fight that I was able
to stop standing there, as I had also stood in the night,
with no meat to cover me. The coats
left against the barricade,
as we had hung them the night before,
were full of arrows. Yet none of us
were either hit or hurt. The best of us
had spotted their leader within half a musket shot,
protected by a tree and giving us full blast.
We took full aim at him, and made the bark and splinters
fly about his ears, so that after which
he gave an extraordinary cry, the same cry
we'd heard now twice, and leapt
away. We took up eighteen of their arrows.

I still keep them, as I picked them up,
exactly there, my father
allowing me. Many more, no doubt,
were shot. It is the thing about it,
as it was about the night, how thick
it was. I hate the night's
mementoes. I want the day to yield
likewise. I want that beach
to be the same. It's why I still say,
Billerica.

We gave God thanks
for our deliverance,
we took our boat
and went on our journey.
We called this place
the First Encounter.

Thoughts of the Time

The fields of the sky.

A hot moon low in the west.

In it, as in a net a knife
might sit, not gleaming

as a fish in the day in a gull's beak.

not caught. Gone into it.

In it. Sittin there.

"Who slays the Spanish sun . . ."

Who slays the Spanish sun
the Russian hill, makes born
what Monterey was the farthest (Larkin
all that the American has been there until)
Duncan

(sutters basques or my friend Facci
driven out, as a newspaper man, by Musso-
lini gangs, his press wrecked, the dull

radicalism of the town, as dull as the local–
ismish way San Franciscans reduce anything
to their size
except their streetcars

    On Potrero Hill a wisp of a girl cries
    "Mother" who will kill
    her father her husband her children.
    Is a flower
    the streets did not sprout
    until Duncan broke through
    the curtains

    The infestation the sun
    doesn't breed, what you can't put down,
    San Franciscans, washing your hands
    and your minds. What he won't let you
    wash, Laodicea

    Nor enlarge

    Or sell. Who teaches you what

    to enjoy. To enjoy

              what he got there
    out of your clean clothes. Cruel
    was your loveliness until your loveliness
    fell into his cruel hands, his aimed
    aimlessness. His love

who slew the old sun,
new North Beach, was shrewder
than the Sacramento Irish (none got as far
as Duncan

The Business

so much slipping by
ain't getting in

it has to at least be
the equal of or

you're not in, you get out of
the business

Hate

Hate any least millimeter,
or gram, of possession. It's the killer
of life. And it isn't
security, it's death. No one needs
to be secure. It means
they're dying

Who sd:

"for free"

the greatest

words

Who

A decadent people, they fight
with their feet, but their minds
thank god for them they're so
neat

Long Distance

pink tits, or grace of white thighs,
roll me your ass, lift me up your knees,
woman

your beauties, whose hair is long or
small, whose hands are method for
me

whose belly is the place in which time
is, to stay except that it leads
down

into upending, reversing, crossing, doing
the rest of it: fucking, she said, goes straight to the
heart

"You know, verse / is a lovely thing . . ."

You know, verse
is a lovely thing.

It issues,
like the vapors,

from the rock

The Loves of Anat, 1

Anat and Acbat
Said Anat
loan me your

Said Acbat
you sneaky female

At which Anat
was wrought

and went to the Lord God
That Acbat

won't let me borrow his
he called me a virgin

El, will you give him
hell?

The Librarian

The landscape (the landscape!) again: Gloucester,
the shore one of me is (duplicates), and from which
(from offshore, I, Maximus) am removed, observe.

In this night I moved on the territory with combinations
(new mixtures) of old and known personages: the leader,
my father, in an old guise, here selling books and manuscripts.

My thought was, as I looked in the window of his shop,
there should be materials here for Maximus, when, then,
I saw he was the young musician has been there (been before me)

before. It turned out it wasn't a shop, it was a loft (wharf-
house) in which, as he walked me around, a year ago
came back (I had been there before, with my wife and son,

I didn't remember, he presented me insinuations via
himself and his girl) both of whom I had known for years.
But never in Gloucester. I had moved them in, to my country.

His previous appearance had been in my parents' bedroom where I
found him intimate with my former wife: this boy
was now the Librarian of Gloucester, Massachusetts!

              Black space,
              old fish-house.
              Motions
              of ghosts.
              I,
              dogging
              his steps.
              He
              (not my father,
              by name himself
              with his face
              twisted
              at birth)
              possessed of knowledge
              pretentious
              giving me
              what in the instant
              I knew better of.

              But the somber
              place, the flooring
              crude like a wharf's
              and a barn's
              space

I was struck by the fact I was in Gloucester, and that my daughter
was there—that I would see her! She was over the Cut. I
hadn't even connected her with my being there, that she was

here. That she was there (in the Promised Land—the Cut!
But there was this business, of poets, that all my Jews
were in the fish-house too, that the Librarian had made a party

I was to read. They were. There were many of them, slumped
around. It was not for me. I was outside. It was the Fort.
The Fort was in East Gloucester—old Gorton's Wharf, where the Library

was. It was a region of coal houses, bins. In one a gang
was beating someone to death, in a corner of the labyrinth
of fences. I could see their arms and shoulders whacking

down. But not the victim. I got out of there. But cops
tailed me along the Fort beach toward the Tavern

        The places still
        half-dark, mud,
        coal dust.

        There is no light
        east
        of the Bridge

        Only on the headland
        toward the harbor
        from Cressy's

        have I seen it (once
        when my daughter ran
        out on a spit of sand

        isn't even there.) Where
        is Bristow? when does I-A
        get me home? I am caught

        in Gloucester. (What's buried
        behind Lufkin's
        Diner? Who is

        Frank Moore?

The Writ

The place of clear concepts is taken by images, *anima telluris*

Kepler supposed the secret of the correspondences to be, the earth

is animated. The earth shapes ships, fishes, kings, popes, monks,

soldiers. The practice of geometry—she produces

the five geometrical bodies, six-cornered figures in crystals.

And all in independence of the reflection and ratiocination of man.

He has his own abundance: mentation behind creation. The dogwood . . .

Empty, to fill.

The six-petaled blue flower alone at the end of the row of jonquils

not yet out, is the toy sergeant of the graduation ball the green-dressed

jonquils will dance (tomorrow? He lifts himself as though his arms

were no longer stiff and with the drumsticks in his hands he plays

a cakewalk.

        On the wind, catching her, she says, That's what I need,

a little of the romantic.

At this time, when the earth smells, my sweat leaves me sweet. The odor

is a state of grass. It smells like my father's hat-band. It smells

like spring. A man smells like spring. A woman tastes

like a six-cornered cup. The dogwood which last month bore berries.

The constant temperature below the surface, the peculiar power

to produce metals, minerals and fossils. Therefore every kind of natural or living power in bodies has a similitude. I grow

a beard, behind my round face I feel the confines. The domain

of the infinitely small, Riemann supposes, is where the laws do differently

than that God does arithmetic. The dogwood and I

have not lost a month.

As ordering operators and image-formers. The Art of Punctation

is in my throat, or the gentian's, on a clear day. Today

the dogwood sticks out anther-bearing filaments all over

my eyes.

These primary images which the soul can perceive are called

by Kepler *archetypalis,* and as ordering operators and image-

formers . . .

        I make no more of it than the sensation that the earth . . .

on a day in the year when the dogwood shows forth anther-

bearing filaments all over itself, in a matter of weeks

after it has been red . . .

        I am as quiet, behind my beard,

as the six-petaled flower, and take her arm

to show her the flower. I am as willing as she

to have the correspondence

of the tempting earth.

The Writ

I

    The place of the clear concept is taken by image. *Anima telluris* is the secret of correspondences. The word has gone out: empty, to fill. The earth shapes ships, fishes, kings, popes, monks and soldiers. The practice of geometry is also known to her: she produced the five geometrical bodies, six-cornered figures in crystals. She did this in independence of the reflection of man. Or his ratiocination. The dogwood . . .

The six-petaled blue flower alone at the end of the row of jonquils not yet out, is the toy sergeant of the graduation ball the green-dressed girls will dance (tomorrow? He stands there as though he wasn't stiff and plays a cakewalk.

                On the wind catching her, my girl says, That's what I need, a little of the romantic.

II

    At this time, when the earth smells, the odor of my own sweat is a state of grass. It smells like my father's hat-band. When a woman tastes like a six-cornered cup, a man smells like spring. The dogwood which last month bore berries . . .

He adduces a number of proofs. Among these are: the constant temperature below the surface of the earth, the peculiar power of the earth-soul to produce metals, minerals, fossils, therefore every kind of natural or living force in bodies can be said to have a divine similitude.

I grow a beard. Behind my round face I feel confines. The domain of the infinitely small, the man supposes, is suddenly much more to him than the astonishing fact that God does do arithmetic.

The dogwood and I did not lose a month.

III

The primary images are called *archetypalis* . . .

I make no more of it than that the sensation . . .

On a day in the year that the dogwood shows forth anther-bearing filaments all over itself, in a matter of weeks after it has been red . . .

I was quiet. I took her arm. I found myself as willing as she to respond

"I weep, fountain of Jazer"

When there were no depths
I was born, when there were no sources
of the fountains of the sea

At hand's length I grapple
to confine
the overlapping flaking
of the core, no waves
I am left with the fine edge
of my amulet fingered
in my pocket, if I shaved
any longer I'd try
the neolithic razor
on my hair, the sea
is postcard
of my fountain

Out of the dry sea,
Dr. Moon. And tears
now that the fountain,
O Jazer: raise up your breaths,
monkeys. Let us look on
the windshield, the mirage
of the sun, the rain-slick
petrol-ridden

    Diesel-dewed
    is my rain-slip,
    dark is my glass-
    es, I'm following
    a truck

I am full, to overbearing
I play pocket–pool
with sources whose edge
cuts my finger
                    Look Jazer:
it weeps

She Who Hits at Will

(*Descensus spiritus*, No. 1)

with dog and catalpa, panicles
streaked
yellow and brown purple, she

was treetops, we floated
entwined, she tossed
her blossoms while below

her dog floated
in the Hudson, precious to her and I was surprised
she had a dog

I said to her, the flower
and the dog are equal, equalized
as creations of you, you snow, you are streaked, you

gentlest water

Anniversary

on the north side of the telephone pole wet snow stuck
the nation
is all right,
Walt

fire-engine-red truck alongside less-interesting-red of De Soto convertible, Walt
they're still making things, WW
and have a Dept
of Commerce

a boy paints watery pink from 5 & 10 Cent Store palette,
and the sweat in his hair from the kitchen oil stove and his exertions
suggests
he can grow up to be a very attractive street car conductor,
if we had street cars,
which we don't   (the Open Road's
the Ford Company's)

No one today would say Ontario's shore is
blue, that is, one doesn't pay that sort of
attention—nor the house, or owning
anything; even not even staring
into the faces or windows on F St, braving
the storms
of the nation

They'd pay attention to you,
to snicker
in Peoples
Drug Store, at the size of your
eyes, Walt—little old foxy gas station
wisdom. You front. We—we

you know, you're
bracing? "Big,"
says the boy, I want the biggest
saucer
the most corned beef, the
precious
cup ("Cute," sd the sister god help us the nutmeg
holder on the wall's from
Adasko   . . .   atiskit NantASK-
et (oi, Valt!

Believe me, Walt
they do

Only, you wouldn't
sense it

from the color
of their cheeks

Or the tissue
for their noses

or the menstrual
blood

The Company of Men

for Phil Whalen for Christmas 1957

both, the company of men,
one, in front of my eyes, bringing in red fish, the other
the far-flung East India Company of poets whom I do not
even know

tons of fish against which to assert pinholes (I punch
the music I want out on rolls of paper to be played on
anyone's parlor harmonium   (the particles
of speech as multiple as those dull repeating patterns
of fish (nature runs to pattern; man, said Lawrence,
cannot afford to repeat

           I mean the finances
           of men (who gave us a haddock

           True Numbers
           are the usableness (how fishermen

           pay their bills. The catch

           repeats but the generosity
           can come only

           from those
           who have fish

In the company of men
what jingles

in his pocket
on Main Street

                    The South Sea
                    or Oaxaca

                    is a Bubble (what blew

                    John Law, why Campion

                    kicked rhyme in the face: Humphreys
                    has resigned knowing

                    the nation
                    will go boom

I mean Phil
Whalen

who brings his girl
a stalk

torn off
a rhododendron

in the public
park

Or my dragger
who goes home with

arete: when his wife
complains he smells like

his Aunt who works
for the De-Hy

he whips out
his pay

and says, how does this
smell?

One Word as the Complete Poem

dictic

Obit

The quail, and the wild mountain aster,
possess the place

"It was a place of blood" sd the mother
of two daughters whose husband
is buried here, and who at seventy

was a woman. "It's hell
to be here," sd the southerner
who founded it

Now the animals, and snakes,
have come down in. I saw a fox
cross the road last night

The mountain lion
is rumored
in the hills. The last man of the place
dreamed
of 14 persons on this hillside
like the mountain in the Chinese classic
to whom all those repaired who were useless,
the empire had become that good it was impossible
it was so dull, the court had no use
for the imperial instructor in fencing,
the greatest wrestler in the nation
with his tight beard
was on the roads picking fights
at bridges, the mistress of the tea house
was also wandering, all of them, 400 of them
fetched up in Kwansing

      —all the ultimate Adam of this American place
hoped for, was 14, 14 who could take
a vow of obedience. "Poverty?", he sd,
to the Bishop of Raleigh when the able man noticed
the farmhouse needed paint. I should say. And
a form of chastity? Claritas. But the last vow?
Who knows, any more, what it is that one does
obey to?"

"It was a polis," sd his friend, "no wonder
you wanted to take part in its
creation."

Hm.

What one can say, is, that there are 400 odd human creatures,
more or less, who were here and, according to their powers,
which have a ratio, carry it, carry the October morning,
the soft August moons, the fabulous hailstorm on the lake
whose hails people kept in their ice boxes and are now,
of course, the size of grapefruits, the mist off
the water, or, the night he drank Tokay and did say
to the least likely man to hear it, 14 people. When he walked down
to his pad he didn't set foot
on the earth, he walked right out over
May West, an acre of

Nights, how the wind off
the oldest mountains
can blow the hell out
of clouds: we have seen the sky here
be torn as the sea swept of its peopling
the speed the clouds
have run before it, as there are people
who ran, when others stayed, and some
got down

          "fucking,"
she sd, "is good. It puts one
in touch with
the universe." As the snow lay
on the pine boughs out the all-seeing
window before. And her touch
thereafter

          This is to be sung to the lyre
of quantity as a lute at Kwansing was sung in honor
of honor—for all those few
who left the empire because
they found her not a good
lay. Every one of them, on the roads,

were missing
from the central places
where business had usurped even
religion. There was a pious
man amongst those 14 who
didn't show up. He sat and watched
the yellow hornets nest
in the truck's
grille. And the inheritors asked,
"Are you Christian? Have you the love
of Christ in your heart?" She sd it as the President
might. At the heart of the world, this
is the orange. God give us
hornets

      Those who cannot crawl
along the ground, "You mean,
you can live in a house
without a bath?" The dream
was only worth $50,000. Every 1 second
there is gain
of 2 born versus
1 dead, and yet
we fly about the earth
looking for a home. They have made everything
a gin, and us poor boll weevils

      The requiem is
that this was a
ziggurat

     It was,
now that it closes,
for those who ain't here,
pain

     It isn't,
for him who sings,

in this case not the dead,
but those who had honor,
who have it, who have left the kingdom

who took this place through their toes or slam-banged

(I remember everything but murder)

A HYMN

to the 400

in the old classic (Chinese, or American,

not greek or roman or british

who weren't wanted

because they knew how to live & love & die

Sing songs

for this one

who signs off

And is now over-

grown

Love, signed

the last one

"Beauty / is to lay hold of Love . . ."

Beauty
is to lay hold of Love
is the leave
to

Moonset, Gloucester,
December 1, 1957, 1:58 AM

Goodbye red moon
In that color you set
west of the Cut I should imagine
forever Mother

After 47 years this month
a Monday at 9 AM
you set I rise I hope
a free thing as probably
what you more were Not
the suffering one you sold
sowed me on Rise
Mother from off me
God damn you God damn me my
misunderstanding of you

I can die now I just begun to live

What's Wrong with Pindar

The pearl. It's baroque. Regular–irregular. A bad dialectic.
Nature. Will not do. A bump is better than mere error
of round. We grow, and act, away from
the mother, turn as well east as south to catch
concupiscence in our pants. Reasserting imagination
and sentiment obscures the classical lying entangled
in what changes the wharves and spires of the city
by shoving masts and engines in its face. The alternate
rising and falling, and of gulfs bays rivers twice
in each lunar day—in the statement itself the juice
is moved onto the wire. The history and functions
vivify the coming into being of anything. Without the season
of structure modes lie like gods thrown down helpless
before the newness upsets genesis when young men
pour in. Exhibiting characters peculiar to living organisms
drags the past—which was, $\frac{1}{50}$th of a second ago, a
present: Saturn, on his elbow, looking over Rhea done in
on the ground, is a pearl better stay in. The oyster.

"Without the Season
of Structure, Modes
Lie Like Gods Thrown
Down, Helpless
Before the Newness
Upsets Genesis When
the Young Men Pour In"

The pearl better
have stayed in the oyster

Just Inside
the Vigil of Christmas

Swinging
the colored afghan
around me—

    my dearest mother,

    in the grave

The Treatment

She smiled as,
lying on her, she

kissed her lightly
(as I kiss her

with the same feeling)
on the right

collarbone

"It isn't my word but my mother's . . ."

It isn't my word but my mother's,
how he and herself were once one,
but split, and stayed apart, plenty
distance from each other

It was when they re-wed that the stuff
really spilled out. Everything
looked good. There wasn't anything
wasn't itself.

—Nauck, *Frg.* 484, Euripides

433

Poemless Rhymes for the Times

I

among
fucks

directly
expect

the worst

II

afterwards
towards

evening
go

carefully
into

their streets
Wistfully

murder
any of them

fathers
mothers
daughters
sons of

bitches
buggers

whores

III

That done,
go into

their homes.
Clear out

the rest.
Then only

may you
sleep

"With what I got out . . ."

With what I got out
of that slot machine,
send me South
—for the winter!

And if that proprietor
and or his son and two cops

come after me, I'll
not be there

This time I'm going
where nobody
stops me—
Watch my smoke!

All Havens Astern

I'm going to swim for my life
to another shore. The human shore's
too much

You can speak. You're on safe
ground, you mandala, you. I'm
getting out of here

"I just passed / a swoony time . . ."

I just passed
a swoony time on earth. I did not dig
that there was more

Of the United States

I'll go and sit down a few minutes with my soul. Hello,
are you there? and if so, what have you got to say?

Like when they ask you, how do you write poems, Mr. Olson,
what do you say? that if they come out, they come out, and

if they don't come out, they don't. Walk out with a resound-
ing tread, if you don't want to walk out, stay, the objectification

is all, the relevance is all, all is included, all does move,
sitting down, if it has the capacity. The bear, or Pencil, the

greatest of all the catfish of all the rivers of the South, of
the United States, is desired, and if you think you can catch him,

or shoot him, without going through the formulas, and concerning
yourself with his relatives, I do believe you are on the thin side.

There are those who are vulgar, and they increase. There are those
who obey, and there's more obedience at the same time that gall,

from the fact that people now live in cells, is most noticeable.
It's the flagrant, and the sensitive, who are now most at war,

the flagrant walking the streets, the sensitive all bundled up,
in their homes. This is the new war, and you could say that Yakuts,

who know bears best, ought to be imported to establish rites and
encourage warnings for those who want to know what they are up against,

when they go out these days. And the sensitive? what can we do for
them? Is there anything which helps a person arm themselves? Is there?

My soul, it's your turn. Have you any answers? Have you anything to say,
today, to those who suffer the present condition of mankind? Have you?

What do you say?

In your dream, let sensation
marry the girl in the long hair,

who admires herself. At the bottom
of the vas deferens, the skin of the animal,

which lies there, is the mirror. In the world,
you can shine yourself best

off a facet of the solid stone. One drop,
of the liquid of creation, is the burning

matter on your skin. Fear not the outrage
of any thing or any body, there is no

desperation, if the goo is what your fish–line
is made up of, bubble of on bubble of: Pencil

is caught, in the rivers
in the South

of the United States

"tenementy twilightish landscape . . ."

tenementy twilightish landscape
into which motorcycle with
scorpion tale-tail

passes

438

"I was stretched out on the earth . . ."

I was stretched out on the earth   so that a wild geranium
was looking down into my face
at a wild geranium

The Year Is a Great Circle or
the Year Is a Great Mistake

Capricorn (of sizable thirst)
stumbles up first—cold dry street, with ladies, and night

shoves aside the year (Boob of the movable cardinal and not melancholic
daylight) bears on his back an ass and the exaltation
of wars

He and his son and his son's son (Water Boy)
butt their way in and out of every
place of creation. They're all
knees

In a sort of reverse apocatastasis, that is, the tail's
where the head ought to be, these
Long Ears

though being locked up does not prove
(they missed the stakeout to bag junkeys)
they don't shove. They shove

all all directions

439

Measure

a vessel blatting
its foghorn

fog bells religious
by the distance

of the island,
double bell

as if bell–buoy
wave-made to sound

the vessel flatting
the graver

measure

The Mind's Notice

The fog blows
by the window

the bell
began
sometime ago

was not heard
except
like tires
in the street

The autos
sizzle
The bell
does not blow
The rain

has loosened the mind's
notice

Rosy, It Was

"Come aboard" the old man used to say
and it was summer night. But this
is February in latitude 43
degrees   Northern lights
sheer from west to zenith
last quarter moon is bright
on harbor, Saturn Mars
are out are in by snowsheets
pile over but clear as soon
as they hide the stars, the sky
one Minnesota of pink
sheathes an unbeginning
unending unfixable storm
of light

                        while a fleet
—10, 12 vessels—put out
at 3 AM
                              Diesels
shoving each plank
of a ship fast and as lit
as flat-car -locomotive, masthead
lights fore main wheelhouse deck
aft as bright

the ship asleep as quiet
as the harbor in the moon

and winter only
in the veil-gale sky

A Six Inch Chapter—in Verse

Don't stand out there, man, in all that howlllllllll

ing

You don't look good keeping up that preeeeeeee

tending

All that talk about you wouldn't be caught crawlllll

ing into any old craven old leeeeee

shore   Sure enough?

Easter

       I

Holy Saturday night
the tide
was almost full,

the Emp
of Empire Clothing
threw

a dry green light
upon the harbor but the moon
was warmer,

and a rose
light fell between them, reflected
by a street lamp from Colonial

brick. The trick
of Christian theologians
to have simplified

the Lord's mortality
by making it ad–writing,
He took it on

Love
to be possessed
independently

of the beloved
(Ten Pound Island
a brawl

of gulls
unsettled
by the brightness

of the night, screaming
at each other, a world
of souls

The full tide said,
woman
has to be as free,

perhaps,
in the world,
as man

perhaps,
more easily
is, the tide lapping

the boards we stood on,
and filling
the artificial

boat haven,
squared out of
granite,

so full, and toiling,
she said, "It's
the ocean"

II

Undazzled, keen
love sits
hungry to redeem

All moon
and fullness
only rule

which follows, evil
not a fact
of nature, nature

only one
of the facts, no soul
solely innocent,

nor one,
by nature, impenitent.
The implicated character

of everything

He whom the mother
bore is first
in death and in the world

But to him whom love rebears
the cosmos
is an ornament,

harmony
is for the stars,
and freedom

is the ogdoad,
the Christian
said, 7

is the society of women,
a place of rest, but 8
is woman

She
is no rest

The liturgical
eighth day
approaches

The ignorance,
and darkness,
which spreads

like a mist,
breaks. The universe
is a sleepless

light, and endlessness
walks naked out, the Mother,

and Magdalen,
looked at,
through the fingers

The Gonfalon Raised Tonight

I don't know
where we'll be at,
23 year old Stoney
is quoted, former gang member,
now married and with job,

who was jumped himself,
tonight. All good people
in block Westerveld
Avenue to Parkinson Street grieve
the death since 9 PM

of considerable portion
of sd block's population
by sudden extension
of what was, previously,
limited to members of

They turned, in strength,
to cut across, whipped
citizens with automobile
aerials, poured gasoline, made Ward
12, their demands include

the restoration of entail,
and primogeniture, the possibility
of mothers succeeding to leadership
when a son with heart is mutilated
in rumbles which will probably cross

state lines. No one
is to teach except
who is listened to
by everyone in the room
for three hours without

disturbance of any kind.
Neither man nor woman
shall exercise
authority whose eye
does not contain the ability

to put down any least action
movement thought or
desire of anyone
under or in their
care which

in their best judgement
is not the equal
of the occasion or
the necessity of that moment. The claim
of these combined units
of 11−17 year old
men and women is
for a wholesale

cleaning out of the
city. No one
in present possession
of any part of any
kind of thing or place or

personal matter through which
the street can't move and
no disturbance either
way—they will flush,
they say, anyone as they have passed through

city block on to the next
until there is clearance
of all hands on all
sides, until some several
scrupulous businesses

which they observe among themselves,
one to one and among each other,
become daily and average
in each home and on the part
of each individual. They declare

no interest whatsoever
in the state of the world,
demark the nation as a turf
on which it will be as they say
or it won't be any longer

allowed to go undisturbed by
their active attention. The pursuit
of segregated
experience is hereby abolished,
the vote is widened

to include 3
year olds, and woman's suffrage
is denied. Women, however,

are to lay and to carry
all weapons until further
notice, with pleasure
and with the same strict attention
demanded of everyone

to the things which properly
belong to them—for example,
their own lives as inclusive of
(1) what each is up against;
(2) what is reasonably asked of them;

and (3) by what they can at all times be
judged. Which is what they mean by
the immediate end of every
social and individual privilege;
and the substitution,

without any further delay,
of public and private
intensities. The alternative,
they insist, is such a passage
as they made through one street

tonight. The endlessness of reality
as the consequence
of the closeness of persons,
and the end of loneliness,
between or within persons,
is declared

And the warning given that
no man or woman shall be allowed
to linger in any least fatuity
of happiness, all to be charged
to move wherever and when

in the privacy of themselves, on
the street or in their most tenuous
dealings with each other
as though they had no time to
indulge, is made

with the previous order on ownership,
and the vote, the
minimum they will be satisfied with. Or
they will continue to assert
the pressure they have already

shown. The speed with which
what has been done
is demanded is noticeable
in the carriage of each
of these club members. No one who has yet

reported has given any indication
that what has now been introduced
into the situation is anything
but what those who make the proposals
care, and are capable, of carrying out

"Rufus Woodpecker . . ."

Rufus Woodpecker visited the President
today. The subject of their discussion
was foreign policy. He advised

that bi-partisanship must be replaced
by symbiosis, or else. Citing
his own experience with

the Black Tree Ants (they live together
despite mutual self-destruction) he showed
how the whole sub-continent changed,

between dawn and dusk, grubs reigned
where states previously boasted
they had democratized creation. The President,

impressed by the visit, showed his guest
from Up Over the condition of his own
condition and proposed to do anything

he could about the partnership
situation. Rufus Woodpecker,
when asked how he found the

President said simply a White House
is as good a rest home as a Mayor's
Nest; and he went on to speak of

four times the Four Fold principle.
When asked what this was all about, his
answer was, You can go anywhere

if you go out. All reporters were
one in thinking that there is no end
to what may follow. The chief

of the head of the Confederacy
for The Doubles to End the World's
Troubles was quick to support

the visitor, saying, Nobody
has ever denied that you can eat
with false teeth, but no one

has said you can see with a
glass eye. All the women
of the nation are reported

to be ready to give up beer
with breakfast if the outcome
of these chains of meetings,

which promise so much and have
already alleviated considerable
concern for what is the condition

which has caused such loss
of what was previously con-
sidered to be so attractive

a way of spending Friday nights
in town, that merchants everywhere
are prepared to offer fashion

colors for any elements found wandering
(four were, yesterday) within the city's
walls, their happy hands stained brown

from the amount of yours they'd pick up
coming from Loftoland into the massed
arrays of our forces arranged (as agreed

upon four years ago in the treaty of
the Vast Moths, at Genoyen). They assert
that you can hardly get through the Lowest

Tundra from the weight of the numbers of the
people buying whatever
is offered to them, no one, apparently,

considering at all the outcome of the
supreme meeting which took place here
today. On all hands there is

the thought that though normally,
and normally, the, and in certain
seasons, not eat, and actually

the young are born,
Rufus Woodpecker wouldn't
come near these shores, there isn't

a woman who wouldn't rather naturally
appear on Main Street shopping nights with her
hair in curlers, but now that the whole

question of overseas improvements has been
decided in favor of the formula for
home improvements, that they do involve

the whole family, Dad Mom Sis and Brother
are safe anywhere, the New Zealand Tuataras
and the Sooty Sheerwaters combining

a night shift and general
domestic cleanliness so adequately
there can be no question at last that union

is possible, the world can be one,
the Mites lie down with the Mrs,
everyone, keeping permanent shape,

having built-in fairness of cooperation and
chirping excitedly at the approach of each other

       Or,
          as today,
              at tea

at the Capitol where three nurses
and a dog drove happily off backing
into the car behind at the sight

of the representative of the rest of creation
nesting inside the Mouth of the nation, and pecking
broccoli out of it, clearly concerned

that if he went any deeper he was apt to find more
foodstuff buried in the Defrost

Stone and Flower Series

I

I banged it out
of stone
long enough

The lily pad
sits flat
on the water
level

Its tail
hangs down
from it
to the bottom

Then one morning,
like pert eggs, the flowers
are there, too,
at the point

And the dull pond
has the fulgor appropriate
to it

2

The tile pavement
of the pool, the tesserae,
are in use

After five centuries
& with Tedeschi,
and American

trucks since,
the city's
squares, and adjoining

streets—some
superintendent plus
the Council and *fabbri*

think of it, before
nothing, or dirt
then suddenly the commercial

supremacy. And to this day
streets, which last, and are slippery
as well as gleam when wet:

it is a bird's tail, or blue
China, the amplitude of,
like saucers, the eyes

of his generosity, like plates,
she said, the way his element
shows above the other
elements, he strode

the Mediterranean world,
the Mediterranean world
did. Taut

is the surface, it will snap
if you draw a file fast
across it. Only trucks,

and heavy armament, crowds
on festival days, fireworks
bounce on it, and at night

the watch, or a man and his girl
click, as they go along. It's
a firmament

3

Candor also
is a character
of the wet light

In this respect
stone & water
have another

placement one
who has used the hammer,
done his time,

knows, beat it out without
ending it. The noumenon
of the pool (or Chief Sun Dance

sd, the stone
is enough
of itself; it won't

break up, it is round,
and stone). We will draw out
the meaning, we will

4

Grease, *ganos*
is plain grease,
too. When the sun's wheels

were stuck,
and day hung
unfreed,

and no one,
and the earth
couldn't get out

from the cold he killed
a bear & busted it
open, to put its fat

in the axle and light
sprang
over the hill with a grin

of appreciation. Everybody,
finally,
moved, got unwrapped

from being bundled
up. It was a morning

5

Like in summer, or
in the Gulf or Molucca
straits, when the wind

is west, southwest
the hardened arteries
which will bring death

cease upon the first
breeze which flutters
the tail of the toc

bird who picks off
redundant feathers
with his bill,

to make an eye
which glows
like the pavon (ficus

mirabilis).
Whom he envies.
An end to envy,

toc. You look good enough
skating up the walls
of the old cenote,

a resplendence
against the dry
limestone

And the water
is your resonance,
into which they threw

the prettiest virgin any of them,
and they knew a good looking woman
when they picked one. She fell

but only in the National
Geographic colored
plate (as silly as the toc

to beautify itself). Dredged up
there is no maiden pelvis, an assortment
of drunks and old people who must have

stumbled getting home
after dark. What the breeze
blows over is best

itself. Like the sacrificial
maiden who married
the farmer

6

The streets of the burned city,
even the railroad bridge
whose supports

were burned, supported
the passengers working their way
along sidewalks no two persons

could get by on but had to
because ice, thin but there,
had settled on the water

left all over from the fire-fighting
had gone on to save, or not very
effortfully, the stores

and houses, but mainly Main
Street, where the business places
are, for which the cops,

and fireman, are actually
hired. Otherwise the street lamps
are supposed to save girls

from rape hurrying home,
in the old days,
from the social,

or whatever. Those
were other times. Now
there is no

fear. There are
no bodies. The spirit–body
has gone off

with the fire, they are living
in sin in
another city. No one

speaks of them
any more. Or does,
all the time, spreading

the story

7

It isn't a matter
of waves. It's rather
where what issues which

one notices, in fact anything
on and in its own enough to be
light and invisible

And the soul,
working heavily,
fixed and visible,

attends, from behind
the square inch
between the eyes

which look backward
from the ancestral
face. I banged it

out of ignorance.
Old Spearfish said,
Regardez, man

has his place
in nature
as his wife

hers. Three sons,
and his daughter,
on a beach experience enough

of the built-in rage
to be. They,
distracted,

from growing, he,
and his wife, differently
interested.

Memorial Day

Memorial Day flowers
were spread on the waters

Woman Mayor Corliss,
the florist's wife, made

a speech. A helicopter
dropped a wreath. The paper

carried the usual veterans'
pension plug (they died, without

etc.) etc. A
parade. People

fainted. Children
got trampled on. But none

of the dead rose
to the occasion

I Mean, No

by the eleven
naked
varsity football
players strewn
in the station wagon

—no!

"I hang on by . . ."

I hang on by
It is as though
the cliff I might fall
put out its belly

half
Around the World
you said. It
was. The night

was. I do not doubt
the flower
exists. Simply,
it isn't

there. So half
and not half mine,
To hell
with you, you

said (as I clamber
on the wall

Afica

Hard water (water-
falls) in the sheet
of the waterface
a clambering
gnat

hard water (water-
falls) the cliff
holding
the streaming
of the loving flesh
up

Across
the valley, I
the lover, and
she,
the beloved, view
each other

I hold her as hard as I can
in my arms

To Try to Get Down One Citizen as Against Another

to bug: an act of intelligence
where other less persons will
disorganize the air for city blocks with
their compulsions

"the Flower grows / from the roots . . ."

the Flower grows
from the roots of the Sea

      the Great God of the Sea

the Flower grows
from the roots of Earth

      the Great God Earth

under the Flower
hides
      the Great God Hell

"The liturgical / eighth day . . ."

The liturgical
eighth day
approaches,

The ignorance,
and darkness,
which spreads

Like a mist
increases. The universe
is a sleepless

light, and endlessness
walks naked
out

"Undazzled, keen, / love sits . . ."

Undazzled, keen,
love sits,
disposable, a sun

And all moon fullness
is a rule
follows from

No soul
is only innocent
Nor, contrawise,

unpenitent. The implicated
character of everything
is love

by self possessed

"Sit by the window and refuse . . ."

      Sit by the window and refuse

      my father, crying Curtains

      instead

(as of father's visit, & Thanksgiving!

anyway

      Contesting his authority &

claiming a calendar of your own

Winter Solstice

I'm going to get
the hell as far
south as I can to
stay the hell out

of the darkness. And
when I turn (as
I'll have to, the
laws being

what they are) I'll
hesitate a day in
order to scare the piss
out of the useless

ones who pine
for less than
the Great *One* who

hides in
the rose as
the fire does

in me

Christmas

dirty Christmas
which Origen
and Clement
both showed up

for the junk it
is—as though,
sd O, he was a
mere Pharaoh. Or,

says Clement, do
we have here some
child baptism to
go gew-gaw over?

in long favorably
embroidered gown,
a boy? instead of
a man standing

in desire in the
Jordan, with green
banks on either
side, a naked man

treated by another
adult man who also
has found out that
to be as harmless

as a dove is what
a man gets as wise
as a serpent for,
the river,

of life?

The Song

more than the sennet of the solstice pipe,
lovely though a hautboy is, now that the season
is indoors

Now that we are driven
and all outdoors
is no good

and the season
nor the hautboy
cover the tune,

we talk, pell-mell.
And when, for a moment,
nothing is said,

in this season still (and so forth
And it is
indoors)

And small as the group. Then,
more than the sennet of the solstice pipe,
lovely though the piping is,

and the season
still is cold

Being Altogether Literal, & Specific, and Seeking at the Same Time to Be Successfully Explicit

1.

Cant first attacked as such, 1596, Count Francesco Cenci (source: Stendhal)

America outproduces the world in steel, Pittsburgh March 14, 18–
97 (choice of the significance of the date, Brooks Adams') The Ameri-

canization of the world may then proceed, predictably, to conclusion.
Still proceeding. Cant

uber alles. The American word is
confidence. Coca-cola

is my name.

2.

Coca-cola speaks: "Sassparilla was my frontier grandmother.
A root. Mildly alterative. A tonic. Against me, there

has only been
Moxie. And Ted Williams

has taken the stick
out of that. Diabetics

may drink us both
without any harm. I am pause. I am two–color

harmony. I am with anything. I am
taste. I am the cup

which pays. I am syrup, in big bottles. I am gas.
You can run any human being on me. I am carbonated

water. I am what Life began from. I am juice. I am as it was
in the beginning. I've got it all back

where it came from. Drink me, teenager. Don't have a thing
without me. I am Jim Farley. I maybe didn't make the Presidency but

I'm
all over

the world. Follow me. Leave yr cars, outside. Ma said Grandma said
Topeka. When you say that, she said they all said:

smile. (He also told me the handsomest boys in his outfit, all from
Nebraska, North Dakota and some from Iowa—artillery unit—writing home

to their mothers when in England would
date

the cripples
of the towns,

the women
whom none

but these
boys

473

from the States
would take out on

dates. Nadir, the guy
made the advertisement read

for the imported
fruit from

Araby—the nation's
finest. And the son

of the first cousins in
the Jewish orphanage

Vienna, 1912, to his
"I was Hitler's

Buddy" the title
reads (source, New

Republic, 19something
or other) said, "Sell in July

stuff to keep frost
off of windows. And I'll

conquer the world in May, by
changing the weight of iron

to feathers. (The record,

on the juke-box, to
the end, of, the cooling

of the peoples
of the world by

refreshing them, from
Amere–icka. Who took Beauty

on his knee
and found her

sour: amère
is the French letter
for it

II

If you begin again you come to another nexus at the same
point of time: Europe just then was being drained, 1590

or abouts by the ravage of what Columbus's sailors, wasn't it,
are supposed to have picked up from sheep, isn't it, and thereafter

syphilis has made Puritans
of us all? Said date "Adventurers,"

not using their wealth as Francesco
did, to stay at home and hold parties

at which he'd sneer as Timon had but
Timon was Platonic, Cenci was (as de Sade

made real revolution in
1792) concentrated on

flesh: he raped his daughter to test
how far righteousness might

be pushed. And he found out: the Fugger
newsletter told it

475

like the outbreak
of war: in 100-point it screamed

Mother
and Brothers

expiate Sister's
honor. (Thus death

got sour among
Elizabethan

poets who
thereafter impose love

upon us. As only now,
as William Carlos Williams puts it,

fornicators can,
and not lose their minds, go

for it as the flies
do. And horses. Sassafras

was the only known previous
answer. And thereby

America
got started. The cure

for the pox, and worth more
in the return of confidence

to Elizabeth's
young blades

than Drake was,
to her—1200

to one on her
guilder—but Pring

Purenose whoever
would take a ship out of

Bristol and hunt the root the sheep
perhaps did not scramble their brains

therewith, could get joint stock capital
to carry shovels

to dig the shores hereabout for
SAXIFRAGE was his flower

said the poet above mentioned who
the Doctor who

has celebrated the return
of love

        (the gift,
        fr the C.:

        the dried bark
        of the root

        of S. varii-
        folium yields

        an aromatic volatile oil
        used in perfumes . . .

                (source,
        Webster)

III

Or the third, Tawney, the source (who credits,
as all do, some German) who read it into

the Western record: Protestantism,
and the rise

of Das Capital: Brownnose or whatever
date Shakespeare-Jonson the

character first showed
on the world stage, the birth

of the Commercial
Traveler, "Homeward Bound,"

USA. 300 years the world
has had nothing

better. Sour,
is the round,

around rights
is junk

the Age
of Cant. Sour

are we. And junkeys
all, around

your hung-up
skins. By the mother,

stuck among the boughs,
from the old frontier,

whose handsome son,
running for a hammer, cried "Christ, you'll never

be able to move from there," the baby
in a carriage on the right woke up, and says

                (his face
                wallowing

                from sleep) "Aren't we
                supposed to be

                revolutionaries?"

Conversation galante

I   She dreamt of a lady in light green
       who said, "Well, why don't you go see

       where he is?" In a field of flowers
       to wander. To walk out all free

       in a meadow. Focussing quite naturally
       on the smallest, she was easily

       surprised by him as he took her,
       wide-eyed, to his kingdom. A maiden

       is also a form
       of a queen

479

2 Tearing pieces
  out of her son's

  soul the mother
  left him,

  as a man,
  showing

  the shape
  of his calf

  Or another
  wore a homburg

  to impress
  a slant-eyed

  blonde. One half
  belongs

  to the type

3 As harmless
  in the depths

  as the flower
  at the heart

  of the cosmos,
  she who

  opens Eve
  from the shell

of her belly, wild
with desire

to yield
the secret, poised

with the glittering
eye of the free

snake

4   Death
is a grandmother.

The virgin dies
then.

Destructiveness
is a lie.

One woman
was dressed all

in gold.
She pointed

to the turn
of the stairs

The other,
who had always

worn black,
was now

in a red dress
she felt

made her body
as tall,

and as full,
as her monitor.

He had kissed her
as he went down

the stairs. In the room
her son,

with the two
of them,

was as ready
as flesh

as fire
for the world

"the dogwood comes out yellow . . ."

the dogwood comes out yellow
& then flares white
it is so, with each spring

of my soul, the body first
and then, the flare
my body is my soul as
dogwood is yellow
& then white

"right in my eye . . ."

right in my eye the west sun zing saying
level glance dig man I'm setting what are you
doing today

"This man's weakness is straw . . ."

This man's weakness is straw
But it could light a fire

This other man's weakness
is improvidence. But he

is firm as iron while gentle
as his mother isn't and his father

is weak. This man is a woman
incomplete

"My love is also / like . . ."

My love is also
like a sixteen
year old whose blouse
I unbutton like
her old piano teacher

Incunabula, 1958

The Picture

naked, but with my boots on / my son,
to my left

I walked the open piazza / I kissed her
emphatically, my wife
and we, I said,
live here, it is right
you have come

The Words

       love by word of mouth
                       , love,
                             love by mouth

"go / make a bridge . . ."

go

make a bridge

of sand

over the sea

go

make a ladder

of sand up to heaven

and go to god and come down

no more

"It's not / the erotic . . ."

It's not
the erotic
but the
kairotic

But the erotic
's so.
And the other
's not

So who wouldn't,
rather,
than
    ?

Every Man His Own Matador; or for That Matter Any Member of the Family

One wants to say to them: even Florida, if they'd have just left even Florida alone

Or my son says, That's you, Papa, when all there's left in the world, is,
to be a Nuba. One would have to go that far away,
one man on the back of another, they've wrestled, and one of them
has won, and the other is carrying him. Just that. By my own fantasies,

when $4\frac{1}{2}$ or 5, I could have told them how to keep the beaches
so that we could have used them, if we wanted to. Leave them alone.

                                I was cruel enough
to animate the scene. I had pictures of my desire. The thing is,

                LEAVE THINGS ALONE

That's the trick. We'll take care of the rest. Every time my son
breaks something he says, I didn't mean to

May 20, 1959

The moon must be in Perigee the sea
is on the land so I think someone has cut
and no it is the sea is new-mown

Talk to me I say to it from the snap
of it behind me as I walk it
talk to me as a gull did two days
ago rattling off even making duck sounds

And for the first time in my life so far north
by god if there aren't whippoorwills in
Ravenswood Mad May night for distinctly
a bird followed me obviously insisting

he had something to say to me I had said
to myself Antaeus, to his earth
Which had felt right turning my back
on the harbor shining and my own breast

as full It was that bird,
whatever it was, coming after me tree
after tree and pistoling me with his
message—I don't know I still went home feeling

like I was right

The Nerves Are Staves, and When the Tears Come There Is Voice

It got to cost $1,000,000 to kill an Indian
by 1868

Shortly before that date said white men had fought a Civil War was
expensive

Whatever shall come to this continent, like destruction—or
Payne's vision of Chinese farming Illinois land after victory—

there has been already taken a negative, on the plate, is now being
printed

The Intended Angle of Vision
Is from My Kitchen

the West pink
Hammond's Castle
da allure of
smoke clouds German

expressionism
But where I look
—the 'pond' of
Western Harbor,

Stage Head a pure
Tsukiyama-sansui,
the water, at this hour,
silver, and ochre, where

it was once
black,
and gold: the wake
of a boat peels

off the ochre and runs
silver over

"the proper soul / in the proper body . . ."

the proper soul

in the proper body

is mythological

the general soul

in the general body

is theological

the person's soul

in the person's body

is for psychology

The Distances

So the distances are Galatea

                                        and one does fall in love and desires

mastery

                 old Zeus—young Augustus

Love knows no distance, no place

                              is that far away or heat changes

into signals, and control

                 old Zeus—young Augustus

Death is a loving matter, then, a horror

                                        we cannot bide, and avoid

by greedy life

               we think all living things are precious
               —Pygmalions

                                      a German inventor in Key West
who had a Cuban girl, and kept her, after her death
in his bed

                                   after her family retrieved her
he stole the body again from the vault

Torso on torso in either direction,
               young Augustus

                                  out via nothing where messages
are

      or in, down La Cluny's steps to the old man sitting
a god throned on torsoes,

            old Zeus

Sons go there hopefully as though there was a secret, the object
to undo distance?

                                They huddle there, at the bottom
of the shaft, against one young bum

                             or two loving cheeks,

        Augustus?

You can teach the young nothing

                            all of them go away, Aphrodite
tricks it out,

        old Zeus—young Augustus

You have love, and no object

                     or you have all pressed to your nose
which is too close,

        old Zeus hiding in your chin your young
        Galatea

the girl who makes you weep, and you keep the corpse live by all
your arts

        whose cheek do you stroke when you stroke the stone face
        of young Augustus, made for bed in a military camp,
        o Caesar?

O love who places all where each is, as they are, for every moment,
yield

        to this man

                  that the impossible distance
be healed,

        that young Augustus
        and old Zeus
be enclosed

        "I wake you,
stone. Love this man."

"I am so small you can hardly see me . . ."

I am so small you can hardly see me, I am Priapus,
I live on this watch-house neck of shore, not much bigger
than a sea-gull, sharp-headed, footless, such as a boy
might scratch my picture lazying along the sand home from
school, throwing rocks at bottles or gulls:

                           but if anybody needed me I'd
make myself available, I can move fast enough. Likewise,

I see the creatures who live in the wood of the soul,
and all the things which drift or run under water

a translation of Archias (via J. W. Mackail)

"All pink from the bath she slept . . ."

All pink from the bath she slept
while he ate the second joint of turkey
with pretzels and grapejuice in the
kitchen

Assuming the Soul Is a Bitch

That then becomes you Have
no fear

of anything Doubt not except
the one which troubleth

all Ok a Brooklyn gun Place the shot
on the moon Diatomic power, Lady

of my insides—or Crash program
for Mr Big who fucks

all the time Or at least
wants to

          Neither
animal vegetable nor

natural Neither
gender

                    Neither
all this gab

                    Neither
any one else Nor ma nor

Pa Nor
Willy-grand

Upside Nor—one needn't
take any

position—naw, sd the girl,
writhing

on the white iron bed, from the white salesman trying
to force her

                    Neither
sex

nor death

                    Nor children,
except as one's own does

present pride And altogether too much

attention

                    Nothing
but all

"one night Ma / lay with Pa . . ."

one night Ma
lay with Pa
and I was around

That changed Ma

one night Ma
lay with Pa
and I happened to

her eyes her teeth her tongue
out her nails clawing him
her hair all over
her look

That changed me

Carrying Water to the Youth in Honor of Sappho Jane Harrison & Miss Duncan If She Had

carrying water to the bear
run down the alder path. The maidens wash themselves
before they approach his ancientness

496

each of us urinate
or defecate naturally
behind the *bocci* bush. The loveliness

of their bodies not because they are young
but by the bear grown into women.
Rising close to the stream the trees

lean over with the rain

The Dance, of the Grizzly Bear

Red Man told me, 'Your father
sent me

to teach you to do two things always
at the same time, to be

of words the speaker and of deeds
the doer, this is the way you were

born'

On All Sides

the cave/wall the cave lion's

SHOULDERS

are rubbing (off

"On the equator east of my son . . ."

On the equator east of my son I Orion bequeath to him my riches
the milkweed the meadowlark and Scorpion his mother

"The Muse / is the 'fate' of the poem . . ."

   The Muse
is the 'fate' of the poem
its 'allotment'
ahead of time

its 'allotment' ahead of time   the face of it
at the end, seen at the beginning

The Objects

So Venus does hang and glitter in the prepared sky
                                                    I kept her for you
while you were south in the city
                              I watched her race

into the west not to set to go shooting off into night's bed or
coming morning somewhere else upon the globe for others like us who
live for love

You make so much of disappointment in your life you cling
like her fuzzy light bedazzles all who ever look at her
                                             And groan
of her diseases
                You said her atmosphere
                must be ammonia

would frizzle us if we were there like hands too long in soap

        She's not moon or sun, Attis, nor mother
        to comfort you   The trio
        of wife and concubine and boy

do not remove some sal of taste upon your tongue
by which you turn away

from her who's sign of love
and war

and the other, that one
whose old Victorian bed you sold

"abt the dead he sd . . ."

abt the dead he sd
he was going to write an obit
about those americans, dead,
who had shaped the world, he sd,
with a more than heavy hand

now she sd, looking up
at the bomb like it was a bird
got between her
and the sun

            I don't know
what she sd about Grant
Phil Whalen
insisted
San Francisco
1957
that everything I ever sd
she sd   But abt Grant

I sd Butcher I read
Kenneth Williams
on Grant I feel Grant
more days in more
of those fall-ins
where the glue, it feels,
of the creation is all
that holds anything
back?

The next turn of the wheel,
what do you think
about the next turn
of the wheel?

"not a rat-hole, a cat-hole . . ."

not a rat-hole, a cat-hole: the knife of time; on the ledge, overlooking
Norman's Woe a mausoleum with Aztec steps up, the Pseudo-Vault inside which

Inside the castle another tomb, of Primus the son of his old age who spat
upon Christ and the young man's modern equivalent called the dog

which he called Christ the bride who turned, said Simon Magus into
the beast who'll eat him until by some shore Christ will walk across

Old Man's Pasture but hasn't yet and in the moonlight the father cries
while the bride eats the boy Come sweet Jesus save us cats who long

for mortality, "I raised this house for you, me whom you will not have
always

with you,"
as I have my cats

gum from Araby to make it smell right, red Cardinal's cloth to eat steak
off of, green dye to make the pool not corrupt, no birds allowed the cats

get em, no live thing allowed to en-ter here except cats, and human
beings, who will slide down my castle door and disappear among my lights

and shadows, pass out from the immortal
world, the dirty bitch of a dog who eats us

gnaws away at us, claiming her bed-right while I bathe
my latest boy

in the green pool: Primus, nod
at our doings, stroke the dog

look at us eating like the Masque
of the Red Death or the Brown Hamburgers

staining the Seven Drawers, the dead cats and rats,
each night, in the hallway of the rooming houses all moderns

live in outside
my sanctuary: here is peace

which can be
preserved, in these rites

of eating, drinking and taking
H2 we shall live with our cats

long enough to have fooled
the One Who Doesn't Come, while the boy

hopelessly
fails to grow,

wanders a non-existent earth
trying to find out if

anyone will tell him what
to do to get the bride out

from under the grave-cloth
of the saviour—"Oh Primus

poor Primus I hold up my arms
in the moonlight" (while Venus

hangs her lamp right in his eye,
sweet Faustus of Radio Control

who dreams a dream dream ends:
    in the fantasy

    of the creation
was the illusion,

not in the building of
the Castle, not shoring up the shore, the knife of time

is not at our throats as the dog bitch woman bride who
was turned into nothing seeking him, to tear him, Simon Magus said,

until Christ does come, the saviour. When you have said,
the soul of a dog

    you will live with cats
    and you will bury nothing

    on your private grounds except
    cats, time's monsters who stare

    in the ennui of time occupy always
    the point of cynosure curl up

    as though what never was is
    sitting on the hearth: it was never

    there. The mausoleum,
    is as the castle, as the castle

    is as the mausoleum capped
    by Primus, the Cardinal's

    hat, the Pseudo-Phrygian
    ears: on this site I

    who had four bills placed
    before Congress in my behalf, do hereunto will

    what I accomplish
    each night and am

    a wafer. I have built,
    and invented,

    a Way of Cats,
    and a Poison of Time

I will only leave you,
at the last possible moment,

and even after Primus is eaten,
if possible, if there is any desire

I can get stimulated to offset the enormity
that flesh is not eternal. In this faith I bequeath

to no one leaving it to lawyers to dispose
both my castle and my position

What I will is a grave
of three cats and a castle

so described:

As Cashes a ledge a sea-marke on which all may fall, my Castle a horn
of a different order, the stones diamonds from Afriky, the hangings

as soft as my mother's
my cats to lie

as I did, my jeweled hands
presented

to my father (I was Primus
then! Then fate came to push me, stone by stone the Finnish masons raised

my castle on the Woe (Rafe's Slit
was once my plan to set Mont St Michel inverted

on this shore Christ has not yet come to: Christ
does not come and only someone else makes Venus

rise in the eastern sky at 4 AM to swing her evil lamp and
stick me in the eye of the jealousy of where my newest Primus is

Out into the night out of my carefully heated spaced and newly used
nave altar clerestory to seek him, and get him away from the bitch dog

the cloths of the grave of the Soul of a Dog leads him away from the way
of the cat—o whatever thing substitutes for what one might once have

believed in, to turn, I this wafer of my own hands and love cry out to
nothing, what joy do you throw down when all is as swift as and thin

lovely flesh of youth, make us die: I am nothing, all I've done, nothing,
in this maltese cross of mesons coming in on a third tape to mock and show

the form of spiritualism pouring from outer space and radio stars of cruelty
I never have matched my sentimentality over you by—I love my cats, and bury

them more than I wld myself, give me nothing but yr loveliness you
third rate fool. This is my will. I bequeath to whatever does end the

impenetrable stupidity of man except for desire all my equipment. I have my wine
from Guyenne,

fat steaks
from Brown's, my cats

eat ground
mice sent from

New York City, there was some
indignation expressed

in the Press, why was
this waste made

but I said, "Let me alone
for the dogs are yours,

but you will have me
not always

as Cashes a shoal
Abbadia Mare

my spikenard—the Na-
dir

of me

      (the daring
       of the darling

        to imagine
        a contravention

        of the Way

        the shy one
        the sexual alone

        allowed

the expensive stones,
the arts of Europe

adorn my air, my restlessness
rustles

in silks, my beds adore
the unworthy bodies

of men

Across Space and Time

If the great outside system—species and stars—proceeds
successfully across great time, and curves to return to
stations it was once in before, and the belt of the ecliptic
slides like her cestus in months of a great year taking
25,725.6 years, what wonder that any one of us may be inflamed
with love at birth and spend a lifetime seeking to take the tail
into one's mouth, the disaster or augury of the shape and voluntas
of one's person, cast out of the combinatorial, substance the real
at the moment of birth, and one's own love *the affectiones* to cause
all of it to swarm, to know that as those beasts wheel variously
onto the point where night and day are equal one now does approach
the date at which man will pour equally from left to right out of
the pitcher of his portion of creation?

                        Hail Aquarius,
                        who is coming in

The Fish swam in on the back of Christ, by 1180 Christ was catching
the fish, by the 19th by carbon test (plus or minus 157 years) the fish
was sailing off, the Renaissance was over. Now the 2nd, and the 20th
were like (analogues) of a different source and of a different struct-
ure, presenting a small Renaissance and a great world state to rush in
to petrify the dragging years of the fish bones, limestone for a future
to come up out of the sea on, when water has again made sense out of
things

        Farewell Fish, your bones
        we shall walk on

Before either, Manes, the son of Sargon, swept out
into the Atlantic while horsemen from the Caucasus
came in with Aries to shake the dead temple world
and awake self and reason, the soft Aries people who ride
horses backward, brilliant riders who only know the back
is an engine of will to be sacrificed if the sons
will have wives, they ride on into battle until all
is divided between flesh and soul and Greece
is the measure of what they were worth

> Ram long gone,
> you won't come back
> You are hopelessly torn
> by the heels of the bulls

America, you are the end of three months of man. For the third,
which began when your head was turned, already has changed you,
you nation of Finks. Let you rule the world. You are a dead hand.
Man, in his courses, is on the other side: Capricorn is drawing
the threads

Compleynt Blossoms
April to July

the smallest flower
Bluet most
in the whole day

soft old rivers
fresh sun–hit sea
washing

marsh and granite
Peasants
and persons

sitting back on
what they do
Nobody does

what they do

The Disposition

All does draw back

from the Atlantic

There is no hope

for France

The hole

which the moon made

when it pulled out of

the Pacific

is where all people
now properly

should hang, on the edge
of Los Angeles

Paradisio
has nothing

any longer to do
with hell

A Promise

who wants action
can have it. I shall stir
myself up

I don't need to
hold back here
in the union

of forms

The Will To

all living things
transpire: love alone
transforms
desire

the measure
of the black chrysanthemum,
that nothing
is anything

but itself, is
too much: I alone
live in the sun.
How to outrage

creation

I'm With You

At 10 o'clock Haydon
had a copy, thus the one

—and note the bracketing
for the rhymes—that I was looking

at—the tourist guide to Harvard's
Keats collection says, with a rubber

nose—probably the earliest, he came home late
after the something or other—like it sounded

like midnight ha ha 10 hours
to write such a master-

piece? I'm standing there looking
into Keats's Looking

Into Chapman's
Homer?

Cross-Legged,
the Spider and the Web

with this body worship her
if necessary arrange
to sit before her parts
and if she object as she might
ask her for your sake to cover
her head but stare to blindness
better than the sun look until
you know look look keep looking until
you do know you do know

The Inadequate Orderly Simplification. But the Three Natural Units. And Only Arbitrary Constants

If you will sit in the chair of the flower it will bear you

Thy Gleeman Who Flattered Thee

as tomorrow as soon as it is day
you shall go out and lose your
friends and loves and they shall
give you a once over lightly, bare
you'll go and have to leave the
world's altogether, now made poor
seasons and thy castle gone back
to gulls the poor palace of all
life   with worms now shall you
make a stopping place and sleep
will be so coldly built you'll
scratch like those drowned sailors
mewing outside the telephonic hull
to get in, fathoms down hundreds of
miles out, the whole ocean a roof
resting on your chin

King of the Wood

King of the Dead

die in the grain
waste away
in the water

come over
the horizon
to come forth
from the earth

a ramp
is trodden for you
to Orion where he lies
with his eyes out

"Borne down by the inability to lift the heaviness . . ."

Borne down by the inability to lift the heaviness,
        and Zeus walks off with Ganymede smiling

My eyes down cast while talking at too much distance
from my friend,
        and Zeus walks on, and off with Ganymede

The days all the fall of the year and man and woman calling
for a new deal,

> and there Zeus is with his fillet tilted and the tilt
> in his eye,

> and he comes right through, snatching
> the boy as he goes

How light I am if I thought of it and hot
if I were inside one foot distance

> And the boy lets him, gaily
> with a lock falling on his captor's shoulder

> and still holding the cock he had, Ganymede
> lets Zeus walk off with him, smiling

The Lie of 10, or The Concept of Zero

decade only meaningful (decimal death. And decade only
because Aeon (or Sybil) does come in divisions of one thousand (4000
being a Platonic year—cf. Mayan value to a cycle also

10 is nothing anywhere else but handy and boring—dollars,
and tallies, and statistics etc: and overlays and creates bad psyches
and bad verse (Dante was clear 11 syllables etc—and the Alexandrine
stinks, as does 10 in English—the dead pentameter, da dum da dum da dum
da dum da dum

Also (more to the point) conceivably it has hidden the power
of 0 all the time since Gerbert got it in from the Arabs 999 or before:
0 now has the value closed, or the inertial field without metric, and thus
1 has been geometrically empowered—and closed once more got back. The
real is whole, for a change. 1 means two-facing, and negative has been
saved from minus: the Bagatto has a Back. He faces *n*.

     The Cosmos rushes in. All flows, right by my fingertip, which
doesn't raise itself. Therefore nothing enters. If I lift it, wow:
I'm changed. Nothing will be the same again. At least it won't be as it
was. It is.

     There are other consequences. One doesn't speak of them. Let
Zero spread itself in your mind........

                        ....

   ....

            ....

                    ....

  ....

            ....

The One

(all the rest is many)

"Mazdaism / has overcome / the world . . ."

Mazdaism
has overcome
the world

the war of darkness
and light
has obscured

the truth. Sexuality
is loose
by itself, and the most striking victims,

women,
are organizing themselves
to further

the light. While scratching
what is hidden, the men
stay home

in gloom, deteriorate
further
toward matter while their wives

and the mothers
of their children
think they're warriors

and Virgins of the Bulb

"In one age or other . . ."

In one age or other, if not in this
fish-time. All cup-bearers come
this evening to dinner we will isolate
ourselves in luxury and talk lie out
separated from desperation and look
from within the rose bowl the light
starting out in all directions all creation
sitting with ourselves in the glow

                          and us

ready dammed up to pour onto the streets onto them
the full flow of the golden unsacrifice of it

A 2nd Musical Form,
for Dave Young

I'm modal, how are you, Nicolas of Cusa?
Only I ain't only modal. I got numbers
in my pants, Pico della Mirandola. Why do anything
these days? The leader,

in voodoo, does many things. He is therefore
an example for us, as is magic drag drugs exhaustion excess orphic
sensation, of the ethical. All exotic instances,
or references now available, shall

be absorbed. It is possible that
one should imagine a sacrifice today
to be literally the inclusion into one's own body of
any mediocrity. What is out is impossible. There are few

who are moral. The community
must be differently based, and religious membership
hopelessly, must probably be world-wide, as Toynbee
argues the Jews, since the Babylonian Captivity, are now the first

example. How socialism (for which, necessarily, read deism)
may join—as the Fifth Wheel or Stain—the muslims
christians buddhists and hindoos over the world
is very dull but will be done. Universalization requires

pitifulnesses. An image of man,
which will meet the single incoming event which hangs
from the future sky so that imagination
may now be met, is your concern,

and mine. An imagination has
obtained. A man now does live
at a point hurrying toward the full knowledge
of the gene. The date of the arrival

has been declared: not this one,
or your child's, or his children but the one
afterwards shall know the 10,000
characteristics. And then God

will burst. We live immense
in rhythm here. The modes

which rush in now from all sides
to enable us are multimillion products

if we do produce. If we get next to
numbers. Numbers.   numbers

A Woman's Nipples Is the Rose of the World

the import, of body a hostess at lunch to my friend a representative
of the interests of the new Dutch East Indian policy her husband
having him to lunch the luxury and pace of the food talk her breasts
a part of her body not swung out there like some dish for Male
magazine bumping like you cld be hit by a house and not also the high
beautiful asses of young African girls shunting their bridal dance to
prospective lean young hunter grooms the one or two of which will
lead the new nations by getting schooling or traveling as labor union
leaders to the U S A and will turn out as American Negroes do on Mont-
gomery Alabama steps normal attractive young American men new African
nations' leaders coming down the aisles between pale white wood of
United Nations Assembly hall on a river brings or carries nothing
of itself to or away all now shining jet planes the policy of my
American friend

drop
nakedness avoid
the nude the world
says while all go to bed at
night cover yourself drop
nakedness

one drop of nakedness
redeems

                    Have lunch with love

Love is the making of bodies God made the world

The Mathematical Secret, and the Apron

weights, the secret
of gravity: when did *vehere*
cease to be operative, so that today
almost anyone is
weightless,
and sodden at once. Copan D
the time-bearers
is as august
as Chartres. There was spirit
in the world in India in the VIIIth
on the banks of the Managua
and among Arabs. It was in Europe
in the XIIth
And in America,
in 1948. But Hitler
won, with his paste
to de-ice windows

if sold in the summer:
the lust,
for the machine,
is copralagnia. One desires to enjoy
what destroys (ah the Munich
niece

"As though there were no flowing . . ."

As though there were no flowing
of opposite to opposite except
in war of classes or of explan-
ation, when the conflict is

the kickoff of love, my son falls
from Tablet Rock, trips, from his usual
overdoing, lands on his head and, I wake
in terror, his neck is broken—was

to break his neck before love's kick-off,
and the man who said his wife was his mother
also dreamt his son was his father! These
pictures on the screen, he said, foretell!

The doom of all is in our dreams—and we
fantasy! Or this man stares, out of his
healthy face, back at his fat black terrier
wife, and says stubbornly I knew the girl

was not a virgin because a dream she had
told me she knew intercourse! Or he picks
bayberries with his pants down to get the
sun, and a woman comes down a hill calling

I see your behind. She does, and reaching
down he pulls up his pants, continuing
to clip bushes on the beach! Self-play is
fantasy or show while all the time the dark

flows and in the tug of its current going
from me to me I am, either I pour, because
I am a man, the nectar into my father's
bowl, or if I were a woman I'd be forced

into darkness by the regularity to be bride
of earth when I am out of the arms of the king
of hell. These are the genes of the soul, the stories
thrown on the shadow of the wall, but the sign,

the hand with the little fingers, which can be read,
bald and flat no more than a perspective of red paint,
stuck on the wall, is about what the paw means, when
one has writ it, here was I. In this forgiveness,

we have our chance

Dylan Thomas, and Now Matthew Mead
—As He Himself, 'To Edward Thomas'

I thought of Alun Lewis
on this wet day walking,
my topcoat steaming in
from the soaking, gulls
chittering like mice

           Italian blue
which had been on the win-
dow sills now plastered on
the great double door, spoil-
ing anew the old brick cod–

          liver oil build-
ing, over my shoulder: war,
and life, and poets sweeten-
ing themselves getting close
to what their self may be, to

sweeten others, to speak
of Gweno as he did, of Aber-
dare, that she lie rustling
in his arms, that Aberdare sags
and he, serious, in He loses

his fate on Goppe Pass: a Welsh-
man to tone the syntax we have
broken, who ask no more questions
which telegraph their answer as
accidentally as pistols go off

                    the squeeks
of new-born things, the supersession
of those billion lives which now
supersede the earth, are closed doors
a man carrying his straw in speech

opens, right through the wet cloth
I am not covered by, as, on like
struck-down streets, long after,
there was in him the wild God's
uttermost intent

                    and it wasn't
his question, or how the teal
goes back and forth, nor death
as anything to do with answer so much
as he who spoke as smoke

                    heats me,
in the recollection of him and of such
who dwell on life and are cut
from under but who draw
to the tip of their tongue

                    as the sugar
is pulled out of the flower

The Yellow of the Mask

Only a few faint elements of order hint
in the yellow of the mask

Not shapes, dimensions or measurability
in the yellow of the mask

What regional quanta shall be atomized
in the yellow of the mask

God does not travel
in the yellow of the mask

I am not divisible
in the yellow of the mask

The mutual perspectives which
any such subdivision brings
into real effectiveness in

the yellow of the mask

The Hustings

under the eyes
of the human race
the great outgoing
of the open-ended
future—which sucks
us all, now. No

history which ob-
tains which equals
the wealth suddenly
in each house: Coca-
cola pimpled youth kick-
ing dead white flesh and

packages of gum fallen
from the hands of a man
in a smart brim of suit and
boy-puss old man at 30 puss
kicking his heels, one craves
the Jewish out-slope of feet

from paddling barefooted af-
ter the descendant of the only
horse pastoral persons had the
donagan ass of antiquity before
Indo-European (Aryan) horse: milky
pap-sucking race of antiquity, kind

creature of too much agricultural suns
all over the earth persons working in
fields always sunup to then falling into
a sleep too necessary to allow that dream
might get us somewhere the lie of dreams
that states and societies offered until

Denison Paper Tape (crepe) Papercraft non-
infecting shots at the Moon don't contam-
inate the other spheres elongate old lives
by passing off youth as front for socialize-
ation in the nation in the antions of the new
radical socialism seeking

the same ice-box called John Fitzgerald Ken-
nedy how plausible wealth is to ease the de-
sire that life is redeemable 100 years out of
Kilkenny: my grandfather was born
in Cork brought up in Gort my aunt was Mary
Hynes a blind poet's love Raftery's girl who

died of the con as I watched Bridgy Higgins'
brother soak his feet in mustard water in the
family kitchen with his mother sisters no father
all around his shoulder the shawl the blankey that
is not sensuality or security equal to the jer-
boa tickling the ass of the beauty of the world a

woman's ass

Ode on the Presidential Election 2

That New England and not California
and that it was Waco county votes
that not to be a bigot is to be a
Nixon: one likes persons who
don't cash in on uproar She said
to Leroi Jones sit down at the foot

of the telephone pole justice was
one's own front stoop in Ireland when
Cormac said the equity is his wool for

his grass when a neighbor's sheep had
eaten off my front yard my grandfather's bald
head whose redhair was all gone when

or was it black like my mother's hair before
her anemia which carrying me and her indigestion
both were relieved by the birth of a son Fire for
gold for life: lies sd Jones this nation is lies on
the face of the people and the Secretary of Defense
shld be George Dillon? when one saves the long view

go to the sanatorium poor John Higgins Olson me and
die of the germ of life which now can be cured you
citizen you go get yr neck get a hole in it so that
you can live long enough to outdo yourself you need
five to six years more She said what's Cuba
or China

or the Soviet Union to you poor creosote running off
the telephone pole of American life into a pool of
suffering in the same color at the foot of I am
the color of the eyes of the consciousness that
in the runoff of the race what life cries with
desire to be turned into complete analysis

of the possibility

3

Contingency danger economic comptometry produces
an incomplete dominance which is John Galbraith
(Irish? what is New England that California (San
Francisco feeling qua sensation shld 'lose' to
feeling qua effect ha ha is New England wealth
Robert Creeley

or John Fitzgerald 35th President of
Sweet Adeline? The mockery of pension funds
and gold slipping back like domestic industry to
the New Fringe of those anticommunist Nations which
by doing all do nothing but supply the Capitalist
Center of Action he sd talking the bullshit Leroi

Jones is enough to drive him his wife his progeny we
look forward to the New Frontier as though Nothing
was what the Open Ended Portfolios yes That's
what China Cuba the Soviet Union Algeria Africa one
Great Business Partnership said Ernst Zander non-Irish
not any problem of the marriage of bachelors

and Irish Maids this nation under god shall now suffer
no telephone poles no improvement of Secretary of The
Treasury the gold for the wares will go to West Germany
and barter shall cease throughout the Communist
Nations and One World Under Adlai Stevenson will
satisfy Irving Layton the Canadian Poet will win the

Douglas Wolf Prize Bank Day and Hypocritic Golf Balls on
the Irish Green on which my grandfather rolled to cool
his hot body backed up from the Steel Mill of Sexuality which
Bruce Conner relieved on Election Day with sensation qua
Effect Blow the girl down with yr Mast Head Sailor on
Election Day nail the U S Flag to her

lovely seeming ass

Political Ode 4

If one was asked by Ben Smith today on Main Street what
policy do you have poet to free John Burke from a Federal
rap have you anything to say except my name is Cinna Charles

Olson? what foreign policy old talker Charley was young Turk Johnny
Appleseed Turned to Consumption offers today to John Fitzgerald
Honey Kennedy? what do you have to say, Poet? what do you have to

say What do you have to say What do you have to say to Leroi
Jones   to Robert Duncan   to Frances Boldereff who wanted
13 years ago   to go to Russia   Robert Duncan took one look
at the Asheville North Carolina skyline about as impressive as
the penny postcard of it before Willem Dekooning called the Change
Asheville North Carolina L J Johnson of Waco Texas put John FK

in the White House by delivering Asheville North Carolina RED WILLIAMS'
Home Run to   Robert Duncan preferred it to
Barcelona   I said to Leroi Jones the Cost   She said to me Can
you afford   I said no   She said what about driving   I said walk   She
sd let Leroi sit

The Hustings

A poem written to Leroi Jones
two days after the election
of John Fitzgerald Kennedy
to the Presidency of the
United States

the future sucks
all forward, the past
has been removed

by progress   Cuba
wishes to make its own
sugar   The Soviet Union

may have already
contaminated the Moon   China
wants to destroy

the United States   and Leroi Jones
spits out the Nation
for its lies.

I do too
I stay at home   I don't go beyond
the West End

of main street I greet
the cop on the beat
in his topcoat   Ben Smith

the roommate
of the President   Joe at Tally's
makes fun of

my overshoes   The girl at the Waiting Station
says the colors
of my scarf and hat

clash I take em off
I say so she can
see me   I try to kiss my wife

as she boards
the bus and she says No
not on the street and I go off

feeling like the President
to receive the plaudits
of the populace on a day when Leroi Jones

has asked me
it seems to me
to say why

one should continue
to live
in the United States

The new President
says long range
American views   Underneath the eyes

of the human race I see nothing
but the pasty-face of young girls and boys
and the cock lifts

in my pants
to me woman's
behind. The open-ended character of the future Leroi Jones

says stay in the age
of your nation when all the new nations want
is what your own has

And with no abaissement
to the new child
of the President. France also

has been deprived
of itself   the youth of the world
wears wrist-watches. Do you believe

in the promises
of the use
of human beings? democracy

en masse on
transistors? It isn't the moon
which is in danger, it's the singleness

of the sun, which is neither soviet
nor capitalist, that it has been made into
a cheap one   Leroi Jones

my name is Charles Olson
I live at 28 Fort Square
in Gloucester Massachusetts

in the world. I would like to die
with my eyes open as I imagine
God's eyes are, and that we don't have anything,

no matter what a future, except
that we musn't be blinded
by anything. If necessity exists—

and you and I are as much examples
as crowds demanding
youth taking

and the new inventing—

I don't think there is anywhere
where I am nearer, and I wire you

Please come immediately
There is no need to worry
We shall all eat   All is here

"Pente cōst . . ."

Pente cōst   under the body of the gull flying directly over

over head,

feet retracted

sleeve

of the body

(which appears in the dream

100 days, and in the upper chamber the sea of the inside conversation,
the Collect of the persons who have that reason
to talk to their own spirit especially, with confidence, when the earth itself
bangs out its own repeated growth, meets the bird
which dives directly
into one's own breast (entered the room through the open window, sat
immediately on his right shoulder, then, resting, left the perch and struck
straight home against the man's own bird-bone chest, right through his

hands

holding off (like a quickly shaped nest) and failing the invasion of the
Holy Spirit

across the sweeping air, on tracks of purpose, the underbodies
of gulls often crying their own talk as in tracks of air overhead they
pile on to their repeated placings to feed or in the earliest light go
to their Office posts and in that light by the window pass so large are
their bodies that close (not the one who pours in to the man's breast when
Pente cōst declares itself—99 years or 9 foot 9 was the wingspread of
the Holy Spirit in the Upper Chamber

down on the pilings sit the underbodies

and they are feeding mortals but the conversation when the Speech

of the Air

the sleeve

of the repeated immortal Seal flew in to stamp fire on those men's
tongues, if they had not talked before they had the Chance, the repeated
urging possible Chance, to have that conversation thereafter
with any man,

the Dove which dove into my sealed Chest

When One Age Goes with It Suddenly
Its Errors Evaporate

The Indo-European vision said clouds
are the beginning of
mass; and that mass,
is less primitive and universal than
charge. It turns out (date
1957 and or thereafter—1958?) that
charge, which isn't so interesting to deal with in numbers,
is more interesting in the aspect instance
(which equally well has to do with numbers)
because of judgment: who is authority?
          and ad valorem therefore
              instances?
          What moral interest can you
              and to what? (I sd
          Toronto non occupada
      and was heard by Margaret
      Avison. This is only a passing
      occurrence of behavior actually

537

as against what one does mean by meteura
overcoming
all the previous debasements
of the seats so that suddenly the only interesting thing was
the seats
were empty. Now we
aren't even traveling where Wagon-lits
used to go, and don't give a damn
occupied or even that we don't even
travel. The ocean
is free again   And so forth and so Seaforth
we'll
see ya, Old Zeus and Pa this and
in our regimentals
down Queen's Highway we'll look all right
when the crowd comes to see what's
going on

"Sin is inferiority . . ."

Sin is inferiority. The mother's cooperation in the birth of her daughter

when the body which is later loved

　　　　　　　　or the soul entered that body

love begot what love neglected

　　　　　　I kiss you ass hole in the floor

May 31, 1961

the lilac moon of the earth's backyard
which gives silence to the whole house
falls down
out of the sky
over the fence

                    poor planet
           now reduced
           to disuse

who looks so big
and alive
I am talking to you

           The shades
           on the windows
           of the Centers'
           place
           half down
           like nobody else's
           lets the glass lower halves
           make quiet mouths at you

lilac moon

           old backyard bloom

The Allegory of Wealth

a Poem from America still

On the other phone, Persephone: "He crushed me,—he creased my britches,"
and the load, of the Fatman, on a body, the thought
of the bones broken in a body by weight, not by a blow,
crushed. And then, the life goes, the cry, in her voice. My soul
and I rushed to go across the space from one skyscraper office
to the other, to try to help, to see if there was anything
one might do, what the Milliardaire had done to the Maid

There Is No River Which Is Called Lethe

There is no river which is called Lethe
by the ancients. To forget
is to neglect
or to refuse to
hold on to, to fail
to get . . . they should put out to sea
without being discovered by them . . . he protected
the murderer unawares

       it is not unknown to me
       that some god led thee

What remains hidden
is also what forgetfulness
means, the unnoticed, that which hasn't
been seen yet, *lateo* the Latin is, what lies
concealed . . . lest he perish having not known . . .

       lest he perish
       having not accomplished his end

II

Thou thoughtest
to escape the gods' notice
in . . . to let a thing escape, to forget?

             that she might bear
             unknown?

to forget purposely, to pass over? He chose
to forget?

       Caught by the leg
       he went head first
       through the hole
       into the darkness
       where the waters
       roar

       & when he came out
       he needed
       those who could bathe
       him back into
       his memory and
       his forgetfulness: his wits

were sharp enough
when he was on
sugar & didn't remember
all that had happened
in the year and a half
since he had come in barefoot
out of the snowstorm

III

not to hold
not to remember
not to come by
anything got

The Red Fish-of-Bones

The Red Fish-of-Bones
the Blue Fish
& the White Fish

the eye of the Red Fish of Bones
the quick soft turning & yearning of the White Fish
toward the Red Fish of Bones,

tied as she is
to the Blue Fish who comes
over so fast to interfere

places himself majestically
between the Red Fish of Bones
& his lady.

But the Red Fish of Bones
swings the swing binds
the White Fish to the majestic

Blue Fish of Bones
and swinging wide suddenly
the consort, the White Fish of Bones

is back between
the Red Fish of Bones
and the Blue

& the three
swim in the air peacefully
again.

But for a moment
only—the Blue
Fish of the Air

swims in directly
to the eye of the
Red Fish of Bones

and the White consort
is again off alone like the moon
with Venus.

So forever they jockey
in their three estates,
the Red Fish of the Bones

with his eye for her,
the Blue Fish with her
on the same string.

& she in the middle the winsome
wife, caught in her turning
& maybe her yearning

by the Red Fish of the Bones
whose power over each
is not sufficient

against the Blue Fish of the Bones'
majesty, to bring the White Fish Lady
over across from

the delicate turning of all
in the everlasting air
of the currents

which turn
the Red Fish of the Bones
the White Fish and the Blue Fish

together in turning
and in her yearning
if it is yearning

bound to the Blue Fish
but looking
out from under his majestical turning,

at the eye
of the Red Fish turning, in his sweep,
them both but not reaching

her delicate turning,
the White Fish
of the Bones

The Binnacle

The binnacle! the
binnacle—the smallest
fluid in
the ocean: who floats
in what, thus

lends it di-
rection. What sticks
moves, within as
in the world-
ocean, we offer

considerable
resistance, men
and women making
the wind rose (sitted in
the points, not

loxodromes!) Eyes,
& lines. The gy-
res-
copes (a
       continuously driven, whose
spinning is,
so that the earth's
causes it (us) to
point
      (a wheel or disk mounted
       but also free to,

and to any torque which
would try

us

2

Each makes room for itself
and rhumb lines as it moves

To Empty the Mind

      the gracious gods
      the red man
      and the white man
      how deliberately Sam Adams parlayed
      the "Battle of Lexington" as he had

previously set up the Boston
Massacre as well as led his Mohawks
out of Faneuil Hall to bring about
the Boston Tea Party—failing to get a Constitutional
Army

and that the Reverend Jonas Clarke
in whose house the plot was laid
talked John Locke freshly
during the night thus adding
these general ideas:

at 1:30 AM the militiamen's own decision
was not to meddle with those British soldiers
coming down the pike

to leave us
to our own concerns
thus were the parts
of all the parts of the bodies
of the Federal cavalry troop
—Lieut. Fetterman's command—left around
the landscape on and about the dun hills by
Fort Phil Kearny

(for Ed Dorn

What Had to Go

set fire to the City, burn the City down

start the fire in the top floor

of the oldest building,

bring in a suitcase to be sure

you have the materials,

watch your fingerprints and escape

notice by mingling

with the other occupants of the building

when the cry is 'Fire'

from that fire in that one building the whole City

will be burned

it is required, & you shall know,

suddenly, how corrupt

all relations are between

fire departments   building owners   insurance

companies   police   politicians   and

building inspectors   an impossible

web of fact you cannot place your finger on

to say where it begins or who is

culpable

and you will know this only after

you have been landed on the top floor

to set the fire, then you will have

for the first time concern

about your fingerprints

and how you will get down out of there

and that the corruption is true,

organized and distributed

throughout the system

you set fire to the City, burn the City

down

How Things Change

I came back into my own house
to find my wife to take her out
for a drink, and oysters.

I had been in Ireland,
and had thought to stay there
with my friends and have the drink

and oysters but had come back swiftly
to the old house, Worcester, Norman Avenue
lightly desirously quietly, rather to do

this thing than that and had almost
missed the house it had been so changed
the three–decker Norman Bel Geddesized

one corner from top to bottom
sliced off, the roof pulled in
at the edges and the stairways

turned into modern bus or airplane
or ship passageways up the front stairs
as I went I thought why hasn't she

swept them, with the idea we were leaving
the house but then I thought why should she
the Olsons had paid rent so many years

no matter how they left it it had earned
its way. And at the top of the stairs

I realized she was there from her coat
in the hallway and for me to get in
to the apartment there was a narrow squeak

of a door more like a chute for baggage
of an airplane or a mail chute than
a door and I had a moment of suffocation

from my size, that a little bigger & I could never
have made the space. So she wasn't even
asleep as I had figured because no lights

were on & I had the idea we'll make love
& then go out and have whiskey
and oysters

The Americans

the cosmologist says
what ∧ constitutes a society:
an assemblage of atoms
makes the thing go

why the social stinks
—and each American stinks—
is that it is an inadequate
number of cells they are,
        sitting in a room,
to constitute an organism

they aren't cooked
and ruled by information

The Americans

what the cosmologist meant by what constitutes
a society, they are not. The pursuit of happiness
they have achieved. "Christmas lights" said John
Wieners, they and their children after them
have no havens ahead, all 18th century dreams
accomplished in the present. Thus forming units
which are not organic: they sit in a room
each one a certain insufficient number of cells
to be carbon or vital but as such wreaths
you could play horseshoes with, toss them
socially upon Thomas Jefferson. Or John
Adams. It's a social which is missing:
—"I'm on the top of the United States Building
taking a sunrise," sd my son.

The Snow

the snow falls eternally down
into the sea and lovers
rain kisses on each other's
    water is black in the snow

falling in water there is no end
to snow down as up
there is no end to the falling in love

of men and women
        the snow falls in the water so

a million is as snow
children fall out of procreation so
new lovers come to sit on boulevards
and lie on each other in front seats while window-wipers
        call attention to the fact
        that they are there

the snow falls
in the night
the automobiles of lovers
build up their batteries now

they go home to supper
water is black in the snow

"17th century men / who founded this land . . ."

17th century men
who founded this land/
                20th century persons all over the place,
                so many it isn't yet China or India or

masses of human beings thus creating an outside equivalent of
the condition of the seed-water- mass of the soul and creation

American society at least, right now, is a half of something
or nothing, fast solving quantity by establishing wealthy

cell-blocks of men and lovely wandering women delicious manne-
quins of the scene a vicious soft potentiality probably more

rigid than the graceful physical looks of all of the young, male
and female

until they are more and thus once again are thrown on each other
in the close space of hovels and Little Diomedes of shacks called

flowering igloos (made of mud and hard stone and heated by snow
and cooking out of almost their own fat and pleasure of the soup

of human being:

                    avast avaunt anoint you witch-weather come out
                    little children into the half-light half-life of

those who are living as though carbon-
life was the measure downhill elegant slope

                    of soap and hygienic water
                    o the artifactual persons the factual

                    balls of twine in which sd half-persons
                    a full nation of same are balls of metal

                    all one music ridden talk-talk go-go ba-
                    loney

down the metal stream goes the heart of thee earth pfpf and runs over
all Herculaneums/ great moist trees only could have covered

New Hampshire/ so shall the blossoms re-
appear

Examples—for Richard Bridgeman

re-entry, without pillow, dear and the pieces
all melted to drops some passing as carriers, motors
from the air port to Springfield, hubby darling, otors
for fences to drain off the mucilage

                          and let the
life-giving fluids re-enter the evident? cell we
dance? cell we?

Off high in heaven observing the uselessness,
the cracks in Charles' Dish (cf. Callimachus)

                       to the Lady said, "Muse,
the ditch you will always have with you" as he *terere*
down through the transmission wall

Bursts in the teeth the old Cosian drops
bought a net and drew up in it aw gee pa when
do we turn around? in this huge building isn't
there a place to pee? Signed off then
when the cushion at his back flew off
into so many violet river-bottoms

On the Shore

choke cherry blossoms on the Back
shore. The streets
all end up in distribution
Go to the Metropolis
wah wah

women in the automobiles
going out to dinner look over
in high heels from the hot top
the scene around the restaurant

awake or we will break
and you will lose me
wah wah I love you better than you'll ever have it
so good before

go to the centers of the power
wah wah
there isn't any nature
in distribution
there isn't any nature on the shore

Hymn to Proserpine

Each red seed bursts
with a liquid nested

as they are as rooms
of the honey-comb break
in the whole mouth as
a sea
      a halo
of fecundation and around his head
there did spring

clothed in a sac
born in drear December
just after the dead sun
              lingered
a moment to be born

all creation watched
as she put her hand out
for the single flower

and in the moment he
in his chariot spun
as a gore
        tore her
with him into
the shades

and off in the night
on the other side
of the earth
one woman
heard
her caw, "A rape!
A rape!"

but only she
and no one else
not even
the girl's
mother who wandered

thereafter
looking
for her daughter
who was lost
below

Shang Dynasty Oracle Bone 2 Say

neat person
make more uproar
possible

"some partial cloudiness will flow locally . . ."

some partial cloudiness will flow locally, mostly
today the great god Zeus opines

his son Apollo his brother the sea
and Black Zeus who is the earth's

God motor man can look up
and in this grapevine corner imagine

a line comes out of them, to him
he is a T to the great sky god

the sun is only his own activity
the sea the sky and the earth

are his father-uncles, he is the son
and nephew who has time

to recognize
his own

To a Poet Who Read in Gloucester Before the Cape Ann Historical Literary and Scientific Society

There can be no anniversary
and you are your own ignored
adversary, blushing
in your sighted eyes

God is substantive and falls
ahead, authority
is as earned as skill, will
is a principle as well as
a means your nose
is out of line with the cleft
in your chin

A snippet
is a route of occasion
and ladies stand in front of Kresges
their French poodles the subject
of conversation but poems by others
will not walk your own
lashing them as though they were
Mexican hairless

The whippet
who came with you
has also no Vaucluse
and bent bodies hang without use
on old vines
slovenly bellies
or unmonked heads

The soul is a body as long as God's

In an Automotive Store

which is like a stock room anyway
a homely City girl and I

flirted, that is I skated
around in front of her as she stood smiling
too openly

on the other side of the counter
from me. A messenger
came in among the clerks

directly to me
with a piece of rubber
obviously from my car,

a small piece of metal
tieing it together. The police
it seemed had come into possession

of it and wanted me,
the man said,
to come and identify

or take the car away. When suddenly
it struck me
the car was in Connecticut

and wasn't here in the City
at all. As I went out
a salesman,

in the hall which was the entrance
of the store and was like the hall
in a rotunda

was putting up a table
like at a Fair

of new automobile
electrical and battery
items

and my son
had grabbed hold
and wouldn't let go

of these connections
and I had to tear him
literally by ugly strength alone

away from them, ogling meanwhile
the salesman in apology
for this son of mine

who was such a willful
kid and I lifted him
like stiffly up and down

and bore him
out the door

"It is a nation of nothing but poetry . . ."

It is a nation of nothing but poetry
The universities are sties   John Wieners
has suffered the most   Catholics
have a shame of the body   The soul
lives in the body until it escapes   Main Street High Street Court
where my auto
threw itself over
the crosswalk   The sign read

your body
is to drop
its load
                    Your body
is a holy
thing
                    Your body
is a wave
of Ocean
                    Your eyelids
will reveal your soul, your mouth will
                                        your clothes will fall
as you do

"in Wiro language . . ."

                    in Wiro language
                    the son (his mother
                    is Zemelo) was
                    dio(s)nuos

a whole mix-up
of part-men and half-god
sons (twins and mothers
either raped by Poseidon or
by their uncles thus giving
birth to children they are
ashamed of, & either kill

or purposely lose
on some mountainside

start replacing the old jum-jam wind-jam
of the father-gods going around
having children

and his funny brother,
King of Hell,
who doesn't have any
of his seed multiplying
himself

who doesn't even seem
to get around much
in fact has to hide
the one time he does get
the bride he wants,

behind
the irresistible
flower he causes to grow
right up in Kore's
face
        the moment she put her hands out
to pluck it up out of its roots
when she did break it off the Earth
opened a hole and he came out,
in his chariot,

quite handsome were his horses,
and the chariot was gold,
and he was able,
in this specific & special circumstance
to steal Kore for his Queen

even as it was he had to trick out
the capture, in order to make it last,
by getting her to eat a pomegranate,
the seeds of which (? or what reason

contaminated her as any longer,
thereafter, a child of earth
alone she belonged then
somehow somewhat to an underregion
which got called Hell but which precisely
was her husband's realm
                              (as Heaven
had been Heaven's, his was
his

            Hades is
a most different man than
his ramp brother, of Heaven
or his lascivious uncle-brother,
of the sea, part also his likeness
especially by way of horses
they both, in difference from their brother,
have power by—or in his 'uncle's
case use for guise: when Kore's
mother was passing
in lament all over
the earth Poseidon
(again) desired & sired
as horse on Demeter who switched
to mare twin-children who were themselves
horses

            but Hades,
that once, breaking out
from the undersoil, hiding
in the roots of the hyacinth,
behind the flower's single

occurrence,
earned a bride he had to share
each part of each year
with her mother and the light
of upper earth

        and Kore
was a barren bride, if
one ignores the other incest legend
that it was she with whom her father
(his brother) lay

        and she begot
the son who was to be the father's
(his brother's) equal: Pluto

or Hades or Orcus or Hell
fell?   who is this King
Brother of Kings
of Heaven and of Sea,
black brother weak brother
'awful' Hades, unseen?

(when Demeter
went wild
at the marriage
of Peleus

and lay in the mud
of the new-turned field,
with Iasion,

and Zeus saw
the mud on both of them
and slew
Iasion
there in her face and at the marriage
feast,

the child she bore
was Plutos   (the series

of the seeds by which Hell
has names
are these:

                'adein, the King
Unseen; Kore his Bride, barren,
and a 3rd part of each year
on Earth; Kore surely the daughter of Demeter
by Zeus, Hades' brother,
but Hades himself if Pluto probably
his own bride's brother—as she
may well have been the mother
of a 'lost' son greater than
Zeus the Father!

"Shut in   kept off . . ."

Shut in   kept off
in their ships
fair, and safe enough
            the daughters of Ocean only
            dispassionate
The pitiless
will of man
to know his whereabouts

be stiff,
and dour,
or be of water
                 (the children of the sea)

Alion
geron the old One
was unlying
                    3000
daughters   Ocean
had

Keep back stay off
each to his own

there is no need to extend
if you are not one of the children
the children of the sea

Shoot em & bring em
down   subvert
                 the Enemie

Go all the way   by foot path and by whatever other means
of transport you may require,

and pemmican will do,
for food, safe in water or in ice or left
for years where you may choose
to hide it, to leave it for yourself

there is possibly no reason to hurry
back   you may not wish to do
any other thing but this which you are doing,

and when you do
come back
if you ride some one of us

will be the first to report seeing
the thin red sign of the pennant seen
up against the sky on the top of your lance
as you approach us,
having been away so long

"there they were . . ."

there they were
on my grandfather's
bedroom wall, then my
bedroom wall—the Runaway
Match, the chaise flying
in the foreground looking
for repair at the nearby
Inn mechanics rushing
to unwheel the wheel & get
the new one on while Pa
off now in the distance
not too far away, by a bend
coming into the view is whacking
his poor horse to get on dear dear
daughter run off

with whatever this
dashing young fellow
was who on that litho
stood
        holding the horses
rampant whipping with his arrogant

look the workers below while daughter
with arms thrown out in panic
turned to watch Father
coming on
                    sd mechanics
successfully
mounting the new wheel & clearly
despite the Girl's concern
the picture on my grandfather's wall
promised

the taste of the subject was
the Winning Pair

"I saw, from under Him . . ."

I saw, from under Him, the beginning
of the web of God

Even to the exordial colors necessary
for a father to be a male

Ferrini—I

A Study in Ideal Form

Into the pool at 5 AM to freshen
the new year Child (Dewsnap-Ferrini
was his name

Over the nearest hill
the day in rose arises
and, at night, Venus

in white, tell-tale
of evening the woman's song
accompanied by a bell

                        French woman's voice
as women on a hillside in Greece
rent Pentheus

and a bell counts two prime numbers
out of which arose the World—the World

is composed of two prime numbers, Alpha
and Epsilon

Formed into two
the organ
of the eye

        scoptophilia
        will make the new one
        blush

while at the window
in the dawn a woman
in all the beauty
of her naked body
looks out and does not know
the man behind her in the bed

regards her in a burst of joy

Welcome,
the morning of the World

The unceasingly gentle One
has come to put his arms around you

Dawn fell
and in the next instant
already pregnant with the boy
espied another was to the liking of her eye
and took him down upon her as the crow
set to watch her in her loveliness
flew up helpless in the light
to warn his master who already knew
and said why did you not, white crow,
tear out the lover's eyes? and turned him black
and flew himself to kill
the mother of his child
and quite forgot
until she lay before him cold
that this was she whom he
had found so much
and in her grave cut out
his unborn son

The eye
shall hold us
to the course

the eye
which holds us in the mind

Apollo's son by Dawn
he who wouldn't marry many women
but got them all by child

a kiss beneath
an oak-tree
the cherry lips

rub her belly
she liked you to kiss
her rosy tits

then ground the body
in a selfish dance
in the middle of the room

in the night

Or his own Boeotian mares tear
Glaucus into pieces
and both men and women shriek aloud

hysterical or
he implored loudly
so that the house was full of his voice
as the air was with his hands
his hands were the healing plants
of his body
the actions
of his days
the preventative
of his troubles
the carvings
of his hours
and minutes
all which was not expelled
all which was formally kept
that which did count
as epsilon
in the creating
of the world
a epsilon

Purity
is an intensifier
not a state

    The eye sees
    instantly—not a delay

    Alpha,
    and Epsilon

        the sound
        is immediately
        on the air

              alpha
          and *epsilon*

nothing need be spit out
as though it were a seed
passed in the urine

                pursing the ass
                or the mouth

                        the ideal
                creates the fluent organ
                or it is not worth the thought

and the child suffers
as a man he can say ai–ee

                if in his time he chooses
                or because he finds out

                            His friend said
that he saw him walking
on the opposite side of the street
but he didn't stop him
or ask him if he wanted a lift
because he noticed
that he was walking talking
to himself
with his hands

                If he should find out
                what his hands are

II

an organization turned toward two worlds at once

                                        requires

a cognitive means which supplies both motive and

                                        direction

originary and essence

                wash yourself

in the pool to begin the morning

                so that you may know what it is that you are doing

in the latter part

of the day

                Dewsnap-Ferrini

was born of a pretty mother

at 5:30 of

a frosty morning

                and he was lucky

                for it was after the turn

of the dirty year

the dirty turn

of the year

when those who are born

when the sun has faltered

and not gone down and has not come back

who are held in the year like the crack of a vise

the crack of a vice

time is in

Saturnalia

all holly and anything else

which protects throw in

for the birds who can't get food

against the unholy things which are abroad

in this desperate season

Dewsnap–Ferrini

was born in a pretty picture

on a hospital bed

danger, the snap-shot

danger the year

blue-gray the eyes

blue-gray the hair

The lover
who knew her best
remembered
50 years later
what it was like—something terrifying,
he said,
about her embrace

elemental, archaic.
She was completely amoral
and yet very pious, a vampire
and a child. And Nietzsche,
when he met her: I am greedy
for her kind of souls. In the near future
I am going to rape one.

"I shall never be faithful
to men." And her husband
who knew the only way to get her
stabbed himself, and for 43 years of marriage
never once knew her as his wife

                              Virgin of the

         bad magazines

                    Sacher-Masoch

         writes you up

                    Dewsnap-Ferrini,

         in your care

III

                         Hines-Orpheus comes floating
                         down down the good path-way

                         wants Heaven without Hell
                         good Hines-Orpheus

                         plays on his flute
                         or does not believe

                         or makes music of the squeak
                         of her hair

                         oh where is the good mother
         who will be the bosky girl?

he went into the sea

to get the grass

he swam down from the sun-drenched waters

at the beach-side,

                  Glaucus did

and the Bermuda fisherman

who speaks an excellent English

and as interesting in his pitch and tone

as a native of San Frediano,

has a good ear

                  fished up Glaucus,

found the grass-eater

in his net

Freud who did not know the Germans were

officialdom—and did not therefore properly

interpret dream. Co-kings, Hines-Orpheus and

Dewsnap-Ferrini: Dewsnap means impartial

beauty. We rule, beyond the mares' hooves.

IV

       If I have used
       the serpent's herb
       I have done it
       as Polyidos
       to give life

       And having done it
       as Polyidos likewise,
       because there is good reason
       why we shouldn't know,
       spit into my mouth

       For the day,
       which is that heifer-cow
       that changes her color
       three times,
       from white to red,
       and red to black

       and whoever can say
       as Polyidos did
       what that heifer-cow
       is like, can find Glaucus,
       the Child-Raisers said,
       and restore him even if dead

turn the eye
stem outside
don't look harmful
once more

          make only one announcement:
          I am half a dog-rose

"As the shield goddess, Mycenae . . ."

       As the shield goddess, Mycenae
the Baubo of the belly is a faceless thing
behind which beats a clock like a bomb
power enough to blow the world apart

womanhood, is power enough to blow
the world apart. Let this atomic furnace
be said and shown as such, instead of these
cute demure peddle-pushers and slippers
who don't even seem to know
the 100-blossom thing which makes
their engine go to work, to fall for it
and reach out with both their hands
and toy with it to see
what they can make it do

       So let the woman known as Baby Doll
come on, who stands before you with a single story,
and good enough it is to tell, that here's the body
of a woman thrown from birth alone to entertain
the boys, the freshness of those things,
growing out of the side of her like mountains,
twin-breasted mountains, and showing them off,
manipulating them with her hands squeezing them
as though they'd shoot berry juice,
or a man could get caught in them and lose
his life, the pleasure of the demonstration of those
                      hugenesses
by herself, that she has them grown out
on her there, with all the rest of her
    flat body and simply legs

falling away below—nothing to it
but to come out from behind the curtains
leading with one breast alone,
                    letting it show first
in the glory of it and then following
so the fullness of the thing,
                    the mountain itself,
will fall in gasp upon men gathered
to see the wonder of it

and let their hands slup up her legs
as though this below was the sideshow
to the main attraction she was billed for
the dusted twat a make-up table
to the glories of the pillows and the windows
upstairs

This is the Mycenaean shoved up against the
beasts, holding them under and by her side they
paw the air

"Snow White was always waiting . . ."

Snow White was always waiting for The Prince
And that was the story of Snow White

Snow Red was the one, wasn't she, who was always
pricking her fingers on the needles
she sewed with, and leaving the drops behind her
all over the place?

or wasn't that actually how Sleeping Beauty
went to sleep, and the Prince who did wake her

>   had to arouse his horse
>   to go over a thicket
> which surrounded the whole Castle
>   like a thorn apple hedge fence
> in one leap, and wasn't

>   at all looking for anything and simply
> went in there and idle
>   like somebody poking around
>   sticking their nose into anything
> simply that it does lie around and looks unused and

>   and covered
>   with stuff, ran into

the girl up on the top floor

where she had fallen, straight

from the bite of the sewing machine?

"I had had / a beetle . . ."

I had had
a beetle
on my leg

I must have taken
the leg
off

For the beetle
is now in the air
way up above

my head head

"I met my Angel last night . . ."

I met my Angel last night on Cinvat Bridge
or maybe it was the corner of Reservoir
Road. He was me allright, and I went
right ahead with what I was going to
do, counting him in by asking him,
even though I did think he was blind,
to take this train trip which ran
down this river into the City and,
I had been told, the scenery was
something one ought to see. He easily
agreed and we took the train at the
corner but thereafter the scene was
his, when, inside the train he got
a passenger beside me into shooting
craps with him and was quite clear
that the place to shoot was the aisle
and looked over his shoulder at a
possible conductor in the car behind
as though even if the conductor coming
through might object what was that equal
to doing what was called for straight and
in the open? I observed then, as he stood
there, that he was not the bum I also
thought he was, that even if he seemed
worn and used he maintained himself
and was provably able.
It was again his ability which was
supported later by two men when we were
back at the corner where the restaurants
were (the trip itself never did get to
the scenery) when he and they insisted
against me that a restaurant there had
good food. The two, who were at the moment

eating cheese-cake had much to say about
the cooking, in supporting his opinion,
mentioning specifically the fried partridge
or pheasant penises. My Angel was standing like
a counterman or short-order cook himself,
behind the counter, and at that moment
demanded that I return him
a fish I was holding
as I sat there too.
    The last challenge
was of another sort and it was then I
learned he wasn't blind at all. I was sneaking
for my son a coupon was in a book or it was
part too of the fish, on which was written,
as he pointed out, a name which could have been
his or mine or my son's and which was his claim:
that the coupon belonged in place on the fish
and not torn off as I had torn it along its
perforation—and in addition the name
gave it the ownership he then and there
for us as well as for himself demanded.
I was thus twice refused, and he was himself
three times revealed, and it was clear each
time that he well had himself in care, and
that in his judgement, as of both the restaurants
and the coupon I was wrong and he demanded back
the fish—and name we shared.

"Love is the talk . . ."

Love is the talk
of the organs
to each other
in another
person

"His house / in the branches . . ."

His house
in the branches of
Iggdrasil

      the coral plant
on the bottom of the

pool by the rock I was levered over full tilt
to watch a very small crab make

the good sized mussel wave
in the water while

on a rock in the water busy
barnacles were opening the slit in their horned eye

& letting out the fibres they
use like right Greenland whales have

on the fences in their mouths

A Part of the Series on the Paths

(fr. *West*)

on your feet like paws   and if a board might squeak
on your ass, and with your eyes tripping
any ambush   but before that the mind
already had worked out the next
problem, the city
is a false forest   there is no need
for your care   the darkness
is not real   there is no space
for the day, day has no room
night cannot sit in its silence
                              death the faceless
does not have the chance to meet you
except in the forest glade

"The personality and dourness of winter . . ."

The personality and dourness of winter

As the snow lay throughout the woods it begins

in December travels down between the two Lakes

piles itself in corridors North and South blowing

from the West into the Gulf road balding the fields

at the top of the ridge to clutter the passage of the road

Then the house part to the east is the possible place

to be in and all the East Hill is a platform of angles

in the snow

For Mac Hammond

Parallelism therefore is in fact Black Stone to Footstool of
the Heavenly Heart

round and round the round we go inverting
the swifter silent sun

& the modes of equivalences solely the variants the sd

poet or individual of the poem capable of, approaching the construct?

language the language of both of the feet of God

in appreciation for his Warsaw address on
POETIC SYNTAX, 1960

"—the End of the World / is the Turn-About . . ."

—the End of the World
is the Turn-About:

  After you go backward   After you go backward
after you reach the limit of Ocean,   the Vulture
which picks on Prometheus' liver   (vulcan's artificial
animal–creation, none of Vulcan's inventions
are anything but machines

"Color . . ."

Color is image

2

Color is reflective (the opposite of
                                    primary
        Color should come from
                                    somewhere

        It follows. It is (grammatically)
demonstrative.

3

Color is not the noun or the verb,
the subject or the action. It is
the effect. It fixes
the statement. A statement
requires it. You could not have a statement
without color.

4

        Light is not color, color is not sign.
Color is not social, color is not recognition. Color
is the evidence of truth

it is a very trustworthy thing,
color

Color is the Fruits
or the Four Rivers of Paradise

—William Dorn, 1597

'West'

I've been absorbed by the subject of America all my life. One piece of it has been what the enclosed hopes, in that sense, to set down. Actually as in fact it was reading and playing it out as a child in redoubts we imagined trenches and trees on the foot of Fisher's Hill we were sure had been a part of earlier Indian wars the books of James Altschuler—and I am now convinced there are indeed only "three" American stories—that which was 1st, the one Cowpens actualized (the "line" which the Proclamation of 1763 made the Appalachian Ridge)—and then the West. So I have here a much larger story than would appear.

1966

593

as of Bozeman

Red Cloud (DAB) succeeded
left conf. Laramie 1866 June
& for two years, inc. Fetterman
massacre (Dec 1866) &
at the Wagon Box fight (Aug
1867 (also attack on Hayfield
party near Fort C.F. Smith)
he won: govt, by treaty of 1868,
closed trail & 3 forts abandoned

———————

2nd Ann.
cf. Report of Board of Indian
    Commissioners . . . 1870 (1871)
on visit to Washington

———————

for biblio, cf. next page—
was chief of the Oglalas, the
largest tribe of the Teton Sioux
father: Lone Man; mother: Walks as
                    She Thinks

At same time also investigate
Red Cloud's friendship with
    Othniel C. Marsh, Am.
    paleontologist (see DAB)

(all by
    W. J. Ghent (?)

———————

Was the Bozeman Rd to the gold
fields of Montana??
(cf Ghent
on Spotted Tail)

Gold disc. Black Hills 1874

Bozeman fr Georgia—gold seeker

<u>Crazy Horse</u>

(1849–1877
28!

Two Poems

(fr 'West'—possibly)

men are only known in memory
Red Cloud's mind invested Fort Phil Kearny
and produced the careful form of Fetterman's
troop's dispersion upon the landscape of
those rounded hills creating the area

on which he left their parts, and caps
and uniforms and designed thereby
any other event such as (with Crazy Horse
was it in command Yellow Horse Young
Bull) the removal of Custer and
his several persons in an easy
lay-out. There isn't (after the small
incitement of the scene those yards
was it almost out from the Fort on
Bozeman's gold road) any longer,
thereafter, a connection to agricultural
time. Grant as a supplier and his
Southern counterpart's extraordinary ability
to disengage—one with Washington
as his personal mold the other with none
and so more raw to war, neither Indian
nor inheritor of a measure to abide by
U S Grant is a spasm of time

                                    (Apr,
                                    (LXIII)

The Pedens, who re-walked the trails, hobbyists
or their own model & predecessor who re-walked from Salt
Lake—or then one jumps to DeVoto hauling & lowering
teams up over & down from the Wasatch Range
where the difficulties for the Donners ate 'em like the bites
of the bug which got 'em soon enough, poor
World Travelers of the late
New World, the assembláge
of Californiay—·there was only one way
in any way to arrive where the West was when
she had run out was by sea around or
if German in entourage like observers and watercolorists,
of the Civil War: Port Orford or the slash
country back of it until you get east enough to the comfort

away from the brutalization of the Pacific
Orford is a peninsula none try but Cyclops
who are themselves nothing but caked-eyes
like Salt Lake north where Fitzpatrick crossed
on his mule & with his Indian wife frightful
places lie passively in Edons on Pacifica
no good yet hubris and hybrids or eyelids
against bad light no hope for Sutter slicked
Doner only Sauer—and Duncan who trot-mocs
in with the light of seance and the golden light
of those paintings he knows what the dream
may be carries a fowling piece like the possible
World Travelers imagine Duncan in doe-skin
and with his fowling piece—between
those romantic paintings and not Peter Rabbit Robert
Duncan in fringed jacket against that bad sunset
from all across the intermediary space,
                                        the East
doesn't get home beyond
Sacramento

West 4 and 5

Drummond Hadley

TWO POEMS

THE RANGE

What these sounds were
there among the rocks and trees

when I did not know
in the mountains,
and while I came down
and asked of them,
they stayed
and returned out of me,
to the places
where they had been.

PSYCHE

that each object knew the way for Psyche
as if it were a part of way itself,
her self a tower into sky
and Tartarus which led her there.
What she was before
this winged creature is not known.
She must have lain
as though in the wet earth
she were a place of cave,
before what was within her.

                    5

        Soul, and Psyche, and Animus (Will
        : a man's life to be a continual
        Allegory
                    all which is and happens,
        that one brings about, crushing
        like a herd of frightened elephant anything
        under foot, passing as I did
        on the back of the Elephant altogether puzzling
        to me how we did go between trees through
        everything as a will passed through any obstacle
        he was as anagogic visions in his power to
        pass,
            the Elephant
        on whose back I also was slim

West 6

probably the most important person I met in Vancouver
—and most important
conversation
and event
        so many miles
  up over the Pacific Ocean
    looking down on
    whether those were coots
    or sea gulls
    in
    the evening
    water

    Coolidges present too
    and Rosemary
    Margaret
    did not walk out
    (why not?)

        and Diana Hadley

    gave me her pink sweater

  as I also was wearing Drummond Hadley's

  trench coat (?)

(and who read that night

was it Duncan?)

    that marge

  of the few feet make the difference

  between the West, and the Future

Robin Blaser,

and Duncan

and that dream

    at the same time as I was writing
    about the distance
    between Sacramento
    and the old old West

Robin Blaser and Mountain Meadow Massacre

        one lone Indian
    fishing in the river at the bottom of
    the Barranca del cobre

            charles olson, March 4
                (XIX-LXIV

From The Song of Ullikummi

Translated from Hurrian and Hittite at
Wyoming (N.Y.) in March, 1964, and read
at Spoleto 1965 to honor the presence of
Mr. Ezra Pound

    fucked the Mountain
    fucked her but good   his mind

sprang forward
and with the rock he slept
and into her let his manhood
   go five times he let it go
         ten times he let it go

     in ikunta luli she is three
   dalugasti long
         she is one and a half
   palhasti wide. What below she has
up on this his mind sprang upon

When Kumarbi his wisdom
he took upon
his mind
   he took his istanzani
   to his piran   hattatar
   istanzani   piran daskizzi

Kumarbis -za   istanzani piran hattatar
daskizzi
       sticks wisdom
unto his mind   like his cock
into her
iskariskizzi

   the fucking
of the Mountain
   fucked the mountain   went right through it and came out

the other side

the father of all the gods
from his town Urkiš
he set out
and to ikunta luli
he came

and in ikunta luli a great rock
lies
sallis perunas
kittari   he came upon
What below she has
                    he sprang upon

with his mind
                he slept
with the rock   kattan sesta
with the peruni

      and into her misikan X-natur
andan his manhood
                flowed
into her

And five times he took her
nanzankan   5-anki das
and again ten times he took her
namma man zankan   10-anki dās

Arunas
the Sea

"Memory, Mind, and Will . . ."

for Ed Dorn, and with kudos
for Leroi Jones

Memory, Mind, and Will
: politics,
                    make money
                & assert
              yourself use
            public service use
          the citizen carry out
        public policy sell
      your ideas to the tax payer and
    you can vote in America without paying
    any taxes viz
there are men with ideas
who effect

            public policy via
          politicians including
        leaders of service unions
        who can tie up distribution

there is size
to Union
which is different
than size or
more of same, either of which

in the present state of these States
are no longer as interesting as

the admission of politics

"In celebration of Mitos . . ."

        In celebration of Mitos,

and Krateia

        looked at by Protolaos

and Pais

    the Younger

        Kabeiroi

all the snowfall differentiable

on my overcoat's sleeve

          Blizzard

"the unfinished (raw) hero . . ."

the unfinished (raw) hero—un-
civilized intolerable
Odin—Osiris genuine
sons of the experience truly
dismembered and
remembered reassembled
and placed in power—flew off like an eagle
to carry to heaven
what belongs there

             even Zeus
only knows how
to treat his mother
in a way becoming to
her nature

                       by the instruction
                       of Apollo's priest,
                       Plutarch, March 10th, 1964

Buffalo Ode

As Sir Saltonstall ran over
the Atlantic waves carrying the virus
cut down Arbella Lincoln,

and out on the Western plains Bill Gratwyck
the First, skidded into a stop
at Lake Erie's shore almost burning
his hooves off when the rail
ran into the end of the land,

Tycoonery had a wedding in 1904

Section 2

the Holland Land Grant troubled no one, wolves' pelts drew
5 £ up through 1830, and so one does have to look
at Dutch American History as prior and conceivably equal
in social power swung onto International Affairs
at a date early enough to raise two important questions:
the investment of the Hudson Valley
we do know all about but exactly what the teaching
of wampum value to the Pilgrim Fathers does betoken
of earlier sea-coast venturing by Dutch maritime knowledges
let us look in J G Ryans or Mahoney's Documents of Early New York History
to determine what it did mean to begin this Empire State

Section 3

a dog with a head at each end
the Erie Canal made New York State

and Dutch patroons refused
what Philadelphias had to do

the Albany men had such a good deal
up north at Montreal

so it was proper by William Jennings Bryan
for William Gratwyck I

606

to fly in here by jet
and propel Niagara power
in railroad even maybe shredded wheat
to make the new end of the dog
be head as at the other end
of Hudson River was the city
which even then had not
become Metropolis

draw the lines the Master said

and Massachusetts men sold Dutchmen via Robert Morris
the go of infested Genesee and mouth of Buffalo
Creek where Senecas had been pushed until
Transit Road was the line of future Democratic Power
on this end of the dog   Paul Fitzpatrick State Committee Boss because
Buffalo was worth the State's electoral vote by cancelling
the Finger Lakes and so forth all through the middle of the State

      from Chatauqua country on
      to the Bronx line

Connecticut farm houses dotting
      with Greco–Roman elegance
      right out of Asher Benjamin's
      builders book and gingerbread
      and Victorian as good until
              1904

RR
section 4

New York City was the mart of the State
until the crookedness of the telegraph
reporting the sway
of the losses at Antietam
allowed
such men as Daniel Drew
to make money directly out of blood

previous to that moment he like the Astors
had been butchers or drivers literally of meat
to feed the city originally
from the hills of Connecticut or Vermont down then
from Upper New York State via Fordham Road where Drew
invented watered stock by filling his cattle by
giving them salt and then
he went to the Pennsylvania and there
the Allegheny West went open: Cowpens
of the Mountain Ranges

a piece of the song of the white men

up Lansing went, to Chagrin Falls
just fer enough from the Hudson
to go all the way,   the chaise

the choice out of 28
                on any New York estate

Cowpens—and Gurty, Doones and
Double Men all holed up, at
Indian Town, New York: from
New Haven etc and Brant
and Johnson as the French
had whacked the town, to shake it
loose, to get it off
the Indian and White man's
back-country, the
City-Without, the Hole-in-the-Scheme, the Refuse-
Refuge, the "Paris"-Sewer, the
Otsego

"My belly / sounds like an owl . . ."

My belly
sounds like an owl
hooin on a bough, my shirt

hanging on a chair
makes a hand, with one leg
for the littlest finger,
on the floor. My mind,

rattling at this hour, is as empty, and full of such things

609

"like a foldout . . ."

like a foldout

———————————

as against a bas-

relief. <u>No</u>

relief <u>no</u>

eternity <u>no</u>

story no

<u>Transcendence</u> —the ideal

in the occurrence without any raising

of the issue. <u>Or</u>

the person: the Veil of each

undone.

By what <u>is</u> done. Follow me,

said Epimenides

<u>Said Epimenides</u>
———————————

610

"barley or rye . . ."

barley or rye
blue and white green
after the soaking
of winter snow

      King of the Ravished Bride
      Black One-Eyed King
      who lay with my wife
      in the sleeping bag
      on the living room floor

            gone off my own Virgin Daughter
            seen by the eye of my Angel
            swept by him coming through
            on his black 4-wheeled vehicle

Or lusting for the Blond
of Daylight the One to Keep Her
Asleep—not to take her Away
from her own Mother (as these Mother-Haters falsely charm
the ladies

        Not the Black King he
        covers them with the handsomeness
        of his own black horses   —he is the Brother
        who keeps Hell
        clean. He is Hell   Hell
        is a house-keeping of a woman's
        order

Hating
the other kind
of the Blond lover, those

who idealize or falsely blush
because they pee And shit Who want everything
Clean no scratch on the Mirror   no Death
in the Ground   everything round and full of source for themselves of
Admiration

                          Only be careful: the Black
                          King is the Annual Husband
                          who can Keep
                          the woman he has layed
                          because she does know
                          he has no attitude

because she does pee
squatted down   oh Bride of my Life
                        Whose Secret I do Keep

"Grinning monster out side the system . . ."

Grinning monster out side the system
                      horribly not true
Death is not a mother because
we are born, death is its own
business, fallen egg, bird with newest
               wings back-assing out of
               nest instead of sticking
               like its other members of the
               clutch   its gaping mouth
               out

Bird of horror slams down a wall
of night   a solid second wall traveling
double the speed in the black night
                          all the way
from the top of the blackest sky behind
stars right down through the highway blacktop
                          slicing
          the adjoining
fields—and the nearest house empty
not a sound or a person nor a light in it
on the corner Death otherwise
is running out, seepage
into the assuming earth, persons waiting
for it. Horrible. No good. Impossible
                              Loss
Prepare for it? back out of the nest,
instead of sticking one's mouth out for
the food, for the brought
whatever the barnswallow switches
as rapidly into the mouth as
without a stop in the air
is caught? is slammed
in the night   the being? Her heart
beat 120 but the blood
did not any more
have pressure

"her skin / covered me . . ."

her skin
covered me, illuminated
my nature, a gleam
caught from the penetralium of the mystery
               kept me
(at least at night) free

The Lamp

you can hurry the pictures toward you but
there is that point that the whole thing itself
may be a passage, and that your own ability
may be a factor in time, in fact that
only if there is a coincidence of yourself
& the universe is there then in fact
an event. Otherwise—and surely here the cinema
is large—the auditorium can be showing
all the time. But the question is
how you yourself are doing, if you in fact
are equal, in the sense that as *a like power*
you also are there when the lights
go on. This wld seem to be a
matter of creation, not simply
the obvious matter, creation
itself. Who in fact is any of us

to be there at all? That's what
swings the matter, also—
the beam hanging from

Shenandoah

      event
   a reflection
      of possibility,

that is, the World is
a concrete example of
the dialogue, and it's
entirely possible that
only when the dialogue
is with a 'wife' the
World gets into
position; and the events
are more
'informed.' The expression
does improve the condition
of the event. 'Thought' is a bettering
of action.

"will: termite mothers . . ."

will: termite mothers
and locust's children,
greasy eyed fried poets
from the South: pattern
in Nature, aphids
who couldn't even shift
to a nearby eucalyptus tree
which was as good for them
                    to host on
as the variant tree which died

"will: the rat . . ."

will: the rat
smells
the food

The Grandfather-Father Poem

rolled in the grass
like an overrun horse
or a poor dog
to cool himself
from his employment
in the South Works
of U S Steel
as an Irish shoveler

> to make their fires hot
> to make ingots above
> by puddlers of
> melted metal

> and my grandfather
> down below
> at the bottom of the
> rung

> stoking
their furnaces
with black
soft
coal soft coal
makes fire
heat higher
sooner,
>   beloved
Jack Hines (whose picture
in a devil's
cap—black jack
Hines

and would come home
to the little white house
sitting by itself
on Mitchell Street
        or was then

Middle River Road
and take off
all his clothes, down to
his full red underwear
the way the story was told

and go out there
on the grass
and roll
and roll

                my
                grandfather

                my Jack Hines
                whose picture
                I have lost

I have also lost
the tin-type
of—was it?—my mother's
mother? a severe face
tight actually

her cheeks
colored false pink

nothing like the
limber
of that harsh
grandfather's
face in the picture

loving man
who hated

my father would
'understand'
anyone

    and go stupid
when attacked by like
Irish blockheads to
what also conceivably my
grandfather may
have been gave allegiances to
—like the Church I don't know

        was a whiskey
          drinker
        but no drunk

         stored barrels
          of apples
        in his cellar
           etc

there was nothing
   that I can honestly recall
wasn't
'strict' about him—that is he wasn't

soft, I don't believe. He would my impression is give up
anything to
anyone or any
thing: (impossible to be

accurate about
'memories' in
that generation
unless

      like one's own parents
they live long enough
      for you yourself
      to be able to

judge: on my father
I'm afraid I am
right, that he did fight
rigidly the next generation of
'Irish' in the
U S Post Office to

            mon grand
         Père: Paddy Hehir
            "Blocky" Sheehan
         and the Postmaster,
         Healy, ran a travel agency
            Pleasant Street
               Worcester

killed himself
'fighting'
such men (when my grandfather
rolled right over on the rug
when he was leaning over the window seat
getting some magazine say out of the inside
(with the cushions off) when I
came up from behind
and kicked him

            and I went out in the kitchen
         and sd to my mother Grandpa
            is lying on the floor

      he looked out of the tintype
    like a different type
than my pa

       black walnut
the bed was made of
he put the ridges in
where he missed
when he was giving
my uncle a beating

       my mother used to beg
       to be beaten
       instead

     who knows?
but I make Jack Hines
too mean

  a man and a woman either is only a thing when each
is full of blood

      This is my poem to my grandfather,

        John Hines his name was

        he migrated to the United States

        from Ireland sometime

        (my mother was born

        on this side 1872)

        before

        1872

and was employed

so far as I know only

in his lifetime

on this side by

the U S Steel (retired

as such a night watchman

after (I suppose) having

shoveled coal most

of his life

He had been born "in Cork,

brought up

in Galway," and recently

I figured out he must have been

sent 'home' to

Galway during

the potato famine

(the Hines,

as an Irish clan

were reasonably small

and had their center

around Gort

for my friend

drum upon the table you drum
the Tree of the World

drum the table you drum the point
at which communication between

Heaven, Earth, and Hell is made:

the Tree of the World a horse
is made,

the Tree of the World a bow
is

Fly up, fly out
with your ecstatic fingers

on the flat table made
of the bole of Inanna's

tree. The Tree of the World
is a voyage, the sacred

pillar. Drum
the table. Fly up fly out

just where you are. You drum the point
just where communication is made

between Heaven, Earth, and Hell. Drum
the table

who plays directly into the air

FOR JOHN CLARKE

The Drum World

—God is a mushroom.

In particular one man
drummed in particular he sent waves
immediately
into the
air, he played directly
on to the table he was sitting by,
drumming he drummed
upon the Tree of Life he was drumming
on the wood
of the tree of life,
of Inanna's tree, the Djed
pillar

a time (count)
completely open, and his own
the world open, and counted (Clarke's
                               'clock'

I

Men rode
the plataforma
on the narrow–
gauge track

and acquired
the gold or betel or any other riches they wanted
to take or make out of
the earth

Out of the Earth or of woman, out of the genetic
out of that which comes into being, which forever
will come into being. Which is forever
only one step away from
the originary, only one step this side of
the originary, that near,
from the beginning to the end of time and count,
to the imagined. The World

is only one step this side of the motive
of Creation, these tracks
which run as though through Love, Tartaros, Earth, and Chaos,
each of these motives as flight, which
disappears behind itself in the air, consequence
runs through—makes a complete path for the plataforma

simplest hugging track and vehicle to go through
growth, or wet ground bog—land-rover—or all but lank lagoons petrified

air and sound, horror of still rottenness dankness laziness
                              permanent arrest successful
living deadness with birds muskrats suddenness clanks ripples suckenings
the uselessness of growth without man, woman without man. Man alone is
                              alone capable of being
alone

        The World itself the firmness
    of Earth, of woman, of love—of life,
    is the evidence, is the first instance *after*
    of the perfectness
    of the imagined

        2

            not a sleigh, not a carved wagon
    for forwarding: the fingers, heel of the hand both hands
                                    all fingers
    the blessed air disappears beyond the envelope
    of the earth, it is black
    above sound, the sun
    above sound
    is instant deadly rays, is only a red candy stuck
    upon blackness which kills
    instantly. Beyond the speed of life outside the air of earth
    it is rank creation

men with tools or horses or
standing in the special day's
air accompanied her
as her cart was drawn
in demonstration through people
come to see the goddess

or the boat,
with what he had accumulated
because he was or had accomplished
rule or power or usefulness
for others, drew away
from the wharf or beach of his
kingdom, apparently
putting out
to sea, actually
being guided
(as her careful wagon
her maze
wrought
in the wood or bronze
welding of her
plataforma) his boat
when out of sight of the people mourning
was taken
up river
and not sent out upon the distance of the sea,
was,
by family or by priests—by those who love whom they love, taken
to earth, the boat,
80 foot long is carried one mile inland
to the cemetery where a hole
big enough to enclose it has been dug. And
with all his treasures, even possibly not his body
—or hers, who, Oseberg, is the queen lying
                          in the preserved boat—
hauled up hill,
taken from the sea,
fooled the people at the wharf
—the dream,
of eternity—steered
solemnly, by those in charge or
those closest, up the Deben estuary away from the sea

taken up hill like Djoser imagined his pyramid all his life and had it
built—
and set down inside the sand, which then
was turned in likewise over it
until he—or her—and his ship—or hers
were covered by a hill which stood out over
the ground inland
from the sea (or Djoser
from the Nile

THE DRUM II
(for John Clarke)

"my apple branch . . ."

my apple branch dressed
in her green Isis night gown

standing on her tip-toes to see
how she looked in it in

the window mirror of my own
Seth Thomas wood run clock

Absolutely Vernal

the whole of creation shall come to his funeral,
the snow   the rain   the spotlight of the sun   the smoke
filing up through the hole in the Pantheon's
roof

An 'Enthusiasm'

Lane painted true color, and drew
true lines, and 'View' as a prin-
ciple he had also made true as a-
gainst too easy (Dutch) or even a
more brilliant landscape Turner,
Constable (Guardi, Canaletto, Tie-
polo even behind theirs)
What kept him 'local' or at least provincial
(and patriotic, literally, especially in his
ship scenes, and in fact his introduction of
ships into his scenes, when they weren't there,
and he added them
was rather a weakness of selection,
some selecting necessity his principle
of View called for if his lines and color
were to be like it first principle

Or some proposal or Vision like in fact Parkman
by making France-American his subject grabbed off.
     It would be impossible to say, and from my own point of view
there wasn't anything at all wrong with 'Gloucester' actually
as such a proposal (And my own experience of his paintings
and his drawings is that with the isolated exception of Castine
the contrast is his
Boston Harbor or Beacon Hill
his New York Harbor and
his Savannah and San Juan Porto Rico paintings
his Gloucesters are altogether his best. It is as though
he got as far as Parkman and Prescott and even as far as
Noah Webster (in the sense of the virtue of his colors and
line and choices of views in Gloucester & Castine—as against
Owls Head Camden Hills
     Blue Hill Somes Bay Northeast Harbor—
as establishing objects as definitions as exact today as they
were then)
               but that say
Hawthorne (born the same year) or Melville but this is larger
and Parkman is the better reference and certainly Whitman's
grab-off is far away and it may seem irrelevant for me to men-
tion it. But the thing is to be sure Lane's specificity &
"place" in exactly the Who's Who in America sense be found
out: he rates (1814–1865) only the company of the men, &
Gloucester & Castine, I have mentioned not his regional &
dull school & museum & Collectors place of "Artist" & Marine
Painter. He was one of the
chief definers of the American 'practice'—the word is
Charles Peirce's for pragmatism—which is still the con-
spicuous difference of American from any other past or any
other present, no matter how much we are now almost the
true international to which all bow and acknowledge.

                         In honor of 100th
                         anniversary of his loss,
                         1965

630

This Year

Thank God Life Came For Me, Nerthus Gathered Me Up For Her Annual
Parade

And Sat Me Down Beside Whom I Thought Like Everybody Does Was

Her Old Man

Until I Jolted Him Sick of His Silence the Fucking Long Wagon Ride
                                        of the Celebration
                        of What?
And the Son of a Bitch Was Like She is Only She's a Fucking Witch

Nothing But a God Damn Doll Fixed Up With Teeth and Looking Like a Man

        Which Fell to Pieces Right Beside Me in the Riding Seat
    Was Empty, Nothing Live At All, Not the God Not Even as Much as She

    Something Fixed Up To Represent Her Husband God
    Who Because Such a Big Shit and a Warrior Bold

        Of Course Is Buried Somewhere Else in Truth & Life
                    —Some Foreign Land Of Course

    And Really Is The Guy Whom I & All the People Too
                        Thought Was There, Every Year, Riding
    Beside Such Sons or Kids

—Or Even More a Man, Each Year, To Ride With Him

Because, When We Have Gone Around the Kingdom

Next Year, Lord, God, Save Us All

Her Husband Beside Us Might Turn

Out to be the Real One Home From Wars

"as if Hallam Movius . . ."

as if Hallam Movius had placed a grid over it, and plumb-
lines were dropping from each of the fixed corners across
the grid

and I know a poet and story-teller who is himself already,
or his poetry is, a flavor rises off those poems and a surface
of something as encompassable

as the American Civil War: it isn't
50 miles wide in fact, centering on Centreville or Orange County
Courthouse (Culpepper—Warrentown) and, north and south, 150
miles will take you Etc   Body of Event being
that Central
Region and where
I can have
in this room
as I am writing,
November 12th,

1965, the sharpened
—whittled—
sticks a foot and a half
long. Mind you only little scratched sticks
like that boy in blue had used
to protect
himself or impale
any skulking Rebel creeping
up on his prone position *last*
night or day of *last*
battle of Chancellorsville C.H. or Wilderness
where I found it mounted as that soldier had
died & rotted in back of it or removed himself but
left these whittled sticks sticking
as his own little night's fort
in front of him: I *found* it, 90 years later, I mean whittled sticks
mind you   just as he'd constructed it, one night,
two sticks
made into
a protection

And carried them off,
from that easy
underbrush, astonished
as I still am that
a man's act, of this
slight an evidence, shall
stay raised in the grass
and the change
of the growth of
seasons, just think even snow's weight, nothing
storm or trees crashing or a bird or an animal
using this
useful
thing
until I came along apparently the first person
99 years after that nearly last night of that

long war and saw
as though I had come on new birds' eggs in a new
nest, spotted blue, this
chevaux de frise
                    tells me
we are

A *Scream* to the Editor

Moan the loss, another
house
is gone

          Bemoan the present
which assumes
its taste, bemoan the easiness
of smashing anything

Moan Solomon Davis'
house, gone
for the YMCA, to build another
of its cheap benevolent places
bankers raise money for,

and who loan money for new houses: each destruction doubles
our loss and doubles bankers' gain when four columns

          Bemoan a people who spend
        beyond themselves, to flourish
        and to further themselves

as well made the Solomon Davis house itself
was such George Washington
could well have been inaugurated
from its second floor,

     and now it is destroyed because 70 years ago
Gloucester already could build the Y, and Patillo's
equally ugly brick front and building

     (between them the Davis house, then 50 years old,
     was stifled squeezed in no light on one side a Patch
     of soil like a hen-yard toward Patillo's

        houses live or else why
       is *one room* in 90 Middle Street worth
       $100,000 to the Metropolitan Art Museum?

If taste is capital of this order had not
Cape Ann Historical Scientific and Literary Society
or Cape Ann Historical Association—

if John Babson the historian *founded* both
the abovementioned society *and* the Sawyer Free Library
   —and was a banker too, and wrote, with two others, the
            principal history
of Massachusetts banking to his time,

how many ways can value be
allowed to be careless with, and Hagstrom
destroy? how many more before this obvious
dullness shall cease?

oh city of mediocrity and cheap ambition destroying
its own shoulders its own back greedy present persons
stood upon, stop this renewing without reviewing
loss loss loss no gains oh not moan stop stop stop this

total loss of surface and of mass,
putting bank parking places with flowers, spaces dead so dead
in even the sun one does not even know one passes by them
Now the capitals of Solomon Davis' house
now the second floor behind the black grill work
now the windows which reached too,

now the question who if anyone was living in it
now the vigor of the narrow and fine clapboards on the back
now that flatness right up against the street,

one is in despair, they talk and put flowers up
on poles high enough so no one can water them,
and nobody
objects
when houses which have held and given light
a century, in some cases two centuries,
and their flowers
aren't even there in one month

—the Electric Company's
lights are there, every night, to destroy the color of color
in human faces—Main Street is as sick at night as Middle

Street is getting banker-good in sun light—a swimming pool
is now promised where Solomon Davis sat beside the Dale House
& looked with some chagrin at Sawyer's not as tasteful house
across the way,
I'm sick
of caring, sick of watching
what, known or unknown, *was* the
ways of life . . I have no
vested interest even in this which
makes life.
Moan nothing. Hate hate hate
I hate those who take away
and do not have as good to
offer. I hate them. I hate the carelessness

> For $25,000 I do not think anyone
> should ever have let the YMCA take down Solomon Davis'
> house, for any purpose of the YMCA

"He is the Devil . . ."

He is the Devil. He whores Nature. Love is a word in his Mouth. He has no Mouth, he has no Part of a man, he Hates Woman, he knows Every thing he doesn't want. He wants—Nothing. He wants only to Lead Anyone Else astray. From the Path. He uses Love. He Hates. He uses Words, and Every Person. He believes in No Word, he believes in No Person.

He is brilliant. When he coils he is Handsomer than there is Handsome, Wiser than the Poor Wise. Then He is the Son of Heaven, the Seducer, the Perfect Temptation. When he Coils. He Coils. When He Coils He Tempts. All He Waits For is *His* Moment. All other Time is Preparatory, in a meaning Christianity has Neglected. There is Solely Now Literally Satan. All Generosity, all Love, all Belief is Then His. He Suddenly Coils. He is Nobody, Each Person's Bleeding Heart and Desire. Love. He is Anyone, Everyone, All Persons—Strayers. He Welcomes Anyone, Everyone. He offers. Then He Coils. Then He Is. Then—and it is the Weakest Power Whoever He Then Seeks Which Suddenly Is Also Turned On (they are in their Weakest Power) He Performs.

"As snow lies on the hill . . ."

As snow lies on the hill love's blackness lies
upon my blood and I steer perfectly the sled, tears streaming
from the speed and blinding me as I tear automobiles aside and throw them
away as though they were such toys
who seek to kill me and I go on
to the valley floor frozen to the river's
bank, and the river too frozen and across until I smash
into its further bank, the side the other side of the valley goes equally
the other way from, my heart fully darkened by death's arrival
                                      life's blackness
fallen into my blood as love has
                        fallen as snow
into the river's course before the cold froze her surface and we race
out on her in love's blackness to nothing,
which we came from, clothed now to fall like this faster than
all back into blood

"turn now and rise . . ."

turn now and rise

Wrest the matter into your own

hands—and Nature's laws

"So the Norse / were neurotic . . ."

So the Norse
were neurotic
And the pre-
Hesiodic
Greeks Plus the Earliest
Irischer: one wonders
at this point then,
if neuroses like ice,
and agriculture, were
preparing
modern Non–Neurotic
Man, the
Neue Klasse of
freedom   I quote

a lady
Poet who calls herself
an Artist: no cunt
is not free, my cunt
is not free, my poetry
is my cunt, you Dirty Man you
you won't let me have my cunt because

I *am* free, I *am* an Artist, I am the
Poetry

"Indian trinity . . ."

Indian trinity and my son an Etchimin
at the three places super able
as the tightest stitches on a new baseball

"Not to permit himself . . ."

Not to permit himself to be

a civilized man otherwise entropy will be

irreversible, the damages will not be

returned into the System a man will not become the result of or equal to that

of which or from which by what possibility he

may

"the Heart is a clock . . ."

the Heart is a clock

around which clusters

or which draws to itself

all which is the same

as itself in anything

or anyone else the

power of itself lies

all about itself in

a mathematic of feeling

which we call love

but who

love itself is the container

of all feelings otherwise than love

as well

as the Heart equally

holds all else there is anywhere

in Creation, when it is

full

"A big fat fly . . ."

A big fat fly
lives in my house
and in the air
he goes about
as though in fact the house
were just as much his
as it is
mine

And now
I have to share
what I thought all my own
with this sad truck
which just flew down the doors to my bedroom
like a heavy emperor
he thinks he is—or actor   French movie star
or caveat emptor of some sad reign
this extra inhabitant
of winter's heat
in my house's inside as though
his pleasure palace too and
his own torpid stream
to sail his bulk about in while
I look after, on this juicy intruder of
my own   once mine   domain

And this,
is suddenly
a different house,
that he so bumblingly
uses my air
as though
it were his too

And I am,
suddenly only
a co-dweller here
where I had thought
until he seemed to fly
right out of the wall itself
I was
alone

TEXTUAL NOTES

The following notes offer a date of writing and brief publishing history for each poem, followed by the identification of the text used for this volume, along with the location of other texts available to the editor for collation, including tape recordings. Where an entry says "previously unpublished," it means unpublished by Charles Olson during his lifetime; a number of the poems have been published posthumously in a variety of publications (most notably in *Some Early Poems,* Iowa City, 1978, and *Sulfur,* nos. 11–13, 1984–1985). Finally, variant or uncertain readings are given in cases where the original manuscript remains difficult.

Purgatory Blind   Written ca. spring 1940. Previously unpublished. Undated TS (typescript) among the poet's papers in the Literary Archives, Homer Babbidge Library, University of Connecticut (hereafter abbreviated CtU), along with an original holograph version in notebook "#4 Cambridge & NY Winter-Spring 1940."

You, Hart Crane   Written late 1940. Previously unpublished. TS dated "1940" in Morris Library, Southern Illinois University. Another version included in "2 Propositions and 3 Proof" (q.v.).

Birth's Obituary   Originally written late 1940 or early 1941; revised ca. March 1945. Previously unpublished. Undated TS at CtU, along with another version titled "Space."

Atalanta   Originally written early 1940s, definitely by February 1941; revised 27 March 1945. Previously unpublished. Undated holograph MS at CtU, along with two other typed versions.

White Horse   Originally written early 1940s, definitely by February 1941; revised (or at least retyped) ca. September–November 1946. Previously unpublished. Undated TS (typed with "Fire Is") at CtU, along with two earlier undated TSS, one titled "Mavrodaphne."

Fire Is   Written early 1940s; revised (or retyped) ca. September–November 1946. Previously unpublished. Undated TS (typed with "White Horse") at CtU.

Fable for Slumber   Written early 1940s. Previously unpublished. Undated TS at CtU.

Hymn to the Word   Written early 1940s. Previously unpublished. Undated TS at CtU.

Tomorrow   Written 1941. Previously unpublished. TS dated "1941" sent Frances Bolderoff, 23 May 1949, at CtU, along with another version titled "Ur" and a later untitled TS.

The House   Written ca. April 1941. Previously unpublished. Undated TS at CtU, along with an original holograph version in notebook begun 19 April 1941.

By Cure of—Sulfa   Written ca. 1942–1944. Previously unpublished. Undated TS at CtU.

Law   Written ca. 1942–1944. Previously unpublished. Undated TS at CtU.

A Lion upon the Floor   Written January 1945. Published in *Harper's Bazaar* 80 (January 1946), the text used here. Early version begun in notebook "Key West I January 1945" at CtU, along with two carbon copies of the original TS.

Sing, Mister, Sing   Written 27 January 1945. Previously unpublished. Undated TS (carbon copy) at CtU, along with several early versions in notebook "Key West I January 1945."

The K   Written February 1945. Published in *Y & X* (Washington [1949]), the text used here. Undated TS at CtU, along with an early version titled "Telegram." Read on tape for Robert Payne, Montevallo, Ala., 5 May 1950.

Pacific Lament Written February 1945. Published in *Atlantic Monthly* 177 (March 1946), the text used here; revised as "Lost Aboard U.S.S. 'Growler'" in *Ferrini & Others,* ed. Vincent Ferrini (Gloucester, 1955). TS of an early version titled "In Memory of William Hickey" at CtU, along with another text, clipped from the *Atlantic,* retitled "Lament for a Seaman Friend," and another copy of the *Atlantic* with revisions incorporated in the *Ferrini & Others* version.

She Written ca. 14 February 1945. Previously unpublished. Undated TS at CtU, along with another version titled "Valentine."

She, Thus Written 3 March 1945. Previously unpublished. Undated TS at CtU, along with a later version.

The Night Written ca. 9 March 1945. Previously unpublished. Undated TS at CtU.

A Translation Written ca. 11 March 1945. Previously unpublished. Undated TS at CtU.

Her Dream, Half Remembered Written 11 March 1945. Previously unpublished. Undated TS and carbon copy at CtU.

Ballad for Americans Originally written 1942; rewritten 15 March 1945. Previously unpublished. Undated TS at CtU, along with the carbon copy of another TS.

Key West Written 27 March 1945. Previously unpublished. Undated TS at CtU.

New England March "Rewritten," according to the poet's note, from "Purgatory Blind" (q.v.), 28 March 1945. Previously unpublished. Undated holograph MS at CtU.

Lower Field—Enniscorthy Written May 1945. Published in *Harper's* 192 (April 1946), the text used here. Part of the larger "Enniscorthy Suite" (q.v.), which had been sent to *Harper's,* although only this section was accepted. Original version titled "Field Notes" in notebook "April, 1945 / en route north," at CtU.

Said Adam Written ca. 22 May 1945. Previously unpublished. Undated TS (carbon copy) at CtU, along with original holograph MS in notebook "April, 1945 / en route north."

Burial Ground Written ca. 22 May 1945. Previously unpublished. Undated TS at CtU, along with original holograph MS in notebook "April, 1945 / en route north."

Enniscorthy Suite Written ca. 22 May 1945. Previously unpublished (except for section II, published separately as "Lower Field—Enniscorthy"). Undated TS and carbon copy at CtU, along with original holograph MS in notebook "April, 1945 / en route north."

The Town Written ca. 2 June 1945. Previously unpublished. Undated TS (carbon copy) at CtU, along with an earlier TS and several other TSS and carbon copies.

Afternoon Written ca. October 1945–March 1946. Previously unpublished. Undated TS at CtU.

2 Propositions and 3 Proof Written ca. November 1945, although incorporating earlier material (cf. "You, Hart Crane"). Previously unpublished. Undated TS (and carbon copy) at CtU. "Proof" of title typed twice in singular form (in addition to its appearance in text).

A Lustrum for You, E.P. Written ca. November 1945–1946. Previously unpublished. Undated TS (and carbon copy) at CtU, along with an earlier version titled "Lustrum."

The Winter After Written ca. December 1945. Previously unpublished. Undated TS at CtU, along with two earlier TSS titled "Bitter Winter" and "Winter."

Marry the Marrow Written ca. 1946. Previously unpublished. Undated TS at CtU.

There Was a Youth Whose Name Was Thomas Granger Written 1946 or early 1947. Published in *Western Review* 11:3 (Spring 1947); reprinted in *In Cold Hell, in Thicket* (Mallorca, 1953) and in *The Distances* (New York, 1960), the text used here. Early TS sent Monroe Engel (photocopy provided editor); a later TS at CtU. Read on tape for Donald Allen, San Francisco, August 1965 (at CtU).

Trinacria Written ca. January 1946. Published in *Y & X*, the text used here; early version titled "For K." published in *Harper's Bazaar* 80 (February 1946). Undated TS at CtU; title changed to "Triskele" in one of Olson's copies of *Y & X* (at CtU) and in copy presented to Michael Lekakis (at Archives of American Art).

La Préface Written ca. May 1946. Published in *Y & X*; reprinted in *In Cold Hell,* the text used here. Undated early TS at CtU, along with another TS with minor differences; Olson's copy of *Y & X* with revisions; and version read on tapes for Robert Payne, Montevallo, Ala., 5 May 1950, and Richard Wirtz Emerson, Washington, D.C., 19 August 1950.

The Dragon–Fly Written June 1946. Previously unpublished. Undated TS (carbon copy) at CtU, along with original holograph versions in notebook "Enniscorthy—June, 1946."

Epigraph to *Call Me Ishmael* Written ca. 4 July 1946. Published in *Call Me Ishmael* (New York, 1947), the text used here. Original holograph MS in notebook "Enniscorthy—June, 1946" at CtU.

Lalage! Written ca. September 1946. Previously unpublished. TS dated "1946" at CtU, along with earlier version titled "Ladies and Gentlemen, the Center Ring!" and a later version titled "Lalage."

The Return Written ca. September 1946. Previously unpublished. Undated TS at CtU, along with an early version in notebook "Enniscorthy—June, 1946"; copy sent Ben Shahn and family, ca. 14 November 1946, at Archives of American Art.

Bagatto Written ca. September 1946. Previously unpublished. Undated TS at CtU, along with early versions in notebook "Enniscorthy—June, 1946."

"Double, double, root and branch . . ." Written ca. 7 September 1946. Previously unpublished. Undated TS at CtU.

The Fool Written ca. September–November 1946. Previously unpublished. Undated TS at CtU, verso an incomplete earlier TS.

À Constance, This Day Written ca. September–December 1946. Previously unpublished. Undated TS at CtU.

The Moebius Strip Written ca. November 1946. Published in *Y & X*, the text used here (with "Moebus" of title corrected). TS sent Caresse Crosby, 7 May 1948, at Morris Library, Southern Illinois University; undated holograph MS at CtU. Read on tape for Robert Payne, 5 May 1950. Earlier versions, "Upon a Moebus Strip," published in *Portfolio* V (Spring 1947), and "To Corrado Cagli," published in *Corrado Cagli* (New York, 1947) and, with further differences, in *Cagli* (Rome, 1948).

X to the Nth Written ca. November–December 1946. Previously unpublished. Undated TS at CtU, along with a later version titled "X to Zebra."

The Green Man Written ca. November 1946. Published in *Y & X,* the text used here. Original holograph version in notebook "Verse & Geometry" at CtU, along with an early TS; a later TS titled "Arcana Zero" sent Merton M. Sealts, Jr., 7 June 1950; and a copy of *Y & X* with "a different thing" in line 4 changed to "no different thing." Read (with "a different thing") on tape for Robert Payne, 5 May 1950. Earlier version published as "In Praise of the Fool" in *Harper's Bazaar* 81 (December 1947); a copy torn from *Harper's Bazaar* with title changed to "Go, Fool" and undated TS with "In Praise of the Fool" shortened to "The Fool" also at CtU; another copy torn from *Harper's Bazaar* sent Ezra Pound (at Lilly Library, Indiana University).

Canto One Hundred and One TS at CtU dated "november 22, 1946." Previously unpublished.

Your Eyes TS dated "dec. '46" at CtU. Previously unpublished.

R^2 Written ca. February 1947. Previously unpublished. Undated TS at CtU, along with another, later TS; another TS sent Monroe and Brenda Engel, 7 January 1949 (photocopy provided editor). "Phillippi" (l. 11) in all TSS; here corrected to "Philippi."

In the Hills South of Capernaum, Port Written ca. February–March 1947 (by March 17). Published in *Harper's Bazaar* 85 (April 1949), the text used here. Original holograph MS at CtU, along with a TS and carbon copy.

A Spring Song for Cagli TS dated "3/ '47" at CtU, with final four lines crossed out but here retained. Previously unpublished.

Willie Francis and the Electric Chair Written ca. May 1947. Previously unpublished. Undated TS at CtU, along with an earlier TS.

Move Over Written June 1947. Published in *Golden Goose,* series 3, no. 1 (1951); reprinted in *In Cold Hell,* the text used here. Original holograph MS in 1947 notebook at CtU, along with three undated TSS and a TS sent Henry A. Murray titled "Elegy." Other TSS sent Monroe Engel (photocopy provided editor), Robert Creeley (TS prepared by Creeley among Cid Corman MSS at Lilly Library, Indiana University), and Wilmot Ragsdale (at CtU).

A Fish Is the Flower of Water Written ca. 1948. Previously unpublished. Undated TS at CtU, along with four earlier TSS.

Landscape, Without Color Written ca. 1948. Previously unpublished. Undated TS at CtU, along with another TS with minor variations and an abandoned, incomplete TS.

Only the Red Fox, Only the Crow Written ca. 1948, by May. Published in *Atlantic Monthly* 183 (March 1949), the text used here. Undated TS at CtU, with differences from the *Atlantic* text.

All You Can Do Written ca. 1948–1950. Previously unpublished. Undated TS at CtU.

"Put him this way . . ." Written ca. 1948–1950. Previously unpublished. Undated TS at CtU.

Conqueror Written 9 January 1948. Previously unpublished. Undated TS sent Caresse Crosby, 20 January 1948, at Morris Library, Southern Illinois University; earlier TS dated "January 9. 48" at CtU, along with another early TS.

Conqueror (later version) Revised from previous poem ca. May 1948–March 1949. Previously unpublished. Undated TS at CtU.

February 10, One Year Too Late Written ca. 10 February 1948. Previously unpublished. Undated TS at CtU.

"Elements of clothes . . ." Written ca. April–June 1948. Previously unpublished. Undated TS at CtU, along with holograph MS of an original version titled "a Mirko, Knoedler, 1948."

Igor Stravinsky TS dated "April 4, 1948" at CtU. Previously unpublished. Another TS from same date also at CtU, along with another version titled "Stravinsky."

Troilus Written ca. July 1948. Published in *Right Angle* 2:5 (August 1948), the text used here. Originally part of the mask *Troilus,* written June–July 1948 (see *The Fiery Hunt and Other Plays,* Bolinas, Calif., 1977, pp. 34–42, and editor's introduction, pp. xiv–xv, there), with minor differences in punctuation and line arrangement. Two other TSS also at CtU, undated and titled "From Troilus" and "from TROILUS (A Mask)," respectively.

Siena Written ca. 20–30 July 1948. Published in *Western Review* 13:2 (Winter 1949); reprinted in *In Cold Hell,* the text used here. TS titled "In Those Days" (with "Siena 1948" added in pencil) at CtU, along with another TS titled "Siena, 1948." TS sent Caresse Crosby, July 1948, titled "Siena 1948" (Morris Library, Southern Illinois University); another TS with same title sent Frances Boldereff, ca. 22 December 1948 (at CtU).

Sans Name Written ca. September 1948. Previously unpublished. Undated TS at CtU, along with a holograph MS originally given Samuel Rosenberg, September 1948.

Li Po Written ca. 11 November 1948. Previously unpublished. Undated TS at CtU.

Tanto e Amara Written ca. 22 November 1948. Previously unpublished. Undated TS at CtU; another TS sent Edward Dahlberg, 22

November 1948, at Humanities Research Center, University of Texas.

Name-Day Night Written ca. December 1948. Published in *Right Angle* 3:1 (May 1949). Original holograph MS and four undated TSS at CtU, along with a copy torn from *Right Angle* revised in ink, the text used here.

La Chute Written May 1949. Published in *Goad,* no. 1 (Summer 1951); reprinted in *Artisan,* no. 2 (Spring 1953), and in *In Cold Hell,* the text used here. TS sent Frances Boldereff, 25 May 1949, at CtU, along with three other undated TSS. Read on tapes for Robert Payne, 5 May 1950, and Richard Wirtz Emerson, 19 August 1950.

La Chute II Written ca. 10 July 1949. Previously unpublished. Undated TS at CtU, along with two earlier TSS, including one sent Frances Boldereff dated "july 10 xlix" and a TS (carbon copy) made by Boldereff.

La Chute III Written ca. October 1949. Previously unpublished. Undated TS at CtU, along with two earlier holograph MSS and another, incomplete TS.

Dura Written ca. 26 May 1949. Unpublished by Olson. Included as part of a letter to Edward Dahlberg, 31 May 1949 (at Humanities Research Center, University of Texas), the text used here. An original TS dated "May 26 / xlix" at CtU, along with an early holograph version verso an envelope sent Frances Boldereff, 25 May 1949.

The Kingfishers Written February–July 1949, with later revisions. Published in *Montevallo Review* 1:1 (Summer 1950); reprinted in *In Cold Hell* and in *The Distances,* the text used here. Changes in Olson's copy of *In Cold Hell* not incorporated in *The Distances,* thus here ignored. Several early TSS at CtU: one titled "Proteus," with "The First Proteid" and "The Kingfishers I & II" added; another titled "from PROTEUS," which is part 1 of "The Kingfishers" with minor differences; an early version titled "The Kingfishers I & II"; carbon copy of another "The Kingfishers I & II,"

dated "july 20 xlix"; and an undated carbon copy of "The Kingfishers" on Fox River Dictation Bond (used by Olson, January 1950–June 1952). A portion of the poem sent Frances Boldereff, 26 October 1949 (at CtU), and a TS (carbon copy) sent Monroe Engel, ca. January 1950 (photocopy provided editor). Read on tape for Robert Payne, 5 May 1950; tape for Richard Wirtz Emerson, 19 August 1950; record with Robert Creeley, Asheville, N.C., ca. September 1955 (all at CtU); and, incomplete, at Vancouver, 16 August 1963.

Epigon TS dated "11 11 xlix" sent Frances Boldereff, at CtU. Previously unpublished. Another TS (with carbon copy) among Olson's papers at CtU, apparently prepared by Boldereff.

The Laughing Ones Written ca. 18 November 1949. Published in *Ferrini & Others,* the text used here. Seven TSS at CtU, including an undated TS incorporating revisions from *Ferrini & Others* carbon copy TS; another TS titled "O!"; another "The Tellers (Those Who Brought It In)"; and two others "Otvechai," one typed on Frances Boldereff's typewriter and dated in her hand "November 18, 1949."

The Praises Written ca. May–December 1949. Published in *New Directions in Prose and Poetry,* no. 12 (1950); reprinted in *In Cold Hell* and in *The Distances,* the text used here. Original version part of "Proteus" TSS at CtU. Early version sent Frances Boldereff, 16 December 1949, also at CtU, along with TS sent Henry A. Murray, 29 December 1949, and a later TS (carbon copy) sent Boldereff, 29 December 1949; another TS (part 1 of the poem) sent Caresse Crosby, Christmas 1949, at Morris Library, Southern Illinois University.

The Babe Written ca. 23 December 1949. Previously unpublished. TS sent Frances Boldereff, ca. 23 December 1949, at CtU, along with four earlier undated and untitled TSS.

"all things stand out against the sky . . ." Written ca. December 1949–March 1950. Previously unpublished. Undated TS at CtU.

"hear my prayer my father . . ." Written ca. January 1950–January 1951. Previously unpublished. Undated holograph MS at CtU.

"under every green tree . . ." Written ca. January 1950–January 1951. Previously unpublished. Undated holograph MS at CtU (verso preceding poem).

The Advantage Written ca. 3 February 1950. Previously unpublished. TS sent Monroe Engel with inscription dated "2/3/50" (photocopy provided editor); another TS dated "1/10/L" at CtU, along with an undated TS.

These Days Written 10 January 1950. Published in *Imagi*, no. 13 (1950), the text used here. Original holograph MS at CtU, along with two TSS, one dated "1/10/L." *Imagi* text originally sent in a letter to William Carlos Williams, 12 January 1950 (at Beinecke Library, Yale University), who in turn sent it to editor Thomas Cole. Other copies sent or given by Olson to Frances Boldereff, 10 January 1950 (at CtU); Monroe Engel, 22 January 1950 (photocopy provided editor); Fielding Dawson (see his *The Black Mountain Book,* New York, 1970, pp. 105–106); and Caresse Crosby (at Morris Library, Southern Illinois University). Read on tape for Richard Wirtz Emerson, 19 August 1950.

A Po-sy, A Po-sy Written February–March 1950. Published in *Origin*, no. 2 (Summer 1951), the text used here (with minor revisions from *The Distances* proofs). Revisions in Olson's copy of *Origin* (at CtU) considered tentative and not always clear, except in one instance: "you" changed to "your" in 4.6 (also corrected in *The Distances* proofs). Originally a letter to Frances Boldereff, 28 February 1950; a version sent her, 7 March 1950 (at CtU). Four undated early TSS also at CtU, one titled "The Vessel and the Element," another "The Vessel, Say, and Its Element." A carbon copy of one of the CtU TSS sent Fielding Dawson, 29 March 1950 (at Melville Library, SUNY Stony Brook, with a photocopy among Dawson's papers at CtU); another carbon copy of an early TS sent Caresse Crosby (at Morris Library, Southern Illinois University).

"here i am, naked . . ." Written ca. March–May 1950. Previously unpublished. Undated TS at CtU.

"It's SPRing AgAIN!" Written ca. March 1950. Previously unpublished. Undated TS at CtU, along with two other TSS and a carbon copy of one.

Asymptotes Written ca. March 1950. Published in *Artisan*, no. 2 (Spring 1953). The text used here is a TS sent Vincent Ferrini, 21 March 1950, at CtU, a copy of which had been sent by Ferrini to editor Robert Cooper for *Artisan*. Carbon copy of Ferrini TS sent Francis Boldereff, ca. 29 March 1950, also at CtU.

The Morning News Written ca. 7 March 1950. Published in *Origin*, no. 10 (Summer 1953), the text used here. TS of an early version dated "march 7 '50" at CtU, along with first page of the carbon copy of another TS (with holograph revisions). Extensively revised in Olson's copy of *Origin*, although the revisions are not always clear; whole sections appear to be omitted or transposed, in addition to minor changes such as the elimination of "say" in line 15 or the change to "these friends) these two buddies" in line 1.31. Lines 4.11–21 have the note "*Maximus*" added in the margin, while the following statement was made at the poem's end: "The 'poem' has moments but the 'place' for it was the Maximus—not then (1950) proposed   and it suffers from the same malaise as all those others of that period— special pleading, & 'playful' cute / trying to make up for—& argumentative, instead of declarative (a vicious stupidity to have been guilty of."

A Gloss Written ca. 10 March 1950. Previously unpublished. Undated TS at CtU, along with three other TSS.

Of Lady, of Beauty, of Stream Written ca. 14 March 1950. Previously unpublished. Undated TS at CtU, along with another TS sent Frances Boldereff, 14 March 1950, and a later attempt at revision titled "To the Lady of Those Things."

At Yorktown Originally written April 1949; revised ca. 21 March 1950. Published in *In Cold Hell;* reprinted in *The Distances,* the text used here. TS of original version dated "April 18, 1949" at CtU, along with TS of revised version sent Frances Boldereff, 23 March 1950. Read on tape for Robert Payne, 5 May 1950.

The She-Bear Written 25–27 March 1950. Previously unpublished. Undated TS with carbon copy at CtU, along with five other TSS (and two carbon copies), one of which titled "Against All Suffacators [*sic*]" (changed to "She-Bear"), another sent Frances Boldereff, 27 March 1950.

The She-Bear (II) Originally written March 1950; revised between September 1957 and May 1962. Previously unpublished. Undated TS at CtU.

To the She-Bear: *The 1st Song* A revised version of "The She-Bear," written between September 1957 and May 1962. Previously unpublished. Undated TS at CtU, along with an undated holograph MS titled "The Song of the She Bear" and two incomplete TSS.

Diaries of Death Written 1 April 1950. Previously unpublished. Undated TS at CtU.

"friday, Good Friday . . ." Written 7 April 1950. Previously unpublished. Undated TS at CtU.

Cinos TS dated "april 18–19 / 1950" at CtU. Previously unpublished. An earlier version titled "On Cinos" (undated TS and carbon copy) also at CtU; read on tape for Robert Payne, 5 May 1950.

Bigmans Written ca. 19 May 1950. Previously unpublished. TS (carbon copy) at CtU, along with an earlier TS and another early TS sent Frances Boldereff, ca. 19 May 1950.

Bigmans II Written ca. 8 August 1950. Previously unpublished. Undated TS at CtU, along with an earlier TS and a carbon copy of the original TS sent Frances Boldereff, 8 August 1950.

In Cold Hell, in Thicket Written 23–24 May 1950. Published in *Golden Goose,* series 3, no. 1 (1951); reprinted in *In Cold Hell* and in *The Distances,* the text used here (with "he," line I.12, restored from "be," following *In Cold Hell* and other texts). Original version sent as a letter to Frances Boldereff, 23 May 1950, at CtU, along with two other TSS, one dated "May 23 / L." Read on Boston studio tape, June 1962.

For Sappho, Back Written ca. 25 May 1950. Published in *Montevallo Review* 1:2 (Summer 1951); reprinted, revised, in *In Cold Hell,* the text used here (with one change—"leaf," IV.27—as in *The Distances* proofs and the 1967 *In Cold Hell*). Early TS dated "may 25 L" at CtU, along with a carbon copy of the *Montevallo Review* TS. Read on tape for Richard Wirtz Emerson, 19 August 1950.

"Help Me, Venus, You Who Led Me On" Written late May 1950. Previously unpublished. Undated TS at CtU, along with three other TSS, undated and incomplete, and one holograph fragment.

Other Than Originally written 1946; revised late May or early June 1950. Published in *Golden Goose,* series 3, no. 1 (1951); reprinted, revised, in *In Cold Hell,* the text used here. Two undated early TSS at CtU, along with another TS sent Frances Boldereff, 8 June 1950. Read on tape for Richard Wirtz Emerson, 19 August 1950.

Quatrain Written ca. 31 May 1950. Previously unpublished. Undated TS sent Robert Creeley, 31 May 1950, at Washington University Libraries; another undated TS at CtU.

Day Song TS dated "may 31st" (1950) at CtU. Previously unpublished.

Day Song, the Day After TS dated "june 1s[t]" (1950) at CtU. Previously unpublished. In line 33, a "be" may be lacking in the poet's TS; either "She may be" or "the queen of it be."

The Dry Ode Originally written July 1947; revised June 1950. Published in *Golden Goose,* series 3, no. 1 (1951), the text used here.

651

Original holograph MS in 1947 notebook at CtU, along with another holograph MS on endpapers of Pound's *The Fifth Decad of Cantos,* where it is titled "A Note," and two early TSS, one dated "July '47," the other "july '47–june, '50." Read on tape for Richard Wirtz Emerson, 19 August 1950.

ABCs Originally written May 1946; revised June 1950. Published in *In Cold Hell;* reprinted in *The Distances,* the text used here. Another version published in *Artisan,* no. 2 (Spring 1953). Undated TS sent Vincent Ferrini, possibly 10 June 1950 (a copy of which Ferrini sent Robert Cooper for *Artisan*), at CtU, along with another undated TS.

ABCs (2) Written 10 April 1950. Published in *In Cold Hell;* reprinted in *The Distances,* the text used here. TS originally titled "Experiment in Form" and dated "april day after eostre" (10 April 1950) at CtU, along with "Experiment in Form" sent as part of a letter to Frances Boldereff, 10 April 1950.

ABCs (3—for Rimbaud) Written 8 June 1950. Published in *In Cold Hell;* reprinted in *The Distances,* the text used here. Early TS titled "For Rimbaud" and dated "6/8/50" at CtU, along with another TS titled "Report Rimbaud" (changed to "ABCs (3: for Rimbaud)," another early TS, and a TS sent Frances Boldereff, 8 June 1950. "That" in line 30 marked for deletion in Olson's copy of *In Cold Hell,* but not in *The Distances,* so here ignored.

The Story of an Olson, and Bad Thing Written 5–21 June 1950. Published in *Origin,* no. 1 (Spring 1951), the text used here. TS dated "june 5–6 '50" at CtU, along with two earlier TSS and a carbon of the final version.

Adamo Me . . . Written 11–21 June 1950. Published in *Origin,* no. 1 (Spring 1951), the text used here (with revisions incorporated from Olson's copy of *Origin*). Original version written as letter to Frances Boldereff, 11 June 1950, at CtU. Revised extensively in both ink and pencil in Olson's copy of *Origin;* only revisions in ink incorporated here ("that" in 3:23 removed, "is" in "Conc." l. 6 changed to "it"), the pencil revisions too sweeping, not typi-

cal of Olson's more considered and definitive revisions.

La Torre Originally written October–November 1946; revised ca. 26 June 1950. Published in *In Cold Hell,* the text used here. Original holograph MS in notebook "Verse & Geometry" at CtU, along with seven TSS, one dated "October, '46—June '50" and three titled "The Tower," as well as a dated TS (carbon copy) sent Frances Boldereff, 26 June 1950. Read on tape for Richard Wirtz Emerson, 19 August 1950.

The Cause, the Cause Written 6–8 July 1950. Published in *Black Mountain Review,* no. 6 (Spring 1956), the text used here (with revisions incorporated from *The Distances* proofs). An early TS (with carbon copy) dated "july 6–7–8 50" at CtU, along with two other early TSS, a carbon copy of the *Black Mountain Review* TS, and three TSS sent Frances Boldereff, 6–8 July 1950.

Of Mathilde TS dated "july 21–22 50" at CtU. Previously unpublished.

The Gate Is Prouti Written ca. 31 July 1950. Previously unpublished. Undated TS at CtU, with another TS containing two versions; another TS titled "The Gate Is Called Prouti" sent Robert Creeley, 31 July 1950, at Washington University Libraries (see *Olson & Creeley: Complete Correspondence,* Santa Barbara, 1980, II, 86).

There Are Sounds . . . Written ca. 24 August–28 November 1950. Previously unpublished. TS sent Cid Corman "tuesday" (probably 28 November 1950), at Lilly Library, Indiana University; two earlier TSS (with carbon copies) at CtU, along with another sent as a letter to Robert Creeley, ca. November 1950, and returned with comments (see *Olson & Creeley: Complete Correspondence,* III, 150–153, and photograph following p. 81 there).

Issue, Mood Written ca. September 1950, before September 14. Published in *Origin,* no. 2 (Summer 1951); revised in Olson's copy, the text used here. Two undated TSS also at CtU. TS sent Robert Creeley before 14 September 1950, at Washington University Libraries (photo in *Olson & Creeley: Complete Correspondence,* III, following p. 81). "Hock" written above "stone" (l.39) in Olson's copy, but "stone" not crossed out; thus retained here.

Signs Written ca. 27 September 1950. Previously unpublished. Undated TS at CtU, along with TS dated "Sept (Monday) 27 '50," sent Richard Wirtz Emerson, and another version titled "Il Diavolo, Il Sole."

The Moon Is the Number 18 Original version titled "The Moon" written ca. September–November 1946; revised 8 January 1951. Published in *Origin,* no. 1 (Spring 1951); reprinted in *In Cold Hell* and in *The Distances,* the text used here. TS sent Cid Corman for *Origin,* 12 January 1951, at CtU, along with another TS dated "fall, 1946 / rewrite jan 8, 1951" and a TS (carbon copy) dated "10 January 1950" (i.e., 1951), as well as "The Moon" TS, undated. Both Olson's "working copy 1960" of *Origin* and another copy ("Olson copy" on cover) have revisions not included in *The Distances,* thus here ignored.

Abstract #1, Yucatan Written ca. 5 March 1951. Previously unpublished (in this version). Sent as part of letter to Jean Riboud, 5 March 1951 (photocopy provided the editor); another version, untitled and with minor differences, sent Robert Creeley the same date and published in *Mayan Letters* (*Selected Writings,* p. 101; *Olson & Creeley: Complete Correspondence,* V, 46). Another copy, with minor differences from the other texts, sent in a letter to Bernhard and Mary Knollenberg, 6 March 1951 (at CtU).

This Written April–May 1951. Published as Black Mountain Broadside no. 1 (February 1952), the text used here. Early version titled "Right There in Front of Your Eyes" sent Robert Creeley, 11 April 1951, and returned to Olson (at CtU, photo in *Olson & Creeley: Complete Correspondence,* V, following p. 100); another copy sent Susanna W. Coggeshill, same date (photocopy provided the editor); and carbon copy of final TS, undated, sent

Wilmott Ragsdale, 5 May 1951 (photocopy provided the editor).

He, Who, in His Abandoned Infancy, Spoke of Jesus, Caesar, Those Who Beg, and Hell Written June 1951. A version published in *Four Winds,* no. 1 (Summer 1952), but text here is a TS at CtU inscribed "Lerma Campeche / Mexico," with the final two lines of the *Four Winds* text crossed out and other less significant differences. Another undated TS sent Robert Creeley, June 1951, who questioned the need for the final lines (at Washington University Libraries); see Creeley's 28 June 1951 letter suggesting the lines be omitted (*Olson & Creeley: Complete Correspondence,* VI, 83).

Knowing All Ways, Including the Transposition of Continents Written ca. 24 June 1951. Published in *In Cold Hell,* the text used here; an earlier version published in *Ferrini & Others.*

Concerning Exaggeration, or How, Properly, to Heap Up Written ca. 26 June 1951. Published in *In Cold Hell,* the text used here. TS sent Cid Corman, 22 October 1951, at Humanities Research Center, University of Texas.

To Gerhardt, There, Among Europe's Things of Which He Has Written Us in His "Brief an Creeley und Olson" Written 28–30 June 1951. Published in *Origin,* no. 4 (Winter 1951–52); reprinted in *The Distances,* the text used here. Copy torn from *Origin* and sent Donald Allen (at CtU) has "Us" crossed out of title but not omitted in *The Distances,* thus not here. Read on Boston studio tape, June 1962 (same tape played for Buffalo reading, 4 October 1963, record in Poetry Collection, SUNY Buffalo).

The Fathers Written ca. July 1951–1955. Previously unpublished. Undated TS sent Robert Creeley, date unknown, at Washington University Libraries; carbon copy of Creeley TS at CtU, along with undated TS of earlier version titled "The Tale of Two Men."

Applause Written ca. 15 July 1951. Previously unpublished. TS (carbon copy) dated "july / '51" sent Robert Creeley, at Washington University Libraries; TS of a later version titled "A Man Who Is Not St. Francis" among Olson's water-damaged papers at CtU.

Issues from the Hand of God Written ca. 25 July 1951. Previously unpublished. Undated TS at CtU, along with several earlier TSS, including three titled "A Round, A Cannon, and an Evening," and another "About Rounds & Canons," which includes an early form of "A Round & A Canon" (q.v.).

A Round & A Canon Written ca. 28–31 July 1951. Published in *Origin,* no. 3 (Fall 1951); reprinted in *In Cold Hell,* the text used here. *Origin* TS dated "July, 1951" at Humanities Research Center, University of Texas.

Letter for Melville 1951 Written July–August 1951. Published at Black Mountain College, August 1951; reprinted in *The Distances,* the text used here (with two revisions: "this," line 231, changed to "his," following the Black Mountain and other texts, and "wed" changed to "wedding," line 95, as in Olson's revised copy of *The Distances* at CtU). TS of early version titled "A Letter to Be Read Away from the 'One Hundredth Birthday Party' for Moby Dick . . ." and sent George Kirgo, 21 July 1951, at CtU, along with incomplete carbon copies of two early TSS. A copy of the Black Mountain edition at CtU, with opening passages heavily revised (revisions abandoned after line 38, thus not considered conclusive). Read (excerpts) at Goddard College, 14 April 1962, and on *Melville in the Berkshires* tape for Ann Charters, 1 December 1968 (Portents 13, Brooklyn, N.Y., 1969).

"pitcher, how . . ." Written ca. 2 August 1951. Published in *Neon / Supplement to Now* (August 1958), the text used here. Written as a birthday message to Fielding Dawson (see Dawson, *The Black Mountain Book,* New York, 1970, pp. 111–112); *Neon* TS (prepared by Dawson) at CtU, along with two early TSS (among Olson's water-damaged papers) titled *"For My Lad, for / His Birthday."*

The Ring of Written October 1951. Published in *In Cold Hell,* the text used here, and in *Fer-*

rini *& Others.* Read at Berkeley, 23 July 1965, and on tape for Donald Allen, San Francisco, August 1965.

For Cy Twombly Faced with His First Chicago & N.Y. Shows Written ca. November 1951. Previously unpublished. Undated TS at CtU.

An Ode on Nativity Written December 1951. Published in *Montevallo Review* 1:3 (Spring 1952); reprinted in *In Cold Hell,* the text used here. Undated early TS, given Donald Allen, at CtU. Text heavily revised in *The Distances* proofs, but *In Cold Hell* text read by Olson with approval at Berkeley, 23 July 1965 (see *Muthologos,* Bolinas, Calif., 1978, I, 100–107), thus preserved here.

"At midnight, after hours of love . . ." Written ca. 1952–1953. Previously unpublished. Undated TS at CtU, along with two other undated TSS.

The Clouds Written ca. 1952–1954. Previously unpublished. Undated TS at CtU, along with TS of another version titled "Of the Clouds."

For a Lady of Whom I Speak Written ca. 1952–1954. Previously unpublished. Undated TS at CtU, with original title "Lady of the Night" crossed out and present title substituted.

To the Algae Written ca. 1952–1954. Previously unpublished. Undated TS at CtU, along with an untitled earlier version.

The Civil War Written ca. 1952–1957. Previously unpublished. Undated TS at CtU.

The Connection Written ca. 1952–1957. Previously unpublished. Undated TS at CtU.

The Friend Written ca. 1952–1957. Previously unpublished. Undated TS with original title "The Capitalist" changed to "The Friend," at CtU, along with another undated TS version.

War on the Mind in a Time of Love Written ca. 1952–1957. Previously unpublished. Undated TS at CtU.

A Discrete Gloss Originally written June 1951; revised January 1952, by January 16. Published in *Origin,* no. 6 (Summer 1952), the text used here. TS (carbon copy) dated "Lerma, June 51—BMC, January 52" sent Cid Corman, 19 January 1952, at Humanities Research Center, University of Texas; another TS (carbon copy) titled "A Gloss" sent Robert Creeley, at Washington University Libraries.

Kin TS (carbon copy) dated "april / 52" at CtU. Previously unpublished. TS (carbon copy) of another version titled "Vinal" also at CtU.

The Thing Was Moving TS (carbon copy) dated "may 11 '52" sent Robert Creeley, at Washington University Libraries. Previously unpublished.

"He / in the dark stall . . ." TS dated "may 17, 52" at CtU. Previously unpublished.

Black Mt. College Has a Few Words for a Visitor TS (carbon copy) dated "june 16 52" at CtU. Previously unpublished. Two other undated TSS also at CtU, one titled "Black Mt. College—Dat Ole Sphinx—Has a Few Words for a Visitor," the other "BMC Returns an Ambiguity or Two to a Visitor."

Merce of Egypt Written ca. June–August 1952. Published as "Merce in Egypt" in *Montevallo Review* 1:4 (Summer 1953); reprinted, as "Merce of Egypt," in *In Cold Hell,* the text used here. Read on tape for Donald Allen, August 1965.

A Toss, for John Cage Written ca. July–August 1952. Previously unpublished. Undated TS (carbon copy) sent Robert Creeley, at Washington University Libraries; original TS of final eight lines at CtU, along with three other TSS, one incomplete. "Biblioteque" in line 43 originally "bibliotech" in earlier version, thus the spelling here.

The Leader Written July 1952. Early version published in *Contact,* no. 5 (November 1952–January 1953); final version in *In Cold Hell,* the text used here. Carbon copy of undated *Con-*

tact TS sent Cid Corman, 12 July 1952, at Humanities Research Center, University of Texas.

"The winds / which blew my daughter . . ." TS dated "aug 7 52" (verso carbon copy of another version titled "KWO") sent Robert Creeley, at Washington University Libraries. Previously unpublished. Another TS at CtU.

From the Inca Written ca. 19 November 1952. Previously unpublished. Undated holograph MS, in notebook from October 1952–November 1955, at CtU, along with another copy sent Frances Boldereff, 20 November 1952.

Dramatis Personae Written ca. 1953–1957. Previously unpublished. Undated TS at CtU, revised in pencil throughout. The text here is the original typed version before revisions, which are very extensive and not always legible. TS of another version titled "*The Picture*" also at CtU.

The Collected Poems Of Written 2 January 1953. Previously unpublished. Undated TS sent Ronald Mason verso letter, 10 May 1953, at CtU, along with five other TSS, one dated "jan 2 53."

Common Place TS dated "jan 2 53" at CtU. Previously unpublished.

"It's got to this . . ." Written ca. 23 January 1953. Previously unpublished. Undated holograph MS at CtU.

"my poor dumb body . . ." Written ca. April 1953. Previously unpublished. Undated TS at CtU.

"my poor dumb body . . ." (another version) Written ca. April 1953. Previously unpublished. Undated TS at CtU.

Well Written ca. April 1953. Previously unpublished. Undated TS at CtU, along with two other untitled versions.

The Mast TS dated "april 1 53" sent Robert Creeley, at Washington University Libraries. Previously unpublished. Carbon copy of Creeley TS at CtU, along with another, different TS.

For a Man Gone to Stuttgart Who Left an Automobile Behind Him Written ca. 11 April 1953. Originally titled "For a Man Gone to Strasbourg . . ."; changed by Jonathan Williams for publication in his *Elegies and Celebrations* (Highlands, N.C., 1962), the text used here (with section heading "2" restored from original TS). Undated TS sent Jonathan Williams, at Poetry Collection, SUNY Buffalo; carbon copy of Williams TS at CtU, along with another undated TS.

"The sea / is an archeology . . ." Written ca. May–August 1953. Previously unpublished. Undated holograph MS at CtU. In line 3, "snapped" is possibly "snagged."

Proensa Written 13 September 1953. Published in *Contact,* no. 9 (January–April 1954), the text used here. TS sent Robert Creeley, 13 September 1953, at Washington University Libraries; early TS and carbon copy of Creeley TS at CtU; TS prepared by Creeley and sent Paul Blackburn, at Archive for New Poetry, University of California, San Diego.

Jas Jargon Written ca. December 1953. Previously unpublished. Undated TS sent Robert Creeley verso letter, late December 1953, at Washington University Libraries; earlier TS, also undated, at CtU.

Maya Against Itzas Written ca. January 1954. Previously unpublished. Undated holograph MS at CtU, with another version on flyleaf of Olson's copy of Maud Worcester Makemson, *The Book of the Jaguar Priest* (New York, 1951).

The Boat Written ca. 29 May 1954. Previously unpublished. Undated TS at CtU, along with earlier versions titled "The Feast" (dated "29th/54") and "Persona."

The Soul Written ca. 31 May 1954. Previously unpublished. Undated TS at CtU.

Da Boyg Written ca. June–October 1954. Previously unpublished. Undated TS at CtU, along with earlier TS titled "Why the Boyg Was Mistaken for the Sphinx."

Love Written ca. June 1954. Published in *Origin,* no. 14 (Autumn 1954), the text used here. Undated TS at CtU.

The Motion Written ca. June 1954. Published in *Origin,* no. 14 (Autumn 1954), the text used here.

The Pavement Written ca. June 1954. Published in *Origin,* no. 14 (Autumn 1954), the text used here. Undated TS at CtU, along with another TS sent Frances Boldereff, 7 July 1954.

A Story Written ca. 3 June 1954. Previously unpublished. Undated TS at CtU.

Peograms Written ca. July 1954. Previously unpublished. Undated TS at CtU. Title possibly a typographical error for "Programs."

The Real Written ca. 7 July 1954. Previously unpublished. Undated TS at CtU, along with another version in a letter to Frances Boldereff, 7 July 1954.

I Believe in You . . . Written ca. 9 August 1954. Published in *CIV/n,* no. 6 (1954), the text used here. Undated, untitled TS at CtU; originally written as letter to Frances Boldereff, ca. 9 August 1954 (also at CtU).

Red Mallows Written ca. 15 August 1954. Previously unpublished. Undated TS at CtU, along with an earlier, unfinished TS.

The Death of Europe Written ca. 24 August 1954. Published in *Origin,* no. 16 (Summer 1955); reprinted in *The Distances,* the text used here. Undated TS at CtU, along with unfinished TS of first sixteen lines. Read at Buffalo, 4 October 1963 (record in Poetry Collection, SUNY Buffalo).

Going from Battle to Battle Written ca. October 1954. Previously unpublished. Undated TS sent Robert Creeley, ca. October 1954, at Washington University Libraries; another undated TS at CtU, along with original holograph MS is notebook from ca. August 1954–March 1955.

Small Birds, to Agree with the Leaves, Come in the Fall Written ca. October 1954, by

October 11. Previously unpublished. Undated TS at CtU, along with three earlier TSS.

I, Mencius, Pupil of the Master . . . TS sent Robert Creeley dated "october 1954," at Washington University Libraries; written by October 11. Published in *Black Mountain Review,* no. 4 (Winter 1954); reprinted in *The Distances,* the text used here. Early TS at CtU, along with Olson's copy of the *Black Mountain Review* with text revised throughout and title changed to "I, Mencius, Dog of the Master . . ."

O'Ryan Written ca. November–December 1954. "O'Ryan (2)" published in *Black Mountain Review,* no. 5 (Summer 1955); sections 2, 4, 6, 8, 10 published by White Rabbit Press (San Francisco, 1958); complete sections, 1–10, published by White Rabbit Press (San Francisco, 1965), the text used here. Original White Rabbit TS among Robert Duncan's Olson materials at CtU; also, TSS of sections 2, 4, 6, 8, 10, along with carbon copies of sections 1–10, original TSS of sections 1–10, and TSS of sections 4, 5, 6, and 8. Proofs of O'Ryan 1–10, with Olson's September 1965 note concerning type size and spacing, at Washington University Libraries. Read at San Francisco State Poetry Center, 21 February 1957.

O'Ryan 11–15 Written ca. November–December 1954. Previously unpublished. Undated TS at CtU. "Her's" in line 12.15 of original, here corrected.

True Numbers Written 9 December 1954. Previously unpublished. Undated TS at CtU, along with an earlier untitled TS; copied out in letter to Robert Creeley, 10 December 1954, at Washington University Libraries.

New Poem Written 1955, by May. Previously unpublished. Undated TS at CtU, along with two earlier TSS.

Anecdotes of the Late War Written 1955, by October. Published as Jargon Broadside no. 1 (Highlands, N.C., 1955); reprinted in *The Distances,* the text used here (with "is," line 4.1, changed to "it," as in Jargon text and as corrected in one of Olson's copies of *The Distances*

at CtU). Section 3 read at San Francisco State Poetry Center, 21 February 1957.

The Bride Written ca. 1955–1956. Previously unpublished. Undated TS at CtU, along with two other TSS.

The Picture Written ca. 1955–1957. Previously unpublished. Undated TS at CtU.

"He treads on edges of being . . ." Written ca. 1955–1958. Previously unpublished. Undated TS at CtU.

Sut Lovingood Written ca. 1955–1958. Previously unpublished. Undated TS at CtU.

King's Mountain Written ca. February–May 1955. Previously unpublished. Undated TS (with carbon copy of first page) at CtU, along with the first two pages of an earlier TS. One page of the final TS (end of section I, start of section II) missing, but text supplied here from the earlier TS.

The Post Virginal TS dated "may 24 / 55" sent John Wieners (photocopy provided the editor), the text used here. Published in *Measure,* no. 3 (Summer 1962). Three other TSS at CtU, along with a carbon copy of the Wieners TS and four other typed starts of the poem.

"As I went in and out I heard pieces . . ." Written ca. June 1955–May 1956. Previously unpublished. Undated TS at CtU, along with TS of another version.

De Los Cantares Written ca. June 1955–May 1956. Previously unpublished. Undated TS at CtU, along with TSS of three other starts.

Evil Written ca. June 1955–May 1956. Previously unpublished. Undated TS at CtU, along with an earlier TS of sections 3 and 4.

The Seven Songs Written ca. June 1955–May 1956. Previously unpublished. Undated TS at CtU, along with another version titled "The Old Physics Restored, or, Newton on Man . . ."

A Newly Discovered 'Homeric' Hymn Written 20 August 1955. Published as "A Tentative Translation of a Newly Discovered 'Homeric' Hymn" in *Origin*, no. 19 (Summer 1956); reprinted, as "A Newly Discovered 'Homeric' Hymn," in *The Distances*, the text used here. Original TS titled "The Translation of a Newly Discovered 'Homeric' Hymn" (revised by Olson to "A Tentative Translation . . .") at CtU, along with a carbon copy of the *Origin* TS; text torn from *Origin*, with title revised to "A Recently Discovered 'Homeric' Hymn" and sent LeRoi Jones, at Research Library, UCLA.

The Whole World   Written ca. 25 August 1955. Previously unpublished. Carbon copy of an undated TS at CtU, incorporating revisions from a previous TS (carbon copy) dated "August 25 55," along with an undated and untitled original TS. "Somebody else's," line 18, originally "somebody's else's" in both carbon copies, but correct in original TS; thus restored here. "Dieing," line 24, originally "dying," but revised by Olson in his original TS and kept in subsequent TSS.

Quail   Written ca. December 1955–1957. Previously unpublished. Undated TS at CtU, along with an untitled and undated holograph MS (an offprint of Benjamin Lee Whorf's "An American Indian Model of the Universe").

"Cry pain, & the dogs of yrself devour . . ." Written ca. 1956. Previously unpublished. Undated holograph MS at CtU.

The Alba   Holograph MS dated "1/13/56" at CtU. Previously unpublished.

Love I   Holograph MS dated "Jan 13 1956" at CtU. Previously unpublished. The first "be" in l. 35—"to be wept for"—not present in original MS, but added here.

"The chain of memory is resurrection . . ." Written spring 1956. Previously unpublished. Undated TS at CtU.

"Anubis will stare . . ."   Written ca. 30 March 1956. Previously unpublished. Undated TS at CtU, along with three other TSS, one titled "To Be Sure That Fire Is Known to Be What It Is," another "The Dog-Faced One," and the third untitled but dated "march 30/56."

The Lordly and Isolate Satyrs   Written ca. 5 April 1956. Published in *Evergreen Review*, no. 4 (Spring 1958); reprinted in *The Distances*, the text used here. Four complete TSS at CtU, along with a carbon copy with revisions, a thermofax copy of the final TS, and two incomplete TSS; text from *Evergreen Review* torn out and sent, with lines 35 and 44 corrected, to LeRoi Jones, at Research Library, UCLA. Read at Harvard, 14 February 1962 (tape incomplete), and at Vancouver, 16 August 1963.

As the Dead Prey Upon Us   Written 13–16 April 1956. Published in *Ark II/Moby 1* (1956–1957); reprinted, revised, in *The Distances*, the text used here (with "the," line II.9, substituted for "and," following all other texts, including Olson's revised copy of *The Distances* at CtU). Original TS, titled "To Alleviate the Dream" (changed to "The Mother Poem") and dated "April 13, 14, 15, 16th 56," at CtU, along with Olson's copy of *The Distances* with tentative revisions ("they are the life-giving forces / in ourselves, awake / my sleeping ones I cry out to you disentangle / the nets of being" written next to lines 2–4, and "clinging" added under "hanging" in line 8). Carbon copy of *Ark II/Moby 1* TS dated "April 1956" (with "The Mother Poem" crossed out) among LeRoi Jones materials at Lilly Library, Indiana University. Read at Vancouver, 16 August 1963.

Variations Done for Gerald Van De Wiele   Written ca. May 1956. Published as "(Variations, Done for Gerry Van Deweile)" in *Measure*, no. 1 (Summer 1957); reprinted, as "Variations Done for Gerald Van De Wiele," in *The Distances*, the text used here. Photocopy of *Measure* TS provided the editor; three TSS of "Le Bonheur" section (plus four fragments) at CtU, along with five TSS of "Spring," one of which is titled "Je Sais Aujourd'hui Saluer la Beauté." Read at Harvard, 14 February 1962, and at Vancouver, 16 August 1963.

The Perfume!   Written ca. 1 May 1956. Previously unpublished. Undated TS at CtU, along with an earlier TS.

"The perfume / of flowers! . . ."   Written

ca. 1 May 1956. Previously unpublished. Undated TS at CtU.

"The perfume / of flowers! . . ." (another version) TS dated "may-day FIVE SIX" at CtU, along with three other TSS, one titled "The Celebration." Previously unpublished.

The Encounter Written ca. 8 August 1956. Previously unpublished. Undated TS sent Robert Creeley, 8 August 1956, at Washington University Libraries; another undated TS at CtU.

Thoughts of the Time Written September 1956. Previously unpublished. Undated and untitled holograph MS at CtU, along with four other variants, three titled as here, one of which dated "Sept/56."

"Who slays the Spanish sun . . ." Written ca. December 1956. Previously unpublished. Undated TS at CtU, along with a version sent as part of a letter to Robert Duncan, 31 December 1956.

The Business Written ca. 1957–1958. Previously unpublished. Undated TS at CtU.

Hate Written ca. 1957–1958. Previously unpublished. Undated TS at CtU.

Who Written ca. 1957–1958. Previously unpublished. Undated TS at CtU, along with three early untitled versions.

Long Distance Written ca. January–May 1957. Previously unpublished. Undated TS at CtU, along with three earlier TSS, one unfinished.

"You know, verse / is a lovely thing . . ." Written ca. January–May 1957. Previously unpublished. Undated TS at CtU.

The Loves of Anat, 1 Written January 1957. Published in *Combustion*, no. 1 (January 1957), the text used here. Original holograph MS and undated TS at CtU; TS sent Gael Turnbull, 6 January 1957 (photocopy provided the editor), and a copy included in Olson's 14 January 1957 letter to Edward Dorn (at CtU). Read at San Francisco State Poetry Center, 21 February 1957.

The Librarian Written 28 January 1957. Pub-

lished in *Yugen,* no. 4 (1959); reprinted in *The Distances,* the text used here (with final nineteen lines indented, following all TSS and Olson's revised copy of *The Distances*). *Yugen* TS, undated, at Lilly Library, Indiana University; another undated TS at UCLA Research Library; undated TS at CtU, along with another TS sent Michael Rumaker, 28 January 1957. Read at Harvard, 14 February 1962; Goddard College, 12 April 1962; on Boston studio tape, June 1962; and on NET film, March 1966.

The Writ Written ca. spring–summer 1956. Previously unpublished. Undated and untitled TS at CtU.

The Writ (later version) Written ca. 3–11 February 1957. Previously unpublished. TS sent Robert Creeley, February 1957, at Washington University Libraries; earlier undated TS at CtU.

"*I weep, fountain of Jazer*" TS dated "May 3/57" at CtU. Previously unpublished. Originally written as part of an essay-letter to Robin Blaser, who made copies and returned the original to Olson as requested, 12 May 1957 (TS at CtU). Thermofax copy given John Wieners (photocopy provided the editor), later acquired by Samuel Charters, who partially extracted a text published as Portents Broadside no. 19 (1970).

She Who Hits at Will Written ca. 22 June 1957. Published as "*Descensus spiritus,* No. 1" in *Measure,* no. 2 (Winter 1958). Undated TS sent John Wieners, July 1957 (photocopy provided the editor), the text used here; earlier versions titled "Restorations—#1," of which there are four TSS, at CtU.

Anniversary Written ca. September 1957–May 1962. Previously unpublished. Undated TS at CtU, along with an original holograph MS and another undated TS.

The Company of Men Written 13 September 1957. Published in *Evergreen Review,* no. 8 (Spring 1959). TS sent Philip Whalen, December 1957, at Reed College Library (probably the text given Donald Allen for *Evergreen*

Review), the text used here; three early TSS, one titled "The Forms," at CtU, along with corrected *Evergreen Review* proofs (extensively revised, though unreturned, thus not considered the poet's final text).

One Word as the Complete Poem   Written ca. October 1957–April 1959. Previously unpublished. Undated TS sent Robert Creeley, at Washington University Libraries (misdated in *Olson & Creeley: Complete Correspondence,* II, 91); undated TS at CtU, along with another TS titled "The Poem of One Word in Rhyme."

Obit   Written 3 October 1957. Previously unpublished. Undated TS at CtU. "May West" (i.e., Mae West) in line 50 uncorrected here.

"Beauty / is to lay hold of Love . . ."   Written ca. 2 November 1957. Undated TS at CtU, along with copy sent in letter to Robert Duncan, 2 November 1957.

Moonset, Gloucester, December 1, 1957, 1:58 AM   Written 1 December 1957. Published in *Partisan Review* 26:3 (Summer 1959); reprinted in *The Distances,* the text used here. Early TS at CtU. Read at Goddard College, 12 April 1962.

What's Wrong with Pindar   Written ca. December 1957–March 1958. Previously unpublished. Undated TS at CtU, along with an original holograph MS.

"Without the Season of Structure . . ."   Written ca. 1958–1959. Previously unpublished. Undated TS at CtU, along with an earlier TS.

Just Inside the Vigil of Christmas   Written ca. 24 December 1957. Previously unpublished. Undated TS at CtU.

The Treatment   Written ca. 1958. Previously unpublished. Undated TS at CtU, along with another TS, likewise undated.

"It isn't my word but my mother's . . ."   Written ca. 1958–1959. Previously unpublished. Undated TS at CtU.

Poemless Rhymes for the Times   Written ca. 1958–1959. Previously unpublished. Undated

TS at CtU, with several alternate endings in pencil, including "Then only / may you / get some / sleep," "can you / get going," "Then you can / ball," "have a ball."

"With what I got out . . ."   Written ca. 1958–1959. Previously unpublished. Undated TS at CtU, revised in pencil (including "the" added over "that" in line 5 but not crossed out, thus no change here). Original holograph MS of lines 5–12 also at CtU, written in pencil on verso manila folder designated "Book: text / & Whitehead / Weyl notes" (containing *Special View of History* materials) from ca. 1956–57.

All Havens Astern   Written ca. 1958–1962. Previously unpublished. Undated holograph MS at CtU.

"I just passed / a swoony time . . ."   Written ca. 1958–1962. Previously unpublished. Undated holograph MS at CtU.

Of the United States   Written ca. 1958–1962. Previously unpublished. Undated TS at CtU, along with an earlier TS.

"tenement twilightish landscape . . ."   Written ca. 1958–1962. Previously unpublished. Undated TS at CtU, verso an original holograph MS of the poem.

"I was stretched out on the earth . . ."   Written ca. 1958–1963. Previously unpublished. Undated holograph MS at CtU.

The Year Is a Great Circle or the Year Is a Great Mistake   Written ca. 15 January 1958. Published in *Measure,* no. 3 (Summer 1962). TS sent John Wieners, 15 January 1958 (photocopy provided the editor), the text used here; carbon copy of *Measure* TS at CtU, along with five earlier TSS, numbered consecutively.

Measure   Written ca. 22 January 1958. Previously unpublished. Undated TS at CtU, along with another undated TS verso holograph MS of "The Mind's Notice" (q.v.), containing three untitled early attempts.

The Mind's Notice   Written ca. 22 January 1958. Previously unpublished. Undated TS at

CtU, along with an earlier undated and un-titled TS and an original holograph MS verso drafts of "Measure" (q.v.).

Rosy, It Was   TS dated "AM February 10–11 / one nine five eight" at CtU, along with original holograph MS.

A Six Inch Chapter—in Verse   Written ca. 27 February 1958. Previously unpublished. Undated TS at CtU, along with undated holograph MS. Read on tape for Robert Creeley, December 1958.

Easter   TS dated "April 5–6 / 1958" at CtU. Previously unpublished. Original holograph MS in 1958 notebook "II / A long time to fill the wells . . ." at CtU, where there are several versions of each section. Section II later typed as separate poems: "The liturgical / eighth day . . ." and "Undazzled, keen, / love sits . . ." (q.v.).

The Gonfalon Raised Tonight   Written ca. 7 April 1958. Previously unpublished. Undated TS at CtU, along with original holograph MS in 1958 notebook "II / A long time to fill the wells . . ."

"Rufus Woodpecker . . ."   Written ca. 26 April 1958. Previously unpublished. Undated TS at Humanities Research Center, University of Texas; thermofax copy of Texas TS among Donald Allen's Olson materials at CtU, along with another TS dated "Apr 26/ 58."

Stone and Flower Series   Written ca. June 1958. Previously unpublished. Undated TS at CtU, along with an original holograph MS, an early TS of part 1, and one page from another early TS.

Memorial Day   Written 1 June 1958. Previously unpublished. Undated TS at CtU, along with two holograph MSS, one dated "Sunday AM June 1." "Wreath," l. 6, typed "wreathe" in TS and later of two MSS; corrected here.

I Mean, No   Written ca. 17 June 1958. Previously unpublished. Undated TS at CtU, along with a version included in a letter to Donald Allen, 17 June 1958.

"I hang on by . . ."   Written ca. 21–25 August 1958. Previously unpublished. Undated TS at CtU, along with two holograph MSS.

Afica   Written ca. 21–25 August 1958. Previously unpublished. Undated TS at CtU, with title added in pencil (hastily printed; possibly "Atica," with a mark over the *t*, perhaps to indicate a double *t*, making "Attica"). Two other undated and untitled TSS also at CtU, along with two holograph MSS.

To Try to Get Down One Citizen as Against Another   Written ca. November 1958–March 1963. Previously unpublished. Undated TS at CtU.

"the Flower grows / from the roots . . ."   Written ca. November 1958–March 1963. Previously unpublished. Undated TS at CtU, along with undated holograph MS.

"The liturgical / eighth day . . ."   Originally written ca. 5–6 April 1958, as part of "Easter" (q.v.); retyped as separate poem and sent Donald Allen, 16 November 1958 (TS at CtU). Previously unpublished.

"Undazzled, keen, / love sits . . ."   Originally written ca. 5–6 April 1958, as part of "Easter" (q.v.); revised 16 November 1958. Previously unpublished. TS sent Donald Allen, 16 November 1958, at CtU, along with an earlier TS.

"Sit by the window and refuse . . ."   TS dated "Dec 2/58" at CtU. Previously unpublished. Another TS sent Philip Whalen, 6 December 1958, at Reed College Library. Read on tape for Robert Creeley, December 1958.

Winter Solstice   TS dated "Dec 8/58" at CtU. Previously unpublished. Another undated TS sent Robin Blaser, verso letter 8 December 1958 (photocopy provided the editor).

Christmas   Written ca. 9 December 1958. Published in *Nation* 188 (3 January 1959), the text used here. Untitled TS dated "December 1958?" at CtU.

The Song   TS dated "dec 13/58" at CtU. Previously unpublished. Another TS, also dated "dec 13/58," at CtU, along with an original holograph MS. Read on tape for Robert Creeley, December 1958.

Being Altogether Literal, & Specific, and Seeking at the Same Time to Be Successfully Ex- plicit   TS dated "Sunday Dec 21" (1958) at CtU. Previously unpublished.

Conversation galante   Written ca. 1959. Previously unpublished. Undated holograph MS in 1958–1959 notebook designated "*Index,*" at CtU.

"the dogwood comes out yellow . . ."   Written ca. 1959. Previously unpublished. Undated holograph MS in ca. 1955–1959 notebook at CtU.

"right in my eye . . ."   Written ca. 1959. Previously unpublished. Undated TS at CtU.

"This man's weakness is straw . . ."   Written ca. 1959–1962. Previously unpublished. Undated holograph MS at CtU.

"My love is also / like . . ."   Holograph MS dated "January 26/59" at CtU. Previously unpublished.

Incunabula, 1958   Written 27 January 1959. Previously unpublished. Undated holograph MS at CtU, along with original holograph MS in notebook "fr P-Town, July/October 58 on to Jan–Feb 59" and another version of "*The Words*" section titled "Incunabula."

"go / make a bridge . . ."   Written ca. 1959, February or after. Previously unpublished. Undated TS at CtU, along with another TS and an original holograph MS.

"It's not / the erotic . . ."   Written ca. 10 March 1959. Previously unpublished. Holograph MS at CtU.

Every Man His Own Matador; or for That Matter Any Member of the Family   TS dated "March 15/59" at CtU. Previously unpublished.

May 20, 1959   Written 20 May 1959. Previously unpublished. TS at CtU, along with original holograph MS in notebook "*Working mss* / Feb 13th, 1959 on."

The Nerves Are Staves, and When the Tears Come There Is Voice   Written ca. August 1959. Previously unpublished. TS sent Robert Creeley, verso Olson's 2 August 1959 letter, at Washington University Libraries; undated early TS at CtU.

The Intended Angle of Vision Is from My Kitchen   TS dated "Aug 4/59" at CtU, with another holograph version titled "The Intended Angle of Vision" verso. Previously unpublished.

"the proper soul / in the proper body . . ."   Written ca. fall 1959. Previously unpublished. Holograph MS at CtU.

The Distances   Written 17 October 1959. Published in *Yugen,* no. 6 (1960), and in *The New American Poetry,* ed. Donald M. Allen (New York, 1960), where it is dated 17 October 1959; reprinted in *The Distances,* the text used here. TS dated "Oct 15th, 1959?" at CtU; undated TS prepared by Donald Allen at Arents Library, Syracuse University. Read at Harvard, 14 February 1962; Goddard College, 12 April 1962; and on Boston studio tape, June 1962.

"I am so small you can hardly see me . . ."   TS dated "*Nov 18th or 19th*" (1959) at CtU. Previously unpublished.

"All pink from the bath she slept . . ."   Written 28 November 1959. Previously unpublished. Holograph MS dated "day after / like / Thurs? Nov 27" (i.e., Thanksgiving 1959) at CtU.

Assuming the Soul Is a Bitch   Written ca. November–December 1959. Previously unpublished. Undated TS, heavily revised, at CtU, along with an original holograph MS and another TS. The text here is Olson's TS before revisions, which are unclear and inconclusive.

"one night Ma / lay with Pa . . ."   Written 3 December 1959. Previously unpublished. Undated TS at CtU, along with an original holograph MS dated "Dec 3."

Carrying Water to the Youth in Honor of Sappho / Jane Harrison / & Miss Duncan If / She Had   TS dated "jan 10 60" at CtU. Previously unpublished. Three untitled holograph MSS also at CtU.

The Dance, of the Grizzly Bear   TS dated "jan 10 60" at CtU. Previously unpublished.

On All Sides   Written ca. 12 January 1960. Previously unpublished. Undated TS at CtU, along with two untitled original holograph MSS.

"On the equator east of my son . . ."   Written ca. 13 January 1960. Previously unpublished. Undated TS at CtU, along with an original holograph MS.

"The Muse / is the 'fate' of the poem . . ."   Holograph MS dated "Jan 15th" (1960) at CtU. Previously unpublished. Another earlier holograph MS also at CtU.

The Objects   Written 19 January 1960. Previously unpublished. Undated TS at CtU, along with three earlier TSS (one dated "jan 19/60") and an original holograph MS.

"abt the dead he sd . . ."   Written ca. 3 February 1960. Published in *Neon,* no. 5 (1960), the text used here. Original holograph MS and early TS at CtU, along with TS made from Olson's MS by Gilbert Sorrentino for Donald Allen, ca. June 1960.

"not a rat-hole, a cat-hole . . ."   TS with note, "done as is Friday March 25th 1960," at CtU. Previously unpublished. Single typed page of an earlier ending also at CtU.

Across Space and Time   Written ca. April–November 1960. Published in *Set,* no. 1 (Winter 1961–1962). Undated TS given Gerrit Lansing, ca. February 1961 (photocopy provided the editor), the text used here; another undated TS, with note "Sent to Kenner for N[ational] R[eview] Nov 5th 1960," at CtU. "Proceeds," line 1, originally "procedes" in CtU TS, Lansing TS, and *Set;* here corrected.

Compleynt Blossoms April to July   Written ca. May 1960. Previously unpublished. Undated TS at CtU.

The Disposition   TS dated "May 3, 1960" sent Raymond Souster and Kenneth McRobbie as part of a small collection of poems written upon Olson's return from a reading and television appearance in Toronto, titled "A Day's Work, for Toronto" (original in possession of McRobbie; photocopy provided the editor). Previously unpublished. Original holograph MS at CtU.

A Promise   Written 3 May 1960. Previously unpublished. TS dated "May / 1960" sent Souster and McRobbie as part of "A Day's Work, for Toronto" (see note above); original holograph MS dated "May / 1960" at CtU.

The Will To   Written 3 May 1960. Previously unpublished. Undated TS sent Souster and McRobbie as part of "A Day's Work, for Toronto" (see note to "The Disposition" above); undated holograph MS at CtU.

I'm With You   TS dated "May 3, 1960" at CtU. Previously unpublished. An earlier TS dated "May 3rd, 1960" also at CtU, along with an undated holograph MS.

Cross-Legged, the Spider and the Web   TS dated "May 7, 1960" at CtU. Previously unpublished.

The Inadequate Orderly Simplification . . .   TS dated "June 16, 1960" at CtU. Previously unpublished. Another, undated TS also at CtU, along with a fragmentary holograph version in notebook "Started night of May 27th 1960 . . ."

Thy Gleeman Who Flattered Thee   Written ca. 29 July 1960. Previously unpublished. Undated TS at CtU, along with two other typed versions, one titled "The Gleeman Who Flattered You" and dated "july 29 / '60," as well as an early holograph MS.

King of the Wood / King of the Dead   Written ca. 2 August 1960. Previously unpublished. Undated TS at CtU, along with another TS dated "aug 2 60," and an original untitled and undated holograph MS.

"Borne down by the inability to lift the heaviness . . ."   Dated 21 September 1960 in MS sent Jon Edgar Webb for publication (Webb to Olson, 4 October 1960, at CtU). Published in *Outsider* 1:1 (Fall 1961), the text used here. Four other TSS at CtU, one with note, "Sept 21, 1960 (sent to John Webb Outsider)," and one incomplete.

The Lie of 10, or The Concept of Zero   Written ca. October 1960. Previously unpublished. Undated TS at CtU.

"Mazdaism / has overcome / the world . . ."   TS dated "Sun Oct 2 60" at CtU. Previously unpublished.

"*In one age or other* . . ."   TS dated "Mon Oct 3 60" at CtU. Previously unpublished. Three earlier TSS and an original holograph MS also at CtU.

A 2nd Musical Form, for Dave Young   TS dated "Wed Oct 5, 1960" at CtU. Previously unpublished. Original holograph MS also at CtU. Read at Harvard, 14 February 1962.

A Woman's Nipples Is the Rose of the World   Written 5 October 1960. Previously unpublished. Undated TS at CtU, along with two earlier TSS, one dated "Tues Oct 5 / 60."

The Mathematical Secret, and the Apron   TS dated "Sun October 9/60" at CtU. Previously unpublished. Original holograph MS of final eleven lines also at CtU.

"As though there were no flowing . . ."   Written ca. 21 October 1960. Previously unpublished. Undated TS at CtU.

Dylan Thomas, and Now Matthew Mead— As He Himself, 'To Edward Thomas'   Written ca. 24 October 1960. Previously unpublished. Undated TS at CtU, along with an earlier undated TS and the start of another. "Squeeks," line 26, in both TSS.

The Yellow of the Mask   TS dated "October 31, 1960" at CtU. Previously unpublished.

Several other versions at CtU, including one titled "The Yellow Mask," also dated "October 31, 1960," and another beginning "A direct downward path . . ."

The Hustings   Written ca. 10 November 1960. Previously unpublished. Undated TS at CtU. Olson's spellings of "Denison," line 31, and "Wolf," line III.25, have been retained.

The Hustings (later version)   Written ca. 10–16 November 1960. Previously unpublished. TS at CtU, along with another TS and an original holograph MS, begun in the margin of the TS of the previous version of the poem. Olson's spelling of "musn't," line 74, has been retained.

"Pente cōst . . ."   Written ca. 1961–April 1963. Previously unpublished. Undated TS at CtU.

When One Age Goes with It Suddenly Its Errors Evaporate   Written ca. 1961–1963. Previously unpublished. Undated holograph MS at CtU.

"Sin is inferiority . . ."   Written ca. 1961–1965. Previously unpublished. Undated holograph MS at CtU.

May 31, 1961   Holograph MS dated "May 31, 1961" at CtU. Previously unpublished. Another holograph MS, dated "1961," at CtU.

The Allegory of Wealth   Written ca. 13 June 1961. Published in *Outburst*, no. 1 (1961), the text used here. Original holograph MS at CtU, along with three TSS, one dated "June 13, 1961," one titled "Morgan the Fay" (with "Fata Morgana" crossed out), and the third incomplete.

There Is No River Which Is Called Lethe   TS dated "Wednesday October 11, 1961" at CtU. Previously unpublished. Earlier TS, titled "Not to Let a Thing Escape One" and dated "Oct 11, 1961," also at CtU.

The Red Fish-of-Bones   TS dated "November 24, 1961" sent Robert Creeley, at Washington University Libraries, the text used here.

Published in *Poetry* 100:1 (April 1962). Undated TS prepared by Robert Creeley and sent *Poetry,* at Lilly Library, Indiana University.

The Binnacle Originally written ca. December 1958; rewritten ca. 27 November 1961. Published in *Albuquerque Review* 1:15 (28 December 1961), the text used here. A third, unidentified part was apparently omitted from *Albuquerque Review* for lack of room (Robert Creeley to Olson, 8 December 1961, at CtU). Six undated holograph MSS at CtU, four of part 1 only, including one (through line 19) titled "*Maximus, talking to himself / —and anyone / who might,*" and an undated TS titled "Maximus, home again, crying out, to all" (read on tape for Creeley, December 1958). "Gy- / res- / copes" (pun on "gyre") in all MSS rather than "gyroscope."

To Empty the Mind Written ca. 29 November 1961. Published in *Floating Bear,* no. 16 (1961), the text used here (with "Faneuil," line 8, corrected from "Fanuel," following the poet's holograph MS). Original holograph MS (lines 1–10 only) at CtU, along with a final MS originally titled "A Note on How Much There Is to Empty the Mind."

What Had to Go TS dated "December 12, 1961" at CtU. Previously unpublished. Undated and untitled holograph MS also at CtU.

How Things Change TS dated "Dec 13/ 1961" at CtU. Previously unpublished. Undated and untitled holograph MS also at CtU. "Chute," l. 27, originally "shute" in both MS and TS; here corrected (cf. "chute" in l. 28).

The Americans Written 17 December 1961. Published in *Floating Bear,* no. 17 (1961), the text used here. Undated TS sent LeRoi Jones, at Simon Fraser University Library; original holograph MS at CtU, with note, "written & sent Leroi Sun Dec 27 1961."

The Americans (another version) Written ca. 17 December 1961. Previously unpublished. Undated holograph MS at CtU, along with another, possibly original holograph MS.

The Snow TS dated "Dec 17, 61" at CtU. Previously unpublished. Undated holograph MS (final six lines only) also at CtU.

"17th century men / who founded this land . . ." Written ca. 20 February 1962. Previously unpublished. Undated TS at CtU.

Examples—for Richard Bridgeman Written ca. April 1962. Previously unpublished. Undated TS at CtU, along with two TSS of another version titled "Apoptic."

On the Shore TS dated "May 8, 1962" at CtU. Previously unpublished. Undated and untitled earlier TS also at CtU, along with a holograph MS.

Hymn to Proserpine Written ca. July 1962. Previously unpublished. Undated and untitled holograph MS at CtU, along with three TSS, one titled "Hymn to Proserpine."

Shang Dynasty Oracle Bone 2 Say Written ca. September 1962–June 1963. Previously unpublished. Holograph MS at CtU.

"some partial cloudiness will flow locally . . ." TS dated "Wed Sept 12/62" at CtU. Previously unpublished. Undated holograph MS also at CtU.

To a Poet Who Read in Gloucester Before the Cape Ann Historical Literary and Scientific Society TS dated "October 4th 1962" at CtU. Previously unpublished. Undated holograph MS also at CtU.

In an Automotive Store Holograph MS dated "Oct 30th / LXII" at CtU. Previously unpublished. Three other holograph versions also at CtU, one similarly dated "Oct 30th / LXII."

"It is a nation of nothing but poetry . . ." Written ca. 17 November 1962. Previously unpublished. Holograph MS dated "November / 1962" at CtU, along with five other holograph MSS, one dated "Sat Nov 17th."

"in Wiro language . . ." Written December 1962. Previously unpublished. Undated TS at CtU, along with original holograph MS.

665

"Shut in   kept off . . ."   Written December 1962. Previously unpublished. Undated holograph MS at CtU.

"there they were . . ."   TS dated "December 30, 1962" at CtU. Previously unpublished. Undated holograph MS also at CtU.

"I saw, from under Him . . ."   Written ca. 1963–1964. Previously unpublished. Undated holograph MS at CtU, one of three versions on the same page, this one ringed in pencil by the poet.

Ferrini—I   TS dated "January 4–15, 1963" at CtU. Previously unpublished. The text here is the poet's typed version, ignoring extensive revisions in pencil, including entire sections crossed out and alternate lines in margins, often in several versions and difficult to read. Original holograph MSS (some twenty-seven pages in all) on various size sheets, envelopes, and utility bills, also at CtU, along with an early, undated TS, abandoned before sections 3 and 4.

"As the shield goddess, Mycenae . . ."   Written ca. 17–19 January 1963. Previously unpublished. Undated TS at CtU, along with an earlier TS dated "January 17th & 19th, 1963" and early holograph versions titled "The Alembic" and "The Cucurbit." "Slup," line 38, is "slip" in earlier TS and holograph MSS and may be a typographical error by the poet.

"Snow White was always waiting . . ."   TS dated "January 23rd, 1963" at CtU. Previously unpublished. Original holograph MS also at CtU.

"I had had / a beetle . . ."   Written ca. 31 January 1963. Previously unpublished. Undated TS at CtU, along with two other TSS (one incomplete) and two holograph MSS.

"I met my Angel last night . . ."   Written ca. 2 February 1963. Previously unpublished. Undated TS at CtU, along with undated TS of another version and two undated holograph MSS, one titled "The Angel and the Fish."

"Love is the talk . . ."   Written ca. 28 March 1963. Previously unpublished. Undated holograph MS at CtU.

"His house / in the branches . . ."   Written ca. 29 May–15 June 1963. Previously unpublished. Undated holograph MS at CtU, along with an earlier holograph MS.

A Part of the Series on the Paths   Holograph MS dated "Sat Oct 19th 1963" at CtU. Previously unpublished. Two unfinished holograph MSS also at CtU.

"The personality and dourness of winter . . ."   Written ca. December 1963. Previously unpublished. Undated TS at CtU.

For Mac Hammond   TS dated "December, 1963" at CtU, along with a photocopy made by the poet. Previously unpublished. Original holograph MS also at CtU.

"—the End of the World / is the Turn-About . . ."   Written ca. 1964–May 1965. Previously unpublished. Undated TS at CtU.

"Color . . ."   Written ca. February 1964–February 1965. Sections 2–4 published in *Matter,* nos. 2–4 (July 1964–1968), the text used here, with the addition of section 1, previously unpublished. Undated TSS of sections 1, 3, 4 at Poetry Collection, SUNY Buffalo; original holograph MSS of sections 2–4 at CtU. Originally sent as a series of postcards to Robert Kelly, each signed "William Dorn, 1597." Section 1, typed on an unpostmarked postcard among Kelly's papers at Buffalo, is probably the "lost" postcard-poem of the series referred to by Olson in conversation, and thus has been added here.

'West'   Written 1959 (or before)—1964. Published by Goliard Press (London, 1966), the text used here. The original introductory statement, written May 1966 and sent Edward Dorn for Tom Raworth of Goliard Press, concludes: "It ought also to be added that these are the first seven or eight parts, of which more are intended" (at CtU). In a 31 May 1966 letter, also at CtU, Olson instructed Raworth to excise the sentence. The Goliard TS, with corrections and instructions by Olson, survives at CtU, along with the Goliard setting TS prepared for the printer by Raworth; the Goliard mock-up with proofs corrected by Olson is at Butler Library, Columbia University. Information concerning the individual poems follows.

as of Bozeman   Written 1959 from notes made earlier, possibly as early as 1947–1948. Published in *Yugen,* no. 6 (1960). Undated *Yugen* TS at Arents Library, Syracuse University; original holograph MS, also undated, at CtU. "Paleontolgist" (l. 22) in Goliard text here corrected ("paleontologist" in MS, *Yugen* TS, *Yugen,* and Goliard TS).

Two Poems   Written ca. April 1963. Published in *Wild Dog,* no. 5 (30 January 1964). Undated holograph MS at CtU, along with text torn from *Wild Dog,* with revisions.

West 4 and 5   TS dated "March 2nd 64" at CtU. Published in *Wild Dog,* no. 7 (5 April 1964). Original holograph MS of section 5, undated, at CtU, along with TS of Drummond Hadley's poems originally sent as part of a letter by Robert Creeley, 9 February 1964.

West 6   Written 4 March 1964. Published in *Wild Dog,* no. 10 (September 1964). Original holograph MS in 1964 notebook at CtU, along with another holograph MS dated "March 4th (XIX–LXIV)."

From The Song of Ullikummi   TS dated "March, 1964" at Bancroft Library, University of California, Berkeley, the text used here. Published in *City Lights Journal,* no. 3 (November 1966). Original holograph MS in early 1964 notepad at CtU. *City Lights* TS has the following note to printer: "all *spaces* please—& spacings of lines—to be observed as here—including apparent discrepancies (such as das & dās) left as is   (It has been double-checked, as is)." Read as part of "Causal Mythology" lecture, Berkeley, 20 July 1965.

"Memory, Mind, and Will . . ."   Dated "March 4th 1964" in *Matter,* no. 2 (July 1964),

the text used here. Original holograph MS, undated, at CtU.

"In celebration of Mitos . . ."   Written ca. 10 March 1964. Previously unpublished. Undated TS at CtU. "Blizzard," at poem's end, originally typed by the poet with hyphens and asterisks over each letter to give the effect of snowflakes.

"the unfinished (raw) hero . . ."   TS dated "March 10th, 1964," at CtU. Previously unpublished. Undated holograph MS also at CtU.

Buffalo Ode   Original holograph MS dated "night of Wednesday March 25th 1964" at CtU. Published in *Resuscitator,* no. 4 (May 1965); section 1 in *Resuscitator,* no. 2 (April 1964), with errors corrected in no. 4. Holograph MS of section 1 dated "March 25th 1964," sent John G. James that date, and TSS of remaining sections, sent James 4 September 1964, are the texts used here (photocopies provided by Ralph Maud). Errors in section 1 also corrected by Olson in his copy of *Resuscitator* at CtU.

"My belly / sounds like an owl . . ."   Written ca. June 1964–1968. Previously unpublished. Holograph MS at CtU.

"like a foldout . . ."   Written 6 June 1964. Published in *Wild Dog,* no. 16 (April 1965), the text used here. TS sent Edward Dorn, 6 June 1964, at CtU, along with an original holograph MS dated "Sat June 6 / LXIV" and another typed version dated "Saturday June 6 1964."

"barley or rye . . ."   Written ca. 14 June 1964. Previously unpublished. Undated holograph MS at CtU.

"Grinning monster out side the system . . ."   Holograph MS dated "Wednesday June 24th" (1964) at CtU. Previously unpublished.

"her skin / covered me . . ."   Written ca. 6 October 1964. Previously unpublished. Undated holograph MS at CtU.

The Lamp TS dated "October / 14th 1964" (photocopy at CtU). Published in *Magazine of Further Studies,* no. 2 (October 1965), the text used here. Original holograph MS dated "Wednesday Oct 14th" also at CtU. CtU photocopy has what is apparently a tentative revision or attempt at revision (a final "the" added in the last line after "hanging from"), here ignored. In the original MS—written in blue ball-point ink on a Buffalo restaurant placemat and dated in pencil—the poem's last lines are written along the side of the placemat, next to the body of the text, in such a way that the concluding line ends beside the title, thus completing itself in that manner.

Shenandoah TS dated "Wednesday Oct 14" (1964) at CtU. Previously unpublished. Undated original holograph MS also at CtU.

"will: termite mothers . . ." TS dated "Friday evening Oct 16th / 1964" at CtU. Previously unpublished. Undated holograph TS also at CtU.

"will: the rat . . ." TS dated "Sat Oct / 17th" (1964) at CtU. Previously unpublished.

The Grandfather-Father Poem Written ca. late October 1964. Published in *Poetry* 106: 1–2 (April–May 1965). Undated *Poetry* TS sent Henry Rago, 29 October 1964, at Lilly Library, Indiana University—the text used here, with quotation marks in line 64 added from the original holograph MS. *Poetry* proofs also at Lilly Library; undated original holograph MS at CtU.

for my friend TS dated "March–April, 1965" at CtU. Published in *Magazine of Further Studies,* no. 4 (November 1967), the text used here.

The Drum World TS dated "Sunday April 10th, 1965" at CtU. Previously unpublished. Original holograph MS also at CtU.

"my apple branch . . ." Written ca. 3 May 1965. Previously unpublished. Undated TS at CtU, along with an original holograph MS.

Absolutely Vernal Written ca. June 1965. Previously unpublished. Undated holograph MS at CtU.

An 'Enthusiasm' Written ca. 9 October 1965. Published in *Gloucester Daily Times,* 16 October 1965, the text used here, with corrections from the original holograph MS. Undated and untitled original holograph MS at CtU.

This Year Written ca. 1965–November 1968. Previously unpublished. Undated TS at CtU, along with an original holograph MS.

"as if Hallam Movius . . ." Holograph MS dated "November 12th 1965" at CtU. Previously unpublished.

A *Scream* **to the Editor** Written ca. 3 December 1965. Published (undated TS photoreproduced) in *Gloucester Daily Times,* 3 December 1965, the text used here. An original holograph MS, offered for sale with the original TS and a cover letter sent the *Gloucester Times,* is described in Asphodel Book Shop (Burton, Ohio) catalog 47 (April 1976), p. 13: "The manuscript is written on the fronts and backs of three varied sized envelopes, plus one 8½ × 11 sheet."

"He is the Devil . . ." Written ca. January 1966. Previously unpublished. Undated holograph MS at CtU.

"As snow lies on the hill . . ." Written ca. February 1966. Previously unpublished. Undated TS at CtU, along with several pages of an original holograph MS. Here edited from the poet's typed attempt to transcribe his very confused holograph original.

"turn now and rise . . ." Holograph MS sent Harvey Brown dated "April 14 MDCCC-CLXVI," at Poetry Collection, SUNY Buffalo. "For the Ailing ["Ailing" crossed out but restored] Buffalo Herd," replacing "For Those Ailing Buffalo 'Germs,'" verso accompanying envelope, possibly an intended or suggested title. Published in *Niagara Frontier Review,* no. 3 (Fall 1965 [i.e., Spring 1966]), the text used here. Original holograph MS at CtU.

"So the Norse / were neurotic . . ." Written ca. December 1966–January 1967. Published in *"before your very eyes!"*, no. 1 (1967), the text used here. Undated holograph MS given Tom Raworth photoreproduced in *Gegenschein Quarterly,* no. 5 (1973); Goliard Press TS at Butler Library, Columbia University; another undated holograph MS at CtU.

"Indian trinity . . ."   Written ca. 26 July 1967. Previously unpublished. TS dated "July" sent *Freelance* magazine, ca. 8 August 1967, at Washington University Libraries; another TS likewise dated "July" at CtU, along with an original holograph MS.

"Not to permit himself . . ."   TS sent Robert Hogg dated "October/23rd, 1967" (photocopy provided the editor). Previously unpublished. Two earlier TSS at CtU, one titled

"(FOR, SAY,—GEORGE *MEREDITH*(?))," along with an original holograph MS dated "Mon Oct 23rd."

"the Heart is a clock . . ."   TS dated "Sunday January 21, 1968," photoreproduced for publication as a broadside by Gallery Upstairs Press (Buffalo, 1968), the text used here. Original holograph MS and another dated TS at CtU.

"A big fat fly . . ."   Written ca. December 1968–March 1969. Previously unpublished. Undated holograph MS at CtU. The order of the poem's sections is ambiguous in the MS; an alternate reading would place the last two stanzas after the present first stanza. "Sad" in line 16 could be "such."

INDEX